K9 TEAMS

K9 Professional Training Series

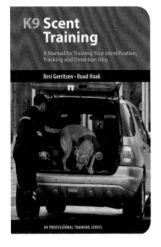

K9 Scent Training
A Manual for Training Your Identification, Tracking and Detection Dog
Resi Gerritsen • Ruud Haak
K9 PROFESSIONAL TRAINING SERIES

K9 Behavior Basics
A Manual for Proven Success in Operational Service Dog Training
second edition
Resi Gerritsen • Ruud Haak • Simon Prins
K9 PROFESSIONAL TRAINING SERIES

K9 Search and Rescue
A Manual for Training the Natural Way
second edition
Resi Gerritsen • Ruud Haak
K9 PROFESSIONAL TRAINING SERIES

K9 Drug Detection
A Manual for Training and Operations
Resi Gerritsen • Ruud Haak
K9 PROFESSIONAL TRAINING SERIES

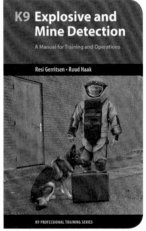

K9 Explosive and Mine Detection
A Manual for Training and Operations
Resi Gerritsen • Ruud Haak
K9 PROFESSIONAL TRAINING SERIES

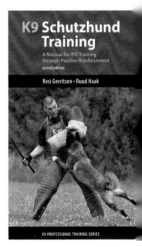

K9 Schutzhund Training
A Manual for IPO Training through Positive Reinforcement
second edition
Resi Gerritsen • Ruud Haak
K9 PROFESSIONAL TRAINING SERIES

See the complete list at
dogtrainingpress.com

To the
Kirk Wells Fire Dept
God Bless

K9 TEAMS

Beyond the Basics of Search and Rescue and Recovery

Vi Hummel Shaffer

Vi Hummel Shaffer

K9 Professional Training Series

An imprint of
Brush Education Inc.

Brush Education Inc.
www.brusheducation.ca
contact@brusheducation.ca

Editorial: Meaghan Craven
Cover Design: John Luckhurst; Cover photo by Lisa Kavakas—pictured are (left to right) Shelly Ulbig, Donna Anzalone, and Sharon Ballweg with her K9 Titan, members of Mason-Dixon Rescue Dogs.
Interior Design: Carol Dragich, Dragich Design

Printed and manufactured in Canada

Library and Archives Canada Cataloguing in Publication
Shaffer, Vi Hummel, 1942–, author
K9 teams : beyond the basics of search and rescue and recovery / Vi Hummel Shaffer.

Includes bibliographical references.

Issued in print and electronic formats.
ISBN 978-1-55059-762-2 (softcover).—ISBN 978-1-55059-763-9 (PDF).—
ISBN 978-1-55059-764-6 (Kindle).—ISBN 978-1-55059-765-3 (EPUB)

1. Search dogs—Training.   2. Rescue dogs—Training. 3. Police dogs—Training.
I. Title.

SF428.73.S53 2018   636.7'0886   C2018-902194-2
                                               C2018-902195-0

Dedication

To Andy Rebmann and Marcia Koenig, whose emotional support and understanding gave me strength during troubled times in my early SAR/R years.

Contents

The Purpose of This Book

Prior to the mid-1990s, no differentiation was made between search and rescue (SAR) and search and recovery K9s. All such dogs were simply considered SAR dogs. There were no distinctive K9 search vests, T shirts, or uniforms that proclaimed "Recovery" as there are today. Due to the increased specialization in and information on training and working with human remains detection K9s, I use the abbreviation SAR/R to include both specializations.

This book is unique because it compiles sound, practical material collected at conferences, seminars, and workshops, as well as an immense array of comments made by instructors and handlers spanning over 26 years. It also offers new research findings, personal experiences, and numerous ideas and methods from across the United States and other countries.

K9 Teams: Beyond the Basics of Search and Rescue and Recovery examines a variety of issues, opinions, and questions that come up frequently in the SAR/R community but are not mentioned in other books. I used only a portion of my accumulated information in writing this book, so all concepts of training, and all facets in SAR/R, are not covered here. However, the sensitive subjects of glory seekers, frauds, "red flags," politics in SAR/R, and credentials have been included to help others avoid some of the pitfalls many have experienced. Learning should come from many sources—no one knows everything, no matter what they claim or how extensive their knowledge appears to be.

> *"It's what you learn after you know it all that counts." – Earl Weaver,* It's What You Learn After You Know It All that Counts

This book is for all levels of K9 detection handlers and those interested in K9 detection work. It is not a step-by-step how-to book, and it does not reiterate what has already been published. Instead, it is meant to generate a broader frame of reference, to entice you to delve into areas related to your search discipline and contemplate what you have learned already. Many books and articles related to SAR/R are quite technical; this book employs straightforward language that is accessible and easy to understand, no matter what scent discipline you work.

The Internet makes it easy to research subjects and enhance training and understanding—though one must be careful about the reliability of the information. Nothing takes the place of an experienced, credible, hands-on instructor for guidance. Although an idea may be good, it may not be right for you, your dog, or the current stage of training.

K9 Teams includes some of my own material and informed opinions based on lessons learned, but the vast majority of the tips and information come from a multitude of SAR/R professionals, K9 handlers, and experts from around the world. Most of the time I do not attach the names of individual handlers to remarks and ideas, for a couple of reasons. First, many ideas in this book come from my notes taken at a seminar or training session where it was unclear who made the sound, viable comment. Second, there is a common expression in the SAR/R community: "The only thing two handlers can agree upon is what the third handler is doing wrong." Therefore, the focus herein is on the information—not the person who said it. In this way, I hope *K9 Teams* will share ideas and open minds to different ways toward and thoughts about accomplishing a worthy goal. Whether you initially agree with the material in this book or not, I hope you will ask yourself: Is it logical? Does it make sense?

> "… *every difference of opinion, is not a difference of principle.*" – *Thomas Jefferson*, First Inaugural Address, *March 4, 1804*

Throughout this book the words "TEAM," and "organization" will be used interchangeably. "TEAM" or "organization" means a group of people that has met preconditions and allied itself with a specific search and rescue organization. However, the word "team" (in lower-case letters) refers to one dog and one handler. SAR/R terminology differs throughout the United States and around the world. The words "indicating" and "alerting" can be particularly confusing. For some, "indicating" means the dog is working in a way that shows he has *detected* the target odor and "alerting" is what the dog does to confirm he has *located the source* of the target odor. For others, the meanings for those words are reversed. In 2006 another term, "final response" (FR), was added by The Scientific Working Group on Dog Orthogonal Detector Guidelines (SWGDOG). While some organizations have begun using this term, others have not. To avoid overwhelming readers with a profusion of acronyms and confusing terms, I use the word "alert" to describe the dog's final action: when he has located the source of the target odor.

DISCLAIMER

While the contents of this book are based on substantial experience and expertise, working with dogs involves inherent risks, especially in dangerous settings and situations. Anyone using approaches described in this book does so entirely at their own risk and both the author and publisher disclaim any liability for any injuries or other damage that may be sustained.

Part I

The Making of a TEAM:
Building a Strong Foundation

The Beginning:
What It's All About

"Good intentions do not make a search team." – Unknown

This chapter will help those interested in SAR/R understand some of the challenges and education involved. Search and Rescue/Recovery TEAMs (SAR/R) are not dog clubs, do not train dogs for other people, and do not search for lost pets. They are serious entities that function in human life-and-death situations.

Although some law-enforcement and fire/rescue agencies do pay SAR/R personnel, most K9 SAR/R teams are civilian volunteers. SAR/R may mean different things to different people, but it is really about:

- changing a lifestyle. SAR/R is a way of life, not a hobby;
- dedicating time to SAR/R study and training rather than pastimes or hobbies;
- leaving your family and friends for a search, even during holidays and special occasions—at all hours and in all types of weather;
- restraining your ego and sense of self-importance;
- the significance of being a team player;

- trust;
- learning about topics you never considered before;
- expanding your comfort levels;
- having a purpose—not for honor or glory but by stepping outside yourself and knowing that your work could mean a profound difference in the lives of others;
- hard, rewarding work—being exhausted and exhilarated at the same time;
- knowing joy or deep sadness that can evoke pride or despair;
- awareness of both physical and emotional consequences; and
- understanding that being a volunteer does not mean being less trained, less professional, and less dedicated than paid workers.

K9 SAR/R professionals need to be honest people who are honorable in their principles, intentions, and actions. They need to be trustworthy people who do not exaggerate their capabilities, qualifications, or level of expertise. In fact, they need to understand their limitations and be truthful about them. They must understand the importance of confidentiality and not disclose sensitive or specific information relative to a search. In addition to honesty, a K9 SAR/R professional should have the following traits:

- commitment—to the mission;
- compliance—with all local government and applicable laws and ordinances;
- ethics—showing up on a search *only* with an official request from the agency, and adherence to moral and ethical principles;
- flexibility—willingness to change without compromising ethics.
- integrity—doing what is right even though no one is watching;
- patience—when training, searching, and interacting with humans or dogs;

- personal accountability—accepting responsibility for his or her actions;
- professionalism—in manner of dress and conduct; and
- respect—for the victim and for others.

Every SAR/R position requires continual training and personal devotion for the duration of involvement. In addition, there is a financial commitment. Almost all volunteer members pay for their own dogs, equipment, training, travel, uniforms, and so on. After the initial cost of mandatory equipment, most personnel spend an average of $5,000 per year on SAR/R-related expenses.

SAR/R is not glamorous. It is exhausting work requiring physical and mental stamina. Not all searches have happy endings. Some searches are unresolved, and the victims are never located. In some searches, the victim is found deceased, and in others, SAR/R teams find the victims alive but in critical condition and they die a short time later. Many searches occur in the worst weather conditions. Wilderness areas and urban environments have their own unique dangers, obstacles, and challenges. You may have to carry a 25-pound (12 kg) backpack for miles on end while working through dense woods swarming with insects or in bone-chilling cold. The search may be in steep, rocky places, in swamps, or in thickly wooded forests inhabited by dangerous wildlife and venomous snakes. Or you may need to search trash-filled alleyways, vacant drug houses, dilapidated buildings, and around hazardous materials. The handler and dog must be properly trained in each type of area in which they plan to conduct searches, so they do not become victims themselves.

"If your vision or dream only involves you, then you should question its intent. A real vision or dream should have an effect on the people. Moreover it should be so big and vast that you can't achieve it on your own. Be Great!" – #pervis principle, Pervis Taylor III

Many new handlers leave SAR/R after 24 months for a variety of reasons. Perhaps they became involved for the wrong reason, usually because they wanted to give their pet something to do or they thought they would become "heroes." Or, maybe they didn't realize the number of training hours far exceeded the number of actual searches. Many would-be handlers underestimate the time it takes to become a competent K9 team, and they become bored with the repetitive training that is needed or with the tremendous amount of in-depth SAR/R-related education they must have and studying they must undertake. Other reasons many potential handlers quit early include overestimating their physical fitness level, deciding the financial burden is more than they care to spend, and interpersonal conflicts within their SAR/R team.

A few of the numerous things the handler must know and will learn through proper training are:

- in the United States, required courses in the National Incident Management System (NIMS), which includes the Incident Command System (ICS);
- proper call-out procedures;
- the roles of the handler and flanker / helper / field technician;
- map reading;
- report writing;
- search strategies;
- lost and missing persons behavior;
- crime-scene preservation;
- legal court testimony and other law-related issues; and
- first aid—human and canine.

Handlers must also learn about scent, what it is and how it is transported, as well as the effect of terrain and weather on scent.

K9 Search Disciplines: An Overview

"If you are setting a goal without understanding the reason for it, then maybe you should re-evaluate the goal in general." – Tina Brown, Setting Smart Goals

A list of 30 types of detector dog disciplines was compiled for an article in the *Journal of Analytical and Bioanalytical Chemistry* in 2004.[1] Since that time, additional types of detection dogs have been identified, but the focus of SAR/R, and this book, is human scent/odor detection, both alive and deceased.

Air scent, trailing, and tracking are the three major search-dog disciplines. Except for tracking, all advanced disciplines are based on air-scenting principles, for example: area/live-victim search, article/evidence search, cadaver search, disaster search, human remains detection, and water search. Each of these advanced disciplines requires specific studying and training. Following are the seven main disciplines in SAR/R.

1. Air Scent General: The K9 tries to detect *any* human scent by sniffing air currents. She works on or off lead and will find anyone in her search area.

2. Air Scent Specific: The K9 first sniffs an object, provided by her handler, which has been in contact with the person she will be searching for. She will ignore all other people and search only for the matching scent. She works on or off lead.

3. Tracking: Some tracking dogs are trained for scent-specific work. Others are trained to search for the freshest track. They work on lead. Some people call this work mantrailing.

4. Trailing: The trailing dog is scent specific and follows wherever the particular scent is—not necessarily where the person walked. She works on or off lead.

5. Cadaver: A "cadaver dog" is a generic term used to describe a dog trained to find the scent of human decomposition.

6. Disaster—Live Victim: In this advanced discipline, teams work within a narrow span of time to rescue live victims trapped in collapsed structures or debris.

7. Disaster—Deceased Victim: This discipline, typically associated with a mass fatality incident (MFI), requires teams with specific training, not just the use of a cadaver dog.

On average, it takes about two years, training at least two or three times per week, to become adequate in one discipline. Proper and frequent training is crucial so that dogs and their handlers are knowledgeable, consistent, and reliable enough to meet the requirements, pass a test for operational level, and be trustworthy for a real mission.

Whatever area of SAR/R you choose, whatever discipline your dog is trained in—*you* have the responsibility to do your very best.

Joining a TEAM

"Dedication requires sacrifice." – Stephen Zempel in Daily Triumph, *by Jeff Pepper*

Researching the current number of SAR/R teams in the United States and other countries has proved to be futile. Previously, a few individuals took on the daunting task of compiling TEAM names and locations to create a nationwide resource website. However, with the continued growth and changes of SAR/R TEAMS, the list has not been updated recently, and other lists created since then do not appear complete or include TEAMs that no longer exist.

As a point of reference, in 1991 there were only five K9 SAR TEAMs in the entire state of Texas—all with cross-trained dogs. In 2017 Texas had over 45 different TEAMs/organizations. At one point, very few teams in the United States specialized in a discipline or type of search situation—handlers and their dogs were simply expected to do it all. But with the increase of information available online, handlers have learned the importance of training for specific areas and K9 disciplines. Advances in science and new proven methods, added to those tried-and-true ones, provide ever-expanding information to those working in K9 scent detection.

After every major disaster, new SAR/R TEAMs are formed. Some are short-lived when the members, even with good intentions, learn what the undertaking entails. New TEAMs also form when a handler becomes disgruntled with the politics and attitude of his or her TEAM, or when:

- a handler decides to start his or her own specialization TEAM;
- a SAR/R applicant is not accepted by an established TEAM;
- TEAMs in the area are questionable or nonexistent; or
- a handler believes his or her K9 should be advanced in status, contrary to the TEAM trainer's views. The handler then forges ahead to create a new TEAM, which may have questionable skills and qualifications.

Any TEAM that lacks the necessary training and education reflects poorly on all SAR/R TEAMs.

"If success comes too soon, a person may think they are smarter than they really are." – Unknown

Before joining a TEAM, it is a good idea to check out its reputation. Consider its ethics, philosophies, training practices, and attitudes. You should go beyond viewing the TEAM website, which can state just about anything for promotional purposes—after all, websites are advertisements. Words like "national," "tactical," and other official-sounding terminology in TEAM names may not be factual but instead used to present the TEAM as "more" than it is. Also note that SAR/R TEAMs that have been in existence for years and have received numerous commendations for members' work and ethics may currently not have those same members. The character, standards, and training of a TEAM can be changed by a new regime that may not measure up to the original TEAM.

After assessing a TEAM located near you, you may decide that joining one farther away would be more suitable. This may mean driving a couple hundred miles each week to attend training sessions—something dedicated handlers are willing to do.

All credible TEAMs have written standards. If they are not published on the website, ask your contact or the TEAM leader if you can read them so you can get a better picture of the organization. Next, inquire about attending a TEAM meeting or a training session or two. Some TEAMs allow potential members to come with their dogs so they can assess both. Others allow attendance only without a dog. Certain TEAMs charge a small fee for evaluating someone's dog, since it takes time away from members' training, or they may feel that payment shows sincerity on the part of the potential member.

If you are allowed to attend a training session, ask about suitable clothing for the type of weather and terrain, and arrive prepared and on time. If you own outdoor gear, bring it, since training may take place in a remote area without facilities—bring water and snacks.

Many SAR/R TEAMs will accept applicants without any SAR-related training—map and compass skills, first aid, and the like—as long as they meet other requirements. Other TEAMs consider only those who have skills relevant to the areas they search. TEAMs that work in mountainous regions, with avalanches, or in high altitudes—which can drastically affect performance—may accept as members only those who are already familiar with and comfortable working in those conditions. Most K9 SAR/R TEAMs require members to participate in whatever non-K9 roles may need filling. All functions in SAR/R are necessary and valuable.

4

The Process of Membership

Several times each year the same questions are asked and discussed on social media, and the same requests are made for copies of other TEAMs' membership processes, dog issues (e.g., type of breeds, selection of dogs, age of dog to start training, certification methods), and standards. The information in this section, compiled from research about TEAMs around the world, should give you comprehensive—though not all-inclusive—answers to questions you might have about the process of membership.

Ordinarily, TEAMs begin the process by asking potential members to complete an application, which may include an application processing fee. The TEAM may also want to interview the applicant at that time. Keep in mind that prospective members might show the desired persona during initial and follow-up interviews, and their true personalities and motivation may only be exposed after they are well into training. While some TEAMs offer applications to anyone interested, others require applicants to attend a certain number of meetings before determining if an application will even be offered. After review and vetting—which is highly advised and can require a background check and fingerprinting, with those costs paid for by the prospective member—a vote is then taken to accept or reject the application. In most cases, a successful applicant enters a probationary period that can range from a few months to one year or more—depending on the TEAM—before final evaluation and another vote on the potential member's acceptance as a full member. Sometimes determination on full membership is undertaken by a management committee; other times the entire TEAM votes. If an individual has an extensive SAR/R or other related background, the probationary period may be shorter.

Some TEAMs' procedures for acceptance of new members are more complex. An example follows.

1. An interview with a committee and a presentation for the prospective member regarding the essence of the TEAM and what is expected of members.

2. A physical fitness test consisting of several field exercises while carrying a 25-pound (12-kg) backpack. If the applicant has a dog, it may be allowed to accompany in the exercises.

3. The first six months of the one-year probation period consist of learning defined subjects and becoming a flanker.

4. After six months of training, the entire TEAM will decide if the probationary member can continue.

5. If the probationary member is approved to continue, his or her dog will now be evaluated.

6. Contingent to the dog's acceptance, the next six-month period has the candidate learning basic K9 SAR/R work. During this portion of probation, the candidate (without his or her dog) may be allowed to go on call-outs, paired with a senior member or in the position of a trained flanker or general helper.

7. After passing the one-year probationary period, the new member and his or her dog must go through extensive K9 training and pass a formal evaluation or in-house certification before being fielded as a search-dog team.

Another TEAM's membership process method has six steps.

1. The applicant attends a mandatory orientation meeting where applications are distributed.

2. The applicant's information is reviewed.

3. The potential member is interviewed to evaluate him/her based on several criteria.

4. A background and driving-record check is conducted.

5. Approved candidates are allowed to start the TEAM's basic search and rescue training program, which requires a non-refundable fee.

6. The applicant's performance, including how he or she interacts with other members and how well he or she learned TEAM procedures, standards, and practices, is evaluated before final determination on membership status is made.

For some TEAMS, a probationary member must demonstrate knowledge in a variety of areas and pass the first responder or SAR technician courses before a vote for full membership. Others require that new members first be certified as flankers (also called field technicians or helpers) or in another position. In England, probationary members must play the role of "dogbody" (victim) for four to six months before they can even *begin* to train their dogs with the TEAM.

"It's not called being picky; it's called not compromising your standards." – Unknown

Although a probationary member may have previous SAR/R experience or certifications listed on his or her application, the member is still only on probation. Most legitimate organizations do not permit members to use TEAM uniforms, patches, decals, or magnetic signs until they have completed all the steps and are full members. Organizations know these are earned items that should be treated with the respect they deserve.

Membership Applications

*"You always have two choices: Your commitment versus your fear." –
Sammy Davis Jr., from "Your Morning Shot," GQ.com, July 25, 2013*

The required information on an application varies from TEAM
to TEAM. Some require only name, contact information, current
employment, emergency contact, any criminal history, and why the
applicant wants to join that particular TEAM. Additional questions might include the following: Have you ever been involved in
search and rescue, and if so, with what TEAM? When? Where?
In what position?

More detailed applications may request other information or
documentation such as:

- work and residential history;
- medical history and doctor's contact information;
- type of vehicle owned;
- type of dog owned and if the applicant is willing to get
  another dog if the present dog does not pass evaluation
  testing;
- copies of all certifications and/or professional licenses,
  showing the types, dates of issue, agencies of issue, and
  expiration dates;
- copy of current immunization record or religious
  exemption;
- applicant release and disclosure form;
- release and indemnity agreement;
- signed copy of TEAM code of ethics;
- copies of military records;
- list of SAR equipment owned;
- parent-signed document if applicant is under legal age;
- an essay on why the applicant wants to be involved in
  SAR/R.

Other applications include a personal skills form so applicants can list their skills—first aid, survival skills, radio operations, heavy-equipment operations, skiing, swimming, and so on—and rate their level of training/proficiency in each skill.

With any TEAM, it is important for applicants to divulge fears or phobias—water, darkness, heights, confined space, spiders, snakes, and so on. Allergies and severe reactions to bites and stings, poison ivy / oak, medications, or anything else be must be disclosed as well. This is not a time to act invincible or be apprehensive discussing these issues—honesty lays the groundwork for safety in everyday and even life-or-death situations. Training can expand comfort levels, and dedication to the work might be the catalyst to overcoming fears.

5

TEAM Standards, Procedures, and Bylaws

SAR/R TEAMs' use of the words "standards," "bylaws," "requirements," "guidelines," and "procedures" may differ throughout the country and the world, but all of these words refer to the same actions or issues: the requirements, rules, or principles of the TEAM. These documents are the core of the organization. Without them there would be no structure and every action from member behavior to qualifications could be decided on whim. Written standards are not only for the members' adherence but also to support the victim, the very reason behind SAR/R.

Training and certifications standards are necessary to address minimum acceptable performance and ensure safety and reliability. A few TEAMs think that simply having written standards is enough to show credibility with agencies and the public. In reality, it is the work behind the protocols and not the piece of paper that affords credibility—if written and not adhered to, standards are meaningless. Just because TEAM standards deviate across the world does not mean that one is necessarily right or wrong. Standards are contingent not only on the TEAM's geographic location and demographics, but also on the types of searches it performs.

Bylaws are the written rules that control the internal affairs and actions of an organization's members. They usually define things like the group's official name, purpose, and requirements for membership; they also govern the way the group must function as well as the roles and responsibilities of its officers. They are the legal guidelines of an organization, and the organization could be challenged in court for its actions if they are violated. United States federal tax law does not require specific language in the bylaws of most organizations. Because some nonprofit TEAMs/organizations have to file their bylaws with the Secretary of State in which they are registered or incorporated, they keep the bylaws as a separate document from their standards, or policies and procedures. Even though a TEAM incorporates all topics under one title, each section is a different matter. Sometimes bylaws are mistakenly called "standard operating procedures" or "policies." Operating procedures and policies tend to govern day-to-day operations and do not have the force of law that bylaws do. Policies and procedures provide the framework for operations. They define what the organization does and how it must be done. Requirements are the distinctive statements of what are necessary and mandatory for the TEAM.

Substance of Standards

Standards are "living" documents that are edited, modified, and updated. "Guidelines" is another word for "standards"—definitive criteria for the actions, operations, and everything relevant to the TEAM for both K9 and handler. Standards dictate the fundamental elements of an organization by establishing consistent protocols. Only through the application of its standards can a TEAM operate fairly and with credibility. Standards can be differentiated by their purpose—for example, codes of ethics, dress, behavior, certification, call-outs and deployment, and training.

Not all states have state SAR/R standards. The purpose of state standards is to develop and maintain high-quality SAR/R resources; to provide coordinated deployment mobilization and accountability, which may help stop people from self-deploying; and to provide an informational network to further professionalism. Organizations may be mandated to adopt their state SAR/R standards if they exist. Others may have the choice to use their state standards or develop their own, as long as they meet or exceed those of the state.

Those states without standards may require TEAMs to submit their written formal documents to the state's emergency services, advisory council, or similar type of authority for review and registration before being recognized as a resource. TEAMs should keep abreast of any state-imposed changes or plans to structure or restructure state standards.

If a state is contemplating establishing K9 SAR/R state standards, reviewing the standards of established SAR/R TEAMs nationwide is suggested. Information derived can be put in matrix form with each row addressing a particular element—process, training, certification, and so on—considering that terminology may differ for each. Emergency service agencies in all statewide jurisdictions can then compare the consolidated elements and decide the degree of necessity and diversity for their particular state structure. With a consensus of user agencies and those most knowledgeable, judicious state standards can be developed.

> *"Remind yourself . . . If you think that it is 'good enough,' then it is not. Good should never be the standard when you are striving for excellence." – Carol Sankar*

Membership Standards

Some TEAMS are always open to new members to increase their capabilities. Others have annual membership drives or accept new members only once or twice a year. Still others are selective, have a limited number of dedicated and skilled members, and only occasionally seek members.

TEAMs may have different types of membership (e.g., junior, supporting, full, associate), each with different roles, duties, and privileges. Not all TEAMs define their memberships and positions the same way, and not all memberships include being active in every type of training and field work.

ACCEPTABLE AGE

The acceptable ages of members vary from TEAM to TEAM. While the majority of TEAMs define 21 years as the minimum accepted age, others allow membership based on the following minimum-age/skill requirements:

- 14 if an Explorer Scout;
- 14 if committed to the Scouts for at least two years and meets other requirements; or
- 16, with restrictions and/or with the approval of the sheriff's department.

Some TEAMs allow younger members only in training sessions, and others set 18 as the minimum age. Regardless, all those under legal age must have written parental approval.

While most TEAMs do not have a maximum age limit because highly trained, non-field personnel may be needed, a few give a maximum age of 55 years for prospective members.

PHYSICAL FITNESS

Physical fitness tests (PFT) also differ from TEAM to TEAM, with most requiring a doctor's approval for the individual's ability to walk or run a distance or complete other physical tasks. The American Society for Testing and Methods (ASTM) Search and

Rescue, Equipment, Maintenance and Training Standards are incorporated in some TEAM standards.

Some TEAMs:

- adopt the PFT standards set by their state;
- utilize an established pack test from another organization that is compatible with their particular location and type of search missions;
- abide by the USDA wildland firefighter pack test, which includes three levels, dependent upon the member's position:
    1. Arduous / pack test: 3-mile hike with 45-pound pack in 45 minutes.
    2. Moderate / field test: 2-mile hike with 25-pound pack in 30 minutes.
    3. Light / walk test: 1-mile hike in 16 minutes for office and occasional field work.
- develop their own PFT; or
- implement other types of PFTs, with aerobics fitness as one example: a 1.5-mile run or speed walk within time frames adjusted according to age and sex.

Physical capability to negotiate rugged terrain may be required of both handlers and dogs. In certain areas of the world, tests might be performed on snowshoes or skis. Whatever the PFT requirements, TEAMs must understand that injuries can occur. Signed liability waivers are routine.

Small TEAMs with a limited number of K9s may structure their PFT standards to accommodate long-standing, experienced handlers who can no longer navigate steep slopes or rugged terrain. Those K9 teams are fielded only in areas within handler and dog limitations. That way the TEAM does not lose a skillful member and an operational K9.

MEMBERSHIP DUES AND EXPENSES

Membership dues may be collected monthly or annually. Annual dues that run from $10 to $100 may change as the need for funds increases or decreases. Some TEAMs that charge an application fee apply it to the applicant's first-year membership dues. Not all TEAMs have annual dues, for a variety of reasons. Some receive funding from their county, state emergency management agency (EMA), or the agency to which they are affiliated. Others receive grants, have fundraising events, or host/conduct seminars that help bring money into the organization. And some TEAMs do not charge membership dues out of concern for retaining members or attracting new ones.

Liability insurance is by the far most prominent expense for TEAMs. Other expenses may be TEAM uniforms or shirts, administrative costs, call-out systems, assistance with costs related to searches, sending members to seminars, and purchasing or repairing equipment. TEAMs that issue expensive, specialized equipment may require deposits from members using the equipment. All equipment, or dogs, purchased with TEAM funds belong to the TEAM—not the handler in control of it.

A TEAM may decide to consider consistent payment of dues along with good attendance records when qualifying members' voting rights—being a "member in good standing" goes a long way in these TEAMs. This policy helps with the politics of a TEAM by keeping decision making within the hands of those who are dedicated to training and doing the work. In the event a committed member falls upon hard times, his or her TEAM may want to consider applying a dues-exemption clause.

OTHER POTENTIAL MEMBERSHIP STANDARDS

Following are a variety of inclusions I have seen in the membership standards of different TEAMs worldwide. The applicant must:

- have family support,
- have considerable resistance to stress,

- have the premise of good sense,
- have own transport,
- live within a reasonable traveling distance to the primary response areas,
- be able to financially cover the costs of uniforms and equipment,
- have good outdoor equipment,
- be a team player,
- not use illegal drugs or misuse prescription medications,
- be available every day, around-the-clock,
- not have alcohol dependency,
- be able to receive permission from his or her employer to respond to search efforts, and
- be a legal citizen of the country in which the TEAM operates.

IMPORTANT ISSUES FOR CONSIDERATION IN MEMBERSHIP AND CODE OF CONDUCT STANDARDS

Besides addressing TEAM officers and their duties, voting rights, membership requirements, new member applicants, certification standards, and evaluator standards, TEAMs should consider the following issues as potential subjects for standardization.

ISSUES IN MEMBERSHIP STANDARDS

- Should a handler and his or her dogs be allowed to become a member of an additional SAR/R TEAM?
- Should a K9 team be allowed to respond to a search independently of its TEAM?
- What length of time should a member be given to train his or her K9 before testing and becoming certified or the dog being washed from the TEAM?
- What are provisions for the suspension or revocation of the certification of a dog team?

- How many training sessions should a probationary member be required to attend during a certain period?
- What are reasons for denial of an application or full membership?
- How long should a denied applicant's paperwork be kept and what happens to it after that period?
- What standards should be in place to address members working under difficult circumstances, in challenging weather and terrain, and for long periods?
- Will members be reimbursed for expenses? If so, which ones?
- What standards should be in place regarding concealed-carry or open-carry weapons at training and on missions?

There are always exceptions to rules that should be spelled out in the TEAM's membership standards. For example, a probationary member who has a trained SAR/R dog may be allowed to take the K9 certification test before advancing to full-member status as long as he or she is active in TEAM training and learning the TEAM's mandatory requirements. In a situation such as this, most TEAMs would still stipulate that the prospective handler and dog be paired with a full member if allowed to search.

ISSUES IN CODE OF CONDUCT STANDARDS

- What are considered unacceptable actions of a member when on a search, at a training session, or at a TEAM meeting?
- What rules should be in place for members drinking alcohol in a public place while in uniform or appearing in uniform in a bar?
- Should there be regulations prohibiting a member to smoke or chew tobacco/spit in a search area or during a training session?
- What rules should be in place regarding members' condition after marijuana use in states/countries where it is legal?

- How should the TEAM code of conduct handle personal hygiene issues?
- What standards should be in place regarding members' use of profanity and racial or ethnic slurs, and engagement in sexual harassment, or with pornographic or obscene materials?
- How much time should pass between conviction of a misdemeanor or felony crime and application or membership status?
- What are the rules related to use of cameras, cell phones, and video- and audio-recording devices during search operations, and what rules govern transmission of such information and data? What behavior is acceptable and what is prohibited with respect to social media, email, photographs of injured or deceased victims, and so on?
- Should a member who receives a citation(s) for driving while intoxicated or driving under the influence be disciplined by the TEAM and, if so, to what degree?
- How should the matter of a member's destruction of another's property be handled?
- Should members be allowed to use emergency lights or sirens when responding to a search? (Use must be in compliance with state and local laws.)
- What actions should the TEAM take when TEAMmates believe a prospective member or full member has exhibited unethical behavior, or inappropriate or grievous conduct, whether it relates to the TEAM or is unrelated to the TEAM?
- What policy should be in place for members collecting any items, matter, or substance visible or tangible—soil, remnants, pieces of remains—from a search/crime scene before it being released by the agency and with or without the agency's approval?
- Should members be required to attend business meetings?
- What, and what number of, events, meetings, and training sessions should members be required to participate in?

- Should members be permitted to attend other TEAMs' training sessions and/or functions? (Some TEAMs do not permit this because of politics, not getting along, or wanting to maintain an elite appearance.)
- What should member conduct consist of during training sessions and searches?
- Should there be disciplinary action for a member who spreads unsubstantiated rumors about a TEAMmate or a TEAMmate's dog?

ISSUES IN MEMBER DRESS CODE STANDARDS

- Should there be rules regarding the wearing of uniforms and what should they be? At all TEAM trainings? Only on searches and at social functions? Other times?
- What are rules regarding the appearance of uniforms, cleanliness, and location of any TEAM patches?
- Should members be permitted to wear certification patches or pins issued by another organization?
- How should standards address specifics in types, colors, and sizes of backpacks, hip packs, and other equipment?

Standards for Training and Certifications

Standards should address all types of training and certifications required for the TEAM.

Understanding the Incident Command System (ICS) should be mandatory for all TEAMs. In addition to courses found on the Internet, many organizations offer a variety of programs based on the American Standards and Testing Methods (ASTM) framework and SAR technician training. Along with local, state, and national organizations, a variety of agencies offer programs worldwide—for example, the Federal Emergency Management Association (FEMA); the National Search and Rescue Program in Canada (NSP); the Royal Canadian Air Force (RCAF); Berkshire Lowland Search and Rescue (BLSAR) in the United Kingdom;

the National Association for Search and Rescue (NASAR); Rescue International (RI); International Search and Rescue Group (INSARG)—and others.

Another course required in some TEAM standards is the Community Emergency Response Team (CERT). Sponsored by FEMA, the course involves 21 hours of training plus a simulated disaster drill. Topics include the following:

- hazard identification and disaster preparedness,
- ICS and team organization,
- fire safety and suppression,
- light search and rescue,
- simple triage,
- disaster medical operations,
- terrorism awareness,
- disaster psychology and emotional impacts, and
- a comprehensive final drill.

While a very good program, CERT does not address all necessary SAR/R elements.

In 2004, the National Incident Management System (NIMS), an outgrowth of the Department of Homeland Security (DHS) in the United States, released required curricula that replaced the Incident Management System and became a national system with Incident Command System (ICS) courses as a cornerstone. These courses are not only for FEMA-activation response, but also so that all involved, at any level, have some idea of resource qualifications. NIMS courses are available online and most SAR/R members must now take the following five courses:

1. ICS 100: Introduction to the Incident Command System
2. ICS 200: ICS for Single Resources and Initial Action Incidents

3. ICS 700: National Incident Management System (NIMS): An Introduction

4. ICS 800: National Response Framework: An Introduction

5. ICS 809: Emergency Support Function (ESF) #9: Search and Rescue

NIMS courses have been "refreshed" several times since their inception, and they may go through other modifications or additional courses may be added. Furthermore, FEMA has developed "Typed Resource Definitions: Search and Rescue Resources."[1] This is a national credentialing system for disasters, based on FEMA's working groups' criteria. This system can document and verify the identity and FEMA qualifications of emergency responders, including their education, training, and certifications. It has been developed to assist emergency managers and responders from different jurisdictions and disciplines to better work together in responding to national emergencies and disasters. Note that complying with the resource-definition qualifications and having completed the above NIMS courses does not grant automatic access to any search location or disaster site.

Characteristics of typical search areas dictate the type of training responders need. Although urban TEAMs may have members skilled in wilderness training—such as low-angle rescue, rope rescue, or swift-water training—their focus will be on specifics encountered in metropolitan and residential locations. That training may be unlike training in wilderness and rural settings.

Some urban training skills may include:

- safety training for handlers working with K9s in traffic- and crime-filled areas;
- working in close proximity to police, citizens, and media;
- working through noise and commotion;

- searching through highly contaminated locations;
- searching biohazardous receptacles and drug houses;
- dealing with constant obstacles and changes in wind patterns;
- understanding building airflow patterns;
- safety training for approaching strange dogs and breaking up dog fights; and
- being educated on search strategies for the vast complexity of places in which a person can hide or be concealed—both humanmade and natural.

In contrast, wilderness-focused TEAMs may list the following types of training and skills:

- mountaineering and wilderness-safety training;
- survival skills;
- low-angle and high-angle rescue and rope skills;
- helicopter safety and rescue techniques;
- water and wildfire search and rescue/recovery;
- avalanche, rockslide, and mudslide training;
- weather pattern behavior;
- animal trap release; and
- predator safety.

In addition, support resources are not readily available in wilderness areas, so advanced medical training, victim extrication, packaging, and transport, as well as confined-space search and rescue skills may also be needed.

In both wilderness and urban areas, being certified in cardiopulmonary resuscitation (CPR) is sufficient for some TEAMs, but an American Red Cross Emergency Response Card for certification in Basic First Aid or Medical First Responder could be required by others. Training in bloodborne pathogens and vector-borne diseases are other possibilities. Searches, wherever they are, necessitate proficiency in a great variety of skills. Some TEAMs have wisely addressed a wide range of prospects and scenarios in their TEAM standards.

IMPORTANT ELEMENTS FOR CONSIDERATION IN TRAINING STANDARDS

Important, and in some cases vital, factors are occasionally overlooked in TEAM training. For instance, training about animal traps and how to safely release them was mentioned as a requirement in wilderness search. However, this knowledge may also be important in rural areas, in addition to safety awareness of poisonous bait that may be scattered or camouflaged for varmints and other destructive wildlife, or pest spraying on agricultural land. Other training issues TEAMs should consider include:

- spotting booby traps and drug sites,
- boat safety,
- emergency response to terrorism,
- dealing with deceased victims,
- dealing with stress reactions and psychosocial emergencies,
- emergency scene evaluation,
- self-decontamination procedures,
- fire-scene safety,
- knowledge of victim psychology,
- visual man-tracking training,
- sign-cutting skills,
- helicopter safety—loading and unloading,
- understanding lost and missing persons behavior,
- critical incident stress training, and
- ability to translate field activities onto a command post map,

Another issue to consider for TEAMs with branches or divisions of their TEAM in other parts of the state or country are standards related to oversight. Monitoring member compliance with training, as well as member proficiency, must be addressed, otherwise branches and divisions can operate independently—by their own rules—and only share the TEAM name.

Note that K9 Urban Search and Rescue (USAR) teams, for disaster situations, require an immense amount of training related to specific subjects that differ from the knowledge required to search for a lost or missing person in a non-catastrophic environment. (See chapter 32 in this book for more information on the requirement for this type of team.)

IMPORTANT ISSUES FOR CONSIDERATION IN TRAINING AND CALL-OUT READINESS STANDARDS

TEAMs may want to address minimum training attendance and meeting requirements before a member is placed on the call-out roster to ensure all teams called are well-informed and prepared for a mission. While some TEAMs require a specific number of training hours each week, monthly or quarterly, others require a percentage of time, which includes participation in events. Following are some issues TEAMs should consider relative to call-outs and training:

- Will all members be included in call-outs, or only certain members?
- How many hours should pass between a member consuming alcohol or smoking marijuana (if legal) and responding to a search?
- What is appropriate dress for training sessions?
- Should members' family or friends be allowed to attend training sessions?

Standards may also address the deployment of a team that has not yet been certified but is almost certified. This provision should state what areas that team would be allowed to search and that such a search would be done only with the consent of the incident commander or agency in charge of the search effort. Note that the requesting agency may not be the agency in charge; this sometimes happens on multi-jurisdictional searches and can create problems.

TEAM Standards for K9s

TEAMs have K9 standards that may include breed type. Some TEAMs are breed specific, accepting only pure-bred dogs—domestic or imported. Others may require dogs based on size, such as TEAMs that require medium-sized dogs, or that stipulate dogs at least 15 inches (38 cm) tall at the shoulders. Certain breeds might be prohibited by some TEAMs, while others allow all types, including mixed breeds. Furthermore, a few TEAMs limit their membership by search discipline or whether the dog will be a single- or multipurpose K9. There are TEAMs that prohibit dogs previously attack or protection trained, or require dogs to be spayed or neutered—though some make provisions for dogs in bona fide breeding programs. TEAM standards should also address whether a bitch in estrus will be allowed at training sessions and on searches. Whether breed specific or not, all TEAMs evaluate prospective dogs for the characteristics and temperament needed for SAR/R work.

In the past, only the larger breeds (i.e., shepherds, retrievers, collies, and Doberman pinscher types) were used for SAR/R. Now, it has been accepted that some smaller breeds have the physical capabilities, a sound musculoskeletal system, essential agility, and do not have any respiratory abnormalities. Small dogs can be especially useful for disaster work when accessing small voids. However, they still must have the drive, stamina, temperament, and other qualities necessary for SAR/R.

It is worth noting that the perception and attitude of law-enforcement (LE) agencies with respect to civilian SAR/R teams are the reason some TEAMs are breed or type specific. Standards may be less about what kind of dog the TEAM likes and more about what LE in the area thinks. Friendly debates exist in SAR/R and LE about which breed is better: Labrador, German shepherd dog (GSD), Malinois, or other. Some LE agencies, handlers, and even K9 evaluators scoff at other breeds, saying handlers should train the type of dog that has been "proven effective." LE, in particular, has been accustomed to the use of traditional breeds—especially GSDs and bloodhounds—for tracking and trailing. Although a lot of agencies have changed their preconceptions, others have not. So the seriousness of the TEAM and its abilities might come into question if it shows up for a search with a dog that is not a conventional SAR/R breed. Staying with recognized SAR/R breeds can be a good decision in such instances.

TEAMs also have their own opinions about the age at which a dog should be evaluated and begin detection training. A few of the combinations of minimums and maximums are:

- at least seven weeks old but no older than four years,
- no younger than six months and not older than one year,
- at least one year old, and
- 10 weeks old but no older than three years.

National Standards

As of this writing, there is no official national certification/evaluation standard for SAR/R dog teams in the United States, although a few major organizations' certification standards, such as those of the North American Police Work Dog Association (NAP-WDA) and the National Narcotics Detection Dog Association (NNDDA) have been recognized in courts of law. FEMA has national standards, but they apply only to the canine search specialists on Urban Search and Rescue (USAR) Task Force teams in the United States. Despite not being members of FEMA, an unspecified number of handlers have duplicated this training, while others have shunned it and created what they think are better or stricter standards.

National standards have been discussed and debated over and over for years. Some people are advocates for one set of national standards, stating it would help establish credibility and interoperability. Others say that the last thing they want is for the federal government to start meddling in local affairs. Moreover, having the federal government in control of these standards would, from the perspective of past experience, create a Pandora's box of bureaucracy. Instead of focusing on proven experience and sound methods, the attention would be on previously established government protocols, terminology, and how the SAR/R TEAM standards would fit into the government pigeonholes current at the time. It would involve a myriad of government departments, directives, forms, regulations, and manuals. In addition, department heads and personnel can change frequently in the government. Regardless if the standards worked successfully, changes could be made when a new person, potentially unknowledgeable in the field, is appointed to oversee the function. In addition, the geographic diversity of the United States and inclusion of all disciplines along with their unique pertinent elements is problematic. What works well in a desert environment would be inapplicable in high-elevation locations or swamps. Although some states have state standards, others do not for various reasons—one of which may be because the counties or territories want to retain their autonomy.

Some handlers wonder if regional testing standards might better reflect the climate and terrain within the deployment range of specific TEAMs. The question then arises: What would constitute a region? FEMA has divided the United States into 10 regions. Five of these have both coastal water borders and far inland states. Regions within a state can have similar matters of contention. For example, California has four main regions that have extremely different terrains—from the Bay Area to altitudes of 10,000 feet in the Sierra Mountains. The same applies to Texas's seven regions, from bayous and swamps to desert and mountains. Would regional certifications require teams to be certified in each of the terrains? Also, who would oversee the correct implementation and verification of compliance with those standards without egos or politics becoming involved? Several states include over 100 counties—Texas has 254—and each county has its own government. With this in mind, agreement on a set of regional standards could possibly be ill-informed and based on subjective opinion.

In 2005, the Scientific Working Group on Dog and Orthogonal Detector Guidelines (SWGDOG), a partnership of local, state, federal, and international agencies—including private vendors, law enforcement, and first responders—was formed.[2] The group worked to establish a consensus of best practices for the use of detection dog teams to improve the consistency and performance of deployed teams. Not all veteran instructors/TEAMs follow every SWGDOG general guideline but have their own excellent standards and certification-testing requirements. However, the working group has publicly given credence to methods and principles embraced by many SAR/R dog handlers and instructors for years but that have been disregarded as misguided by others. Criteria of K9 team certification and proficiency will be addressed in chapter 21, Certifications.

Part II

Canine Abilities and Scent Detection

6

Evaluating Puppies
and K9 Selection

The dog/puppy evaluation process determines whether a specific puppy or dog is suited for SAR/R. It is important that the evaluator's perception of a potential SAR/R dog is based on reality, not merely what the evaluator expects or wants to be true. When selecting a dog, consideration should also be given to the handler's experience in managing and training that type of dog, the dog's size and weight, and the handler's ability to carry the dog back to base camp if it is injured in the field.

All breeds have superior scenting ability to humans and are capable of scent discrimination, but some are not compatible with SAR/R work. The shape of the head, muzzle, and throat of boxers, bulldogs, Boston terriers, and other brachycephalic breeds are prone to obstructive and difficult breathing. Although boxers were used for military work during World War II, their jobs were as messenger dogs, pack carriers, attack dogs, and guard dogs. They were not used for scent work. The breed of dog you choose also depends on state laws and city ordinances, which sometimes conflict. A breed, or even mixes of that breed, may be listed as banned, declared dangerous, potentially dangerous, or vicious. Another vital issue to consider while evaluating a dog for SAR/R is the dog's insurability: your insurance company may designate certain breeds as unable to qualify for liability coverage.

A dog's breed does not ensure she will be suited for SAR/R, nor does a dog's sex. The breed chosen often comes down to handler preference, and it has not been proven that one sex works better than the other. When discussing essential SAR/R dog characteristics, "drive"—the word most SAR/R instructors use to define the dog's level of motivation—comes to the forefront. The term "drive," as it is used in dog training, is a deviation from behavioral scientists' understanding of the dog's desire or impulse to do something. Dog trainers are subjective in their descriptions of what a dog exhibits in her actions, but these descriptions do not usually explain what is motivating the dog. According to some animal behaviorists at Animal Behavior Associates, the terms "instinct" and "drive" have mostly fallen out of use in the scientific community as they have "not added to our understanding of behavior."[1] However, some ethologists (animal behaviorists) disagree with that statement.

Drives

In their article "The Trouble with Drives," Dr. Daniel Estep and Dr. Suzanne Hetts state there are several problems with drive theory as a way of explaining and predicting behavior.[2] The authors go on to say that psychologists and animal behaviorists stopped using the theory to explain behavior 40 years ago. The idea of "drives" as developed by psychologists was to explain how behavior was motivated or energized and how it changed from time to time. The two major reasons this way of thinking has changed are, one, a dog does not store and then release energy for a specific behavior; and two, the use of the word "drive" oversimplifies often-complex behaviors.

Studies of dog temperaments have not identified all-inclusive traits like Prey, Hunt, or Play Drives, and which behaviors in dogs seem to cluster together. There are quite a few differing opinions on what is and is not a drive, and the number of them a dog possesses.

Drive-level interpretations can also be controversial. What one person may consider a very good drive may be described as "low" by another. A dog's ascribed drive level can be inaccurate if only one motivating object is used to test it, and that object is whatever the person doing the evaluation offers rather than what the dog likes. Looking at the situation from the standpoint of judging a human's motivation makes it clearer. A person motivated by money will work for hours on end for a monetary reward. But what happens when the money-motivated person's reward changes to a piece of broccoli? Would the person continue working as hard?

Some instructors and TEAMs insist that a dog without a "Ball Drive" will not make a good detection dog. They may hold fast to this belief although a dog may have a Food Drive that matches the intensity of another dog's "Ball Drive." To be accurate, there is no "Ball Drive," which is really a manifestation of Prey Drive or Play Drive. Prey Drive is evoked by movement—the chasing of a thrown ball or toy in addition to the tug or "kill," the vigorous shaking of the object. In SAR/R, Prey Drive alone—excitement caused by movement—will not be sufficient because in SAR/R, there is no movement for the dog to chase. A dog with very strong Prey Drive may be content to chase something but not pursue it if it disappears from sight. In SAR/R, the dog must also have a strong Hunt Drive, which is the dog's determination to find an object. The type of primary motivation determines the level of Hunt Drive in a given dog. Primary motivators are things like food and water, but once a dog is given a special reward for a behavior (the find), that reward can become a primary motivator.

Hunt Drive can also be exhibited by a dog that likes to:

- rip toys apart (in the wild this behavior marks the conclusion of the hunt—the kill);
- shake toys/objects (this is also a display of the kill); and

- chase objects—including pulling on a leash to catch something (this is interfaced with Prey Drive as going after movement);
- pounce or leap on toys (as in a surprise "attack"); and
- carry things in her mouth (showing she has conquered and possesses the object).

In addition to Play, Hunt, and Prey Drives, dogs have a variety of other drives, including Praise Drive, Pack Drive, and Food Drive. Many of the drives are interlaced with each other. Praise Drive, for example, has also been called both Pack Drive and Retrieve Drive—the desire of the dog to bring prey back to the pack. Dogs displaying a high level of Pack Drive:

- play with people and other dogs,
- catch and retrieve items,
- are social and obey,
- want to please their owner, and
- read their owner's body language very well.

Food Drive is self-explanatory. It is one of the strongest instincts and drives a dog has and is part of both Hunt and Prey Drives. A food-driven dog is not one that has been starved or is given food only when she accomplishes a particular task, but rather a dog that loves food treats at all times and can maintain as high a drive when working for treats as one that wants a ball or toy reward. Thus, Prey or Hunt Drives can be evaluated by the dog chasing or searching for something and being rewarded with a food treat. It is easy to see how these different drives can overlap—and can determine what we use to motivate our dogs.

Whatever motivates the dog must be sufficient to sustain her behavior intensity in adverse conditions. Consider Play or "Ball" Drives after an exhausting search—does the dog really want to run and chase, or does she just want possession of the ball? Does that change the dog's "Ball Drive" to one of being content to simply receive the reward, as a food-driven dog works for her reward, a treat?

While it is necessary to observe these drives in prospective SAR/R dogs, more likely the "outcome" of testing for drives will be determined by what motivator is used and how the tests are carried out. This, of course, does not completely explain why a dog behaves as she does. Kevin George, a world-renowned K9 instructor from Edmonton, Alberta, Canada, had an incredible way of showing dogs how to release a drive that was for some reason inhibited or not evident at first.[3] At a National Association for Search and Rescue (NASAR) conference in the 1990s, Kevin's course began with only a small number of attendees. After each break the attendance grew, until it was standing-room only at the end. A few handlers, brave enough to speak out in front of their peers, said their dogs did not have a strong Play Drive. After only minutes in front of the class with Kevin, the dogs were almost bouncing off the walls with excitement for a toy. His training rules included the following. Handlers should:

- not take the word of just one trainer;
- educate themselves about training;
- "act like idiots" when motivating and praising (Kevin demonstrated what he called "tiger claws," positioning his fingers so they looked like claws to give wild belly rubs and scratches); and
- use what excites the dog to expose what she has to offer.

Sadly, Kevin passed away in 2014.

Puppy or Dog Evaluation?

When conducting puppy tests, we cannot always foretell what the puppy's adult behavior will be. Even with adult dogs, the causes of behavior are complex. This is all really about temperament. A dog's

responses, in the end, are independent of descriptions of the motivation behind her behaviors. Overly simplistic notions of drives
do not make for guaranteed predictions. Regardless of the dog's
age when tested, she may undergo behavioral changes because of
what she is or is not exposed to and how she is trained after being
evaluated. Nothing is absolute.

Dogs also have "drive thresholds" for different categories. These
are the levels of stimulation needed for a particular drive to be executed. The trainer, regardless of discipline, should work to balance
the dog's drives so the dog is not so over the top in one area that
one drive overshadows her other qualities. A dog that is extremely
ball crazy (high drive) may want quick gratification during long,
arduous searches or searches related to mass fatalities where there
are multiple victims or remains. This kind of dog may either false
alert; constantly stop working while she waits for her reward each
time she makes a "find"; or, in training, if the "victim" is holding
the ball, the excited dog may accidently bite the helper's hand in
her attempt to grab it. While this is a training issue, it can result
in frustration for a dog with such an elevated drive. At times, too,
over-the-top, frantic behavior can be due to a medical problem.

PLAYING TUG

A word of warning about playing tug with your dog. You should control the
intensity of the dog's tug, and only tug from side-to-side, not up and down.
Yanking the dog's head by tugging up and down can damage her spine.

The characteristics essential for a SAR/R dog are outlined in
evaluation tests. There are a variety of these tests available, such
as Jack and Wendy Volhard's Puppy Aptitude Test, PAWS Working Dog Evaluation, the Paws of Life Foundation Temperament
Test, and the Scientific Working Group on Dog and Orthogonal

Detector Guidelines (SWGDOG), which is for dogs 12 to 36 months old. Many more evaluation tests can be found on the Internet and elsewhere—some are liked by instructors while others are considered unfavorable.

Some handlers, including some law-enforcement handlers, staunchly believe that a dog should be at least one year old before being evaluated, saying puppies:

- can be too risky—requiring time and money for an uncertain outcome as they reach sexual maturity and may have behavioral changes;
- cannot be adequately judged for drive or nerve strength;
- are too young to show consistency; and
- are too young for elbow and hip evaluations, which are a big concern.

Proponents for testing and selecting puppies suggest otherwise, saying the following:

- Puppies can be molded for SAR/R work from the very beginning.
- When introduced and exposed to a target odor early, dogs ordinarily build commitment to the scent much faster.
- A puppy's problems and fears are usually not as deeply ingrained as those of older dogs.
- When selected early, puppies can be raised in a controlled human-dog social setting.
- When a puppy is selected her type and level of agility training can be controlled to avoid future physical problems—a one-year-old dog may have already been subjected to training that contributes to problems down the road.
- Puppies as young as 10 to 12 weeks old can be examined for their likelihood of developing dysplasia by two reliable

methods: the AIS PennHIP or Ortolani tests. But a good X-ray, even on a one-year-old dog, is not a guarantee that she will remain free of joint problems.

In addition, studies conducted with puppies have shown positive results. One of them states: "Behavioral activity of 7-week-old German shepherd puppies was tested and the activities analyzed if they could be used for predicting police efficiency of the individual. In total 206 individuals sired by 42 sires and 44 dams were used. The activities were divided into 10 tasks in which reactions and behavior of pups were scored from 0 to 5 points. All pups were tested separately from other puppies. Probability that the puppy will pass the certification was tested by a logistic regression. Of the 206 puppies, 148 passed the certification while 58 failed."[4] The study shows a three-to-one positive result validating the beliefs of handlers who prefer starting a puppy and working through the stages of development that assist in molding the dog. However, this study was limited to a few select lines of German shepherd dogs that may not represent the breed as a whole. Still, it shows promising results in some dogs.

An important piece of the puppy/dog-evaluation puzzle is understanding the characteristics of the chosen breed to determine how young that type of dog can be when tested to develop a good picture of her potential. An evaluation checklist covers the requisites, but it does not tell all about the dog. Many highly accomplished handlers look deeper when they perform portions of the tests. With years of knowledge and understanding of detection work, some have developed shortcuts and can usually make sound judgments without completing each step of the test.

Observing newborn puppies as they develop until they are at least eight weeks old and ready for re-homing is enlightening— even if you can visit only once a week. With each visit, you learn something new about each little one, and when the puppies are six weeks old, you can actually begin some evaluations. Evaluations should be repeated until you make your final selection. In other instances, you must rely on what the breeder or litter owner has noticed. Although they may not be knowledgeable in assessing characteristics, they can furnish their observations.

Insights into Stages of Early Development

Puppies raised in a litter atmosphere, with a mother that interacts and teaches them, can develop differently than puppies that have been abandoned, re-homed too early, or whose mother has died.

THE FIRST DAYS

The mother dog begins to help her puppies develop their sense of smell when they are around three days old. Observance of several litters illustrated that from the moment the last pup was born, the mother, after eating or relieving herself, always returned to a position right next to her litter until the third day. On or right after the third day, whenever the mother returned to the whelping box, she would lie down farther away from the litter—in some cases as far as the box would allow her to move. This made the puppies use their sense of smell to locate her to nurse.

THE TRANSITIONAL PERIOD

In the early developmental stages, the puppies' transitional period is between 13 and 20 days old. At this point, they open their eyes, can hear, begin to respond to taste, and are becoming mobile. At this point, they should be picked up, held, petted and cuddled, and talked to daily—admittedly many are held and given affection before that. Different objects like soft toys, knotted towels, and so on should be placed in their whelping box to stimulate their senses.

THE AWARENESS PERIOD

The awareness period, a time of very rapid sensory development and the onset of socialization, begins when puppies are 21 to 23

Figure 6.1 Spirit, in the middle, at five weeks old, staying with the human-remains training aids while others roam.

days old. Still with their mother and littermates, the puppies' learning begins as they use their senses of sight and hearing. During this period, new things may be added for them to explore, but the puppies should not be overwhelmed with changes. Puppies should be allowed to become accustomed to each unusual encounter in their growing world as they experience new areas such as different surfaces like carpet, wood, concrete, grass, and so on. It may be less stressful for each if two littermates are placed together on new surfaces.[5] As early as five weeks old, a puppy can be introduced to the odor of human decomposition if she will be trained for that discipline. Her reactions may vary as some dogs have an aversion to the odor and recoil or refuse to go near it.

LEARNING HER SPECIES

At 21 to 49 days, the puppy learns she is a dog and displays common canine characteristics and behaviors: chasing, biting, barking, fighting, body postures, and playing.

Puppy Evaluation Fundamentals

Along with the various established tests, a different one to evaluate problem solving is worth conducting. Place the puppy in an upright cardboard box or lightweight plastic bin to see her reaction. Does she just sit there and cry, or does she solve the problem and find her way out by climbing on and flipping the box? Another take on this technique is to turn the box over the puppy but put a small rock or similar object down to prop up one edge an inch or so, providing an escape route. Again, does she figure it out and come out confident?

Another necessary trait test covered in the evaluation process is "nerve strength." Drive and nerve strength are two different things. SAR/R dogs must have good nerve strength, which means they should not be skittish. Although they may be startled by a loud, sudden noise, they should not be frightened to the point of not continuing with what they were doing. This is important due to the unforeseen situations with which they will have to contend. However, recent studies by canine behaviorists and veterinarians have discovered that even K9 combat veterans with strong nerve strength may develop post-traumatic stress syndrome (PTSS) if subjected to exceptionally loud noises from traumatic explosions. Some K9 veterans work right through the noise without any effect, while others have to undergo a re-acclimation period to determine whether they can be retrained to return to duty. It seems sensible to expose dogs gradually to loud noises before reaching the volume or intensity of what they may encounter.

The bottom line is that any dog can wash out, develop health problems, or not become a superb search dog despite having passed evaluations, training, and testing. The question then is whether the problem is the training or the dog. In reality, it is probably a little of both. Consider:

- what the dog was exposed to after being evaluated;
- the atmosphere in which the dog is living;

- the handler's character, motivation, and attitude;
- the competency of the trainer (the best dog partnered with a new handler or a poor instructor may not meet expectations); and
- support or oppression from the TEAM. Politics and egos can also play a role in a dog's outcome.

Some handlers—mostly experienced ones—believe a puppy or young dog should be chosen for a specific type of detection work. The definitive traits needed strongly influence their selection during the evaluation process. New handlers may want help to just find a good SAR/R candidate.

There is much talk about selective breeding—choosing dogs to amplify desirable traits and diminish unwanted ones—in an attempt to provide handlers with the perfect SAR/R dog: one with physical and behavioral excellence. While that type of breeding is good, and can be advantageous, it must be noted that behavior is not wholly genetic nor is it absolutely acquired. There can still be problems, even if, for example, before breeding the bitch and sire are X-rayed to screen for subluxation—a deformity of the hip joint that progresses into dysplasia. More than one gene location and interaction is involved and can skip generations, or affect only some of the puppies in a litter. Specially bred dogs can be expensive, and not all handlers have the financial means to purchase dogs from breeders, while many very good SAR/R dogs are rescues from shelters or come to their handlers through newspaper ads. Whatever the age of the dog or puppy, the final selection should be based on sound belief and observations, not only emotions.

Once a puppy or dog is selected, training in a variety of areas begins (e.g., housebreaking, what to chew or not chew, leash adaptation). However, before you begin any type of scent training, be sure you understand how the dog's olfactory system works.

7

The Dog's Nose

Humans are usually not aware of using their sense of smell unless an odor is especially good or bad. It is rarely their main source of information. On the other hand, a dog's world is primarily made up of *layers* of complex odors. When out for a walk and sniffing almost everything in sight, the dog is "reading his newspaper." Pulling him away quickly is the same as someone yanking a newspaper out of a person's hands when she is in the middle of reading an article.

Humans possess approximately six million olfactory receptors. A dog possesses up to 300 million. The portion of the dog's brain devoted to analyzing smells is 40 times greater than that of a human being. The internal fluid dynamics of the dog's nasal cavity are intricate. When he is sniffing, a unique nasal airflow pattern develops that allows for both chemical sensing and respiratory air intake. When the dog inhales, a fold of tissue inside the nostrils separates the air intake into different paths—one for olfaction, which breaks down the odor, and the other for respiration. Exactly how the odor molecules reach the olfactory organ without being filtered by the respiratory airway is not well understood. About 12 percent of the air a dog breathes in travels into a recessed area at

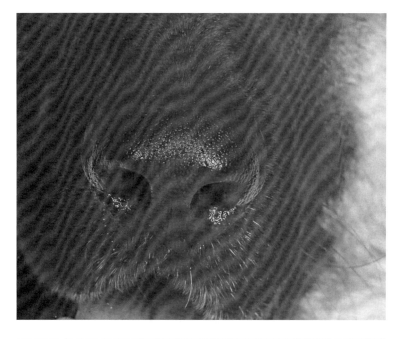

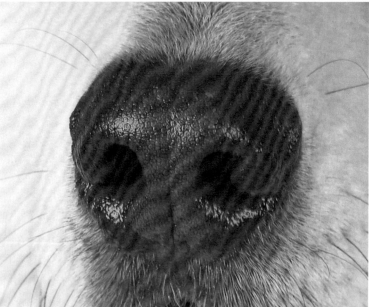

Figure 7.1 Each dog's nose is as unique as a fingerprint and can be used to identify it. (Photos courtesy of John Hnath)

the back of the nose designated for smell. The rest of the incoming air takes a different path and goes to the lungs.

The act of scent detection is a very complicated process that involves odor reception, recognition, and location. When a dog sniffs an object or area, he is not seeking or responding to one specific odor. His olfactory sensors are actively interacting with his scent-brain to create a virtual picture. Detection dogs are trained to find a specific scent picture. Scent molecules trapped in the mucus membrane and olfactory receptors within the dog's nose are identified by shape and send electrical signals to his brain for emotional processing of olfactory stimuli. When the information reaches the brain, it is analyzed for particular odorants and odorant mixtures and either identified as containing the target odor or not. The dog's ability to discriminate between complex mixtures is called "odor layering." It is the reason he can still detect odors that have been masked by more pungent substances. It has been determined that although dogs can detect odor concentrations of one to two parts per trillion, there is a distinction between detection and recognition/identifying an odor.[1]

When humans exhale through their noses, that air exits the same way it was inhaled and forces out any incoming odors. With dogs, exhaled air goes out through the slits on the sides of their noses, making it possible for them to have a steady stream of incoming air for perhaps one minute while searching for an odor. This also allows fewer scent molecules in the air or on the ground to be disturbed. In addition, dogs possess a second olfactory system—the vomeronasal organ, also known as Jacobson's organ. This is a sensory receptor inside the nasal cavity that opens into the upper palate just behind the front teeth. It has two fluid-filled sacs that enable dogs to smell and taste simultaneously. While its primary function is to detect pheromones signaling mating readiness and sex-related details, it is also sensitive for the detection of nonvolatile chemicals and other normally undetectable odors.[2]

Figure 7.2 The Flehmen response.

Jacobson's organ is where chemical messages and pheromones—the chemical substances secreted in blood, glandular discharge, urine, and feces—are received; it sends neuronal signals to the accessory olfactory bulb and then to the brain. When you see a SAR/R dog tasting the water while searching for a drowned victim or chewing a plant in the vicinity of a burial site, he may be using his Jacobson's organ to help detect the target odor.

However, when scenting pheromones, dogs, unlike some other animals, do not usually exhibit the Flehmen response. This is an exhibition of lifting the head and curling the upper lip and is frequently seen in horses and cats. It is referred to as a grimace, smile, or sometimes a "stinky face." Instead, many dogs, male and female, demonstrate a response called "tonguing," which is when they push their tongues rapidly against the roof of their mouths and sometimes chatter their teeth. Profuse foam may collect on the upper lip. This response may help move compounds into the vomeronasal organ and often occurs when dogs lick a urine spot or taste the air.

While there are two passages in a dog's nasal cavity—the olfactory path and the oral path—both are connected to and driven by the lungs, so the dog must close his mouth to sniff. A panting dog cannot produce the air pressure across the nose required for sniffing. As a result, his scenting ability is compromised by as much as 40 percent when he uses the air to cool himself. Scenting capabilities are also affected if the nasal membranes are dry from atmospheric conditions, dehydration, smoke, or other elements. Therefore, it is important to keep your detection dog hydrated. If your dog is licking his nose during a search, he may need water.

Dogs can wiggle their nostrils independently. This ability, along with what is called the "aerodynamic reach" of each nostril, helps them determine into which nostril an odor arrived. Comparing the strength of the scent received in each nostril, they can calculate the direction of increasing concentration. This can be seen when a dog picks up an odor and zigzags back and forth in the scent cone—an action called quartering the wind—and follows the scent to the source.

K9s' Other Senses

Dogs have other senses that surpass those of humans, and others that are not as developed.

HEARING

Hearing is the dog's second best of the five senses. Dogs are better at localizing the direction of a sound than humans. They also can hear much higher and lower frequencies and have amazing sound recognition. Dogs have a frequency range between 40 and 60,000 Hz; humans have a range between 20 and 20,000. Because their hearing range is so much greater than ours, the pitch and amplitude of a sound may be acceptable to us but uncomfortable for dogs. The dog's excellent hearing can deteriorate with age.

TASTE

Taste is the least developed of the dog's senses, although it is closely related to smell. The dog can taste the difference between salty, sweet, sour, bitter, and umami, but they have fewer taste buds than humans. As Dr. Stanley Coren points out, dogs' taste buds for the basic flavors are not distributed equally across the tongue. Sweet is mostly tasted across the front and side portions, while the rear portion of the tongue is most sensitive to bitter tastes. This is perhaps why there can be a problem when trying to give a dog a pill or other medication, since it is usually placed far back in the dog's mouth. While most people will not eat something that has a "bad" odor, dogs are the opposite—they tend to like things that smell bad to most people, and the stronger a food smells, the more they try to eat it, regardless of how it tastes. They often gobble food items down before they have time to chew them or taste them.

VISION

Compared to humans, dogs see approximately 6 percent less detail, and their perception of color is limited. The belief that dogs only see in black and white is incorrect. A 2013 study suggests dogs customarily discriminate between objects based on their hue.[3] However, dogs have only two types of color receptors rather than three like humans. Roughly, a dog sees like a person who is red-green colorblind. Dogs see shades of yellow, blue, and green, but when those colors are combined, they can appear as grayish-brown, light yellow, grayish-yellow, light blue, and dark blue.

The dog's ability to focus on items at different distances is approximately half that of a human's. But his field of vision is wider by at least 60 percent because his eyes are set farther apart. The dog excels in night vision due to more light receptors and larger pupils than humans, and he is also much better at detecting moving objects.

TOUCH

The whiskers on a dog's face are specialized hairs called vibrissae. These hairs are embedded more deeply in the skin and have more receptor cells at their base than regular hairs. Because of this, the dog can use these hairs to detect movement, small vibrations, air currents, and objects in the dark. These hairs may explain why dogs can usually avoid eye injury. Also, the sensitivity of the whiskers may produce a reflexive aggressive response if someone blows air in the dog's face.

Hampered Capacity to Smell

Because of the dog's strong ability to detect odors, certain substances can temporarily hamper his capacity to smell. Fresh bleach, gasoline, creosote, and other strong-smelling chemicals can saturate and even burn the nasal membranes. This can affect the dog's scenting abilities for minutes or hours.

CARBON MONOXIDE AND SCENT

For years it was assumed that carbon monoxide destroyed scent and handlers should make sure vehicle engines on search sites were shut off. However, on August 26, 2002, Bill Tolhurst, chief of Special Services, Niagara County, NY, tested this premise. Tolhurst constructed a pipeline from the exhaust pipe of a vehicle directly to the bottom of a closed box. He then strategically drilled three, 0.5-inch (1.27-cm) holes in the box and allowed pressure to build inside and move the gas fumes around. After he placed a 5 × 9–inch (12.7 × 22.9–cm) freshly human-scented gauze pad on a pegboard-type shelf inside the bottom of the box, the vehicle was started and allowed to run for five minutes. The pegboard and box allowed the carbon monoxide fumes to circulate around and through the holes to saturate the scented pad.

While the box and scented pad were being prepared, three runners had been sent out—the scent target and two decoys. The K9 was offered the scent pad and then ran the trail easily and located the correct runner without a problem. This test was done three more times with different-scented gauze pads, dogs, and targets. The dog in the second test worked the trail off lead and the third one on lead. The last time the vehicle was run for 15 minutes rather than only five before the dog was given the scent pad. The two subsequent tests were also successful. Tolhurst stated this was witnessed by six people. So while carbon monoxide may have an effect on scent, these tests indicated scent is not destroyed.[4] That said, direct carbon monoxide is still a major issue. It can affect a dog's nose for a period, and, more important, it can kill a dog.

A German study was conducted on the effects of pollution on canines' ability to smell with the amount of pollution measured from the ground to 5 feet (1.5 m) high. The study indicated the highest level of pollution was approximately the same height as a German shepherd dog's nose—which is also the same level of 90 percent of vehicle exhaust pipes.[5] Ambient temperatures were not mentioned, nevertheless, the study provides an interesting fact.

Some people suggest that carbon monoxide is the reason dogs cannot trail on busy roadways. The real problem is perhaps the movement of the target scent rather than it being destroyed. Each passing vehicle produces an air current. With multiple vehicles, the scent is propelled with constantly changing air currents, circulation, and concentration. With little or no vegetation or objects for the scent molecules to adhere to, the scent movement continues in all different directions.

8

Developments in Understanding Scent

"The measure of greatness in a scientific idea is the extent to which it stimulates thought and opens up new lines of research." – Paul A.M. Dirac, The Scientific Work of George Lemaître

The words "scent" and "odor" are used interchangeably in K9 detection work to describe blends of volatile chemical compounds.

The 1972 book *Scent and the Scenting Dog*, by William G. Syrotuck, is still cited in articles today. However, Syrotuck's theory that "rafts" shed by humans are what provides scent has been refuted in the article "Specialized Use of Human Scent in Criminal Investigations."[1] In that article, the FBI finds "no supporting scientific basis" for Syrotuck's theory. Current research by the FBI and other organizations suggests that human odor is indeed more complex than Syrotuck hypothesized. Nevertheless, Syrotuck's book continues to help handlers learn how scent moves, even if his explanation of the source of scent is not scientifically supported. In this book, I will continue to use "rafts" as the historically defined word for scent.

The outer layer of skin (epidermis) sheds approximately 50 million dead epithelial cells a day, or about 35,000 to 40,000 skin cells

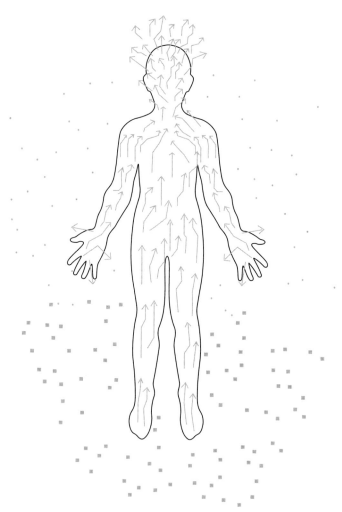

Figure 8.1 This drawing shows how rafts are released from a body into the environment.

per minute. (New studies show that the number of cells shed differs between individuals.) Each one, called a raft or scurf, is composed of bacteria catalyzed by body secretions and surrounded by a minute vapor cloud. These rafts, though dead skin cells, do not produce the odor of human decay.

Rafts are emitted freely from exposed parts of the body, and clothing does not necessarily prohibit them from being distributed. Air currents cause the rafts to escape through neck, sleeves, and other openings that, with movement, act like bellows. There is also a current of warm air, approximately one-third to one-half inch thick, that surrounds the body and travels up and over it at about 125 feet (38 m) per minute.[2]

Science and Scent

K9 scent detection is science. Scientific data validating selectivity and reliability of search dogs used to detect human scent has improved and has begun to identify several of the organic compounds in human scent. Some of the volatile organic compounds (VOCs) that make up human odor include alcohols, aldehydes, alkanes, esters, fatty acids, and ketones. These VOCs of human scent play an important role in scent association between a person and evidence. Differences in human scent have been believed to be due to genetics as well as what a person eats, his or her cultural background, cologne, and personal habits. Because eating foods such as garlic in large quantities can influence a person's body odor, researchers at the Monell Chemical Senses Center in Philadelphia explored whether changes in diet would alter and therefore mask the identity of a person's signature odor.[3] The results of the Monell studies indicate although dietary changes strongly influence odor profiles, chemical analysis can still detect the underlying "odortypes." Thus, human body odors provide a consistent, genetically determined "odorprint," like a fingerprint or DNA sample.

Ongoing research proposes that human scent is much more complex than previously believed. But data are still lacking, as is our limited understanding of how the human body creates scent. Because of this lack of information about using biological detectors (i.e., detector dogs), there have been successful legal challenges against evidence provided by detector dogs in courts of law.

In some areas, odor detection performed by dogs is still regarded as "junk science." However, continued development and implementation for best-practice guidelines for dogs should improve the use of odors as an acceptable form of forensic evidence.

Scent Durability

How long scent lasts is a matter of scientific studies, dispute, and even challenges issued among K9 handlers. Handlers have been taught the duration of human scent is subject to effects of the environment—that moisture and humidity keep rafts' bacterial growth alive and active, and dry conditions minimize that growth. It has been said that scent survives better in grassy, shaded areas than on pavement due to temperature, moisture, and the organic matter onto which scent molecules can attach. It also has been believed that scent will not survive outside for long periods. New studies and case experiences have since determined that human scent is more resilient than previously thought. Following are the results of human scent studies conducted by the FBI in 2001, 2002, and 2003.[4]

An FBI study from March 2001, using the Southern California Bloodhound Handlers Coalition, was conducted to determine the viability of human scent on arson evidence and bomb components, after those objects had been handled and detonated. The handled arson containers were burned for two minutes with 0.5 liters (0.13 US gal) of gasoline before being extinguished with water. Scent was then collected from the items using sterile gauze pads and a device called the STU-100, originally called the Scent Transfer Machine, developed by Bill Tolhurst. Two weeks later those scent pads were used for six fresh, blind trails in a split-trail format. Each of six dogs would have to indicate the presence of the matching scent by trailing to and then properly identifying the person who matched the scent. The overall combined score on trailing was 78.3 percent for positive scent matches. Of the dogs that indicated a positive match, 88.6 percent of them alerted on the correct person. There were no false-positive alerts.

Later that same year, on October 21, 2001, the FBI and Southern California Bloodhound Handlers Coalition did another study. This time it was on the feasibility of determining human scent survivability after decontaminating for biological agents. Separate target odors placed on five sheets of paper were irradiated for one hour at SteriGenics, in Tustin, California. In six tests on six trails, scent-discriminating bloodhounds were able to indicate the presence of matching scent and correctly identify the target odor, establishing that human scent could survive irradiation. Another portion of this same study was also successful when four sheets of paper were sprayed with a 10 percent solution of sodium hypochlorite to ascertain if the scent would survive. Four bloodhounds were used and all were able to indicate the matching scent. Additional test results are astonishing; two examples from these additional findings follow.

In July 2002, a pipe bomb exploded inside a car in Washington, DC, severely injuring the driver. The victim's half-brother was suspected when he left a suicide note, abandoned his car on the top level of a Metro station parking garage, and disappeared shortly thereafter. Seventeen days after the bombing, the Bureau of Alcohol, Tobacco, Firearms, and Explosives (ATF) took the FBI's K9 Human Scent Evidence Team to an unfamiliar neighborhood. With no prior knowledge of the suspect's residence, the K9 team, using scent collected from the pipe-bomb fragments, trailed to the suspect's house and alerted at the front door. The bloodhound team was then taken to the level of the suspect's vehicle still in the Metro station parking garage. In temperatures close to 100°F (37.8°C), the team trailed from the suspect's vehicle to the elevator door where the K9 alerted. When reaching the ground level, heavily contaminated by commuters, the K9 team continued to trail to a bus stop. There the K9 stopped.

Four months later, the suspect turned himself in and pleaded guilty to three felonies. He told investigators he had parked his car at the Metro station, taken the elevator, and then rode a bus out of town. The case indicates that human scent is durable on bomb fragments and in heavily trafficked urban locations.[5]

In May 2003, other blind tests were conducted. This time a bloodhound research workshop was hosted by the FBI at its academy in Quantico, Virginia. One of the tests was to evaluate the viability of aged human scent and determine if a specific subject's scent would still be detectable in his or her long-vacated previous residence. The subject had lived in the house for seven years before moving almost 2,000 miles (3,219 km) away. Six months later, scent was collected from a letter mailed by the subject from the new residence. The letter was sent through the US Postal System and irradiated at the US Army Medical Research Institute of Infectious Diseases. A bloodhound team was given the collected scent, then, starting at an intersection several houses away, indicated a matching scent and trailed to the subject's unoccupied previous residence. The results of these different tests have shown that in the time frames given, human scent retains its unique identity and is viable despite environmental influence, irradiation, heavy contamination, and aging in the field.

These tests, like others with astounding outcomes, have generated much criticism. In general, if results from a study are unexpected, the research is more likely to face criticism. Most people find it easier to accept results that confirm what they already believe. In the face of surprising findings, people often question the credibility of the teams used in the studies. Other criticisms include that there were not enough trials/studies, numbers of dogs used, variety of dog breeds, and double-blind situations, nor enough clear success or consistency. Yet many studies simply report on experiments—typically qualified as to the type—that were conducted and then published, often following a rigorous peer-reviewed, scientific process. Such studies need to be evaluated fairly for what they might contribute to understanding. Before rejecting unexpected outcomes out of hand, take a close look at the study itself to see what might be learned.

The deductions of these tests may sound improbable, but are they impossible? Can the information be used to make your TEAM better? Regardless of your answers to those questions, the new findings on scent durability and existing legal questions produce a conundrum. It is conceivable that vulnerability of K9 teams in court may increase because of unconfirmed alerts, that false hope may be given to victims' families, and that these remarkable discoveries will escalate unsubstantiated claims by glory-seeking handlers. As more studies are conducted around the world, science's answers to questions may change if additional data becomes available.

"He who never changes his opinions, never corrects his mistakes, and will never be wiser on the morrow than he is today." – Tyron Edwards, American Theologian

Part III

Instructors, Training, and Certifications

9

K9 Trainers

"Just 'cause you're following a well-marked trail don't mean that whoever made it knew where they were goin'." – Texas Bix Bender

Some TEAM K9 trainers are simply called TEAM trainers. Others are called TEAM K9 training officer, K9 training director, K9 instructor, vice-president of training, or K9 coordinator. Some titles are delineated according to search discipline—K9 director of air scent (or trailing, and so on). Some TEAMS use law-enforcement or military jargon for titles, such as commander, captain, chief, and so forth, putting emphasis on their positions in the TEAM. Those titles/ranks may sound imposing to people unfamiliar with military titles, but many civilian world titles correspond easily to those of the military: commander or chief = director, senior manager, or division head; executive officer = assistant manager or deputy director. In this book, I use the titles "trainer," "instructor," or "training instructor" to refer to K9 trainers.

Some TEAM training instructors, especially in new organizations, are given their title because they know more about dogs than others on the TEAM—or, they know more about a specific discipline from attending a seminar, so their title may include the discipline. It does not mean they are qualified instructors. This is not a criticism. Everyone has to start somewhere. As long as instructors, who have possibly learned only one way of doing something, keep an open mind and consider comments as suggestions—not challenges—they will broaden their knowledge. If a member who has attended a workshop wants to explain what he has learned but not have the instructor think he is being confrontational, the member could give the instructor his notes from the session. That member may also wish to provide copies of notes from seminars to the entire TEAM. This may open the door to discussions and additional learning opportunities—or debate about what was taught, since some instructors may provide incorrect information they believe is factual.

The question "What is a 'master' trainer and what makes him better than a trainer?" is frequently asked, sometimes with derision. Some handlers, both civilian and law enforcement, believe the "master trainer" designation is ambiguous, to put it nicely. After reviewing many schools and organizations, I find that the title is most often given to an individual who has attained a certain level of training in a specific discipline. The training criteria, however, is not standardized—it is whatever the credentialing organization deems necessary, which in some cases is quite dubious. It is important to verify—not just read—the credentials of the people conducting the courses. Do they have the background and experience to teach in the discipline of interest? Some courses seem to offer no more than the minimum training standards of SAR/R TEAMS. Once again, it comes down to the credibility of the school or organization.

People who have experience training dogs in obedience, at American Kennel Club events, in Schutzhund, agility, and the like, are helpful with some training problems, but they still need considerable training and experience in actually working search dogs before they can be true SAR/R dog instructors. Without experience in search and rescue or recovery, an instructor may not fully understand what she is teaching. She will just repeat what she has committed to memory from books or lectures, and many times that information is lacking—as the saying goes, she knows just enough to make her dangerous. Methods can be taught wrongly and problems created instead of solved. A bad instructor can ruin a good dog. The instructor should know and understand the fundamentals, training principles, and necessary building blocks to establish a strong foundation for the K9 and be able to answer questions regarding the search discipline. Not being able to immediately answer a specific question may not be that big of a problem—but not learning the correct answer is.

"Information's pretty thin stuff unless mixed with experience." –
Clarence Day

Some TEAMs require potential training instructors to provide credentials (certifications) and background about who they have trained under and the proven history of dogs they have trained. TEAMs will need to verify who someone trained under and to what degree, since claims can be misleading. Regardless of the amount of studying completed and training achieved, education ought never end for both SAR/R K9 instructors and handlers. Learning and training creates an informed opinion. What do you think? What do you know? What do you think you know? And do you know how to tell the difference between these? One is fact, one is opinion, and the other merely hearsay.

A "fact" is verifiable evidence or information. But, if not put in the proper context, the fact is meaningless. A fact used properly draws a correct conclusion. An "opinion" is a person's viewpoint or perspective of an issue not necessarily based on facts. (A "belief" is completely different—it is a conviction of personal faith, values, morality, or culture.) "Hearsay" is unverified information—not direct knowledge. However, an "informed opinion" is a judgment established on facts coupled with experience. It is an honest attempt to draw a reasonable conclusion from the facts presented.

There are wonderful K9 training instructors who understand their responsibilities and have the patience and know-how to set up training problems properly to create environments and opportunities that allow K9 teams to learn, solve problems, and fulfill the objective of the exercise. Skilled instructors know that belittling handlers does not encourage them. They know it is not necessary to shout commands all the time because a well-trained dog will respond to a whisper. It must be noted that even if you are an excellent K9 handler, you may not necessarily be a good instructor. While extremely knowledgeable, a handler may not explain things well, creating the need for constant clarification, which causes frustration for both learners and instructor. An instructor must be able to teach so students will understand.

There are many right ways to train SAR/R dogs, and instructors should be flexible and familiar with different training techniques and use what works for individual dogs. However, there are also wrong ways.

Wrong Ways to Train Dogs

Wrong ways to train dogs include rushing dogs through training (there is no fast way to train a SAR/R dog), overlooking problems (because it's "just the way that dog is" or for political or personal reasons), using physical punishment or yelling when the dog doesn't do what is wanted, and incorrect timing for rewards.

Another wrong way to train a SAR/R team, especially a novice handler/dog team, is to change from one search discipline to another in training sessions. An example is trailing exercises in one session, live disaster in the next, and then cadaver detection training in the following session. This kind of program produces confusion and disorganized learning. The focus should be on a specific issue or discipline until both dog and handler are consistent and reliable in the work.

A crucial problem in training is rewarding the dog at the wrong time. Only well-timed rewards will reinforce the desired behavior—wrong timing will not. Equally important is how you praise your dog. How a dog is praised must be addressed in the reward process and the tone of voice used when praising a dog is significant. Men especially tend to use a strong, deep voice that sounds more like an angry command rather than approval—whereas a high-pitched, enthusiastic tone will excite and encourage the dog.

Some handlers say, "the find is the dog's reward" and do not provide anything additional—praise, toy, or treat—because the dog's behavior indicates he is happy with just finding the person / odor source. But, what does the "find" really mean to the dog? Is the find a happy person who excites him, an angry victim who yells at him, or one who does not respond to his achievement? Humans have the capability to understand the psychological rewards in SAR/R work—dogs do not. Is the find or love of the work all the dog wants as a reward? Is that what he prefers? A study unrelated to SAR/R revealed this issue by way of fMRI scanner studies of 15 dogs' brains, and other tests, which have shown a range of responses and the preferences of those dogs when given reward options.[1] Based on the results of these tests, it could be beneficial to offer SAR/R K9s a choice of rewards at the find. The dogs may show what they really want, or they may like two rewards equally. Without options, the handler makes the decision for the dog—relying solely on the dog's behavior and what the handler thinks it means.

Finally, K9 instructors who learn about the different dog breeds they are working with provide better guidance. Some people think

bloodhounds do not need training because they are "instinct certified," and all they have to do is follow their dogs. While herding dogs may test and acquire a "herding instinct certification," a
SAR/R instructor should know that instinct certifications do not
apply to SAR/R dogs. All breeds and all handlers need comprehensive training to work in SAR/R!

10

Basics in K9 SAR/R Training

"There is a vast difference between the serious and the well-meaning." –
Bill Tolhurst, at a training seminar

Despite the volumes of detailed books and articles already in print,
this book would not be complete without addressing at least some
basic training components in a little more depth than what I have
already mentioned in the first section of the book.

Training

It takes two to make a K9 team—handler and dog, working together. Being a proficient and legally defensible K9 team
requires the handler to be trained too. Without that essential
training, the handler is not a SAR/R professional but someone
with a dog that can detect an odor—much as she might find her
ball. It is necessary to learn the fundamentals of SAR/R. After
learning the basics, additional training for the specific search discipline, including the particular types of areas and environments
in which the TEAM will be searching, is essential. Training in
non-K9 related subjects, as defined by each TEAM, is for the
handler's safety and competency. For example, despite global

positioning systems (GPS) being easy to use in the field, training in map and compass land navigation is still vital. Problems can occur with GPS units or GPS smartphone apps, and they may not work at all if there is no reception due to terrain features or battery problems.

The Handler

"If you're not willing to learn, no one can help you. If you're determined to learn, no one can stop you!" – Zig Ziglar, American motivational speaker

A partial list of what is necessary to be a trustworthy, reliable K9 handler follows. As a SAR/R handler, you:

- must have a strong bond with your dog;
- must keep the dog clean, healthy, and in good physical condition;
- must have patience;
- should know how to encourage your dog and properly correct unwanted behavior;
- must understand scent in terms of wind, thermals, looping, and other atmospheric conditions, along with terrain features to work with your K9 effectively;
- must learn to negotiate rough and hazardous areas and change search strategies while maintaining effective coverage;
- must be able to explain your search strategy and translate field activity onto a map;
- must be able to prioritize a search area—referred to as probability of area (POA);
- should be able to determine and articulate probability of detection (POD);
- should recognize when your dog is in a scent pool and apply the proper strategy to assist her at that time;

- should, along with your flanker, define any areas that need to be rechecked by another team and areas that still need to be covered and the reason why they were not searched—and note locations of any hazards in the area;
- must give your dog sufficient water and rest breaks;
- must recognize when your dog is stressed or has shut down and ceased working; and
- must take care of your dog first at the end of a search or training, and check her thoroughly for injuries, thorns, and stickers.

You must also, regardless of how reliable your dog's alert is, learn to read your K9's body language and know her natural alert.

SAR/R DOGS ARE NOT SERVICE DOGS

As a handler, you must be aware that a SAR/R dog is not a service dog, although some states do include SAR dogs in their definition of service dogs and make provisions for them. The Americans with Disabilities Act (ADA), however, defines service animals as:

> dogs that are individually trained to do work or perform tasks for people with disabilities. Examples of such work or tasks include guiding people who are blind, alerting people who are deaf, pulling a wheelchair, alerting and protecting a person who is having a seizure, reminding a person with mental illness to take prescribed medications, calming a person with Post Traumatic Stress Disorder (PTSD) during an anxiety attack, or performing other duties. Service animals are working animals, not pets. The work or task a dog has been trained to provide must be directly related to the person's disability. Dogs whose sole function is to provide comfort or emotional support do not qualify as service animals under the ADA.
>
> This definition does not affect or limit the broader definition of "assistance animal" under the Fair Housing Act or the broader definition of "service animal" under the Air Carrier Access Act. Some state and local laws

also define service animal more broadly than the ADA does. Information about such laws can be obtained from the State Attorney General's office.[1]

Service animals receive special treatment, including flying in-cabin on airlines. Unfortunately, there has been considerable corruption of the term "service animal" by people referring to their pets as such. A few airlines extend in-cabin access to SAR/R dogs when they are being deployed or going to a training seminar—other airlines do not. But the fraudulent use of this classification has caused airlines to enforce new rules in many cases. It is most upsetting that there are K9 handlers who abuse the privilege, some to the extent that they have their dogs sit on airline seats rather than the floor where they belong, and even go so far as to take and post photos of these bad behaviors that are disrespectful and should not occur in the SAR/R community.

Because state laws and airline regulations change, you should periodically research them. Anyone who knowingly and fraudulently represents their dogs as service animals can be punished by imprisonment, a fine, or both, depending on the state.

"You can never make the same mistake twice . . . Because the second time it's not a mistake . . . it's a choice." – Steven Denn

K9 Socialization Training

Socialization is needed throughout the SAR/R dog's life. She will face many distressing situations, and at times nasty people, in her work. The SAR/R dog needs to be friendly and meet people and other dogs in all shapes, colors, ages, and sizes while her handler closely supervises the interactions to make sure there is no rough handling or negative impact. All pleasant interactions with people and other dogs helps the SAR/R dog develop a positive outlook. Understand that just because you tell someone how to approach and pet your dog does not mean that person will not make a sudden or foolhardy gesture. An overexuberant dog lover may try to hug or kiss your dog's nose, which can result in her displaying a defensive or annoyed reaction. Curtailing social interactions because of concerns, however, will neither benefit the dog nor help her deal with what happened to overcome a negative response. Petting should be allowed only with your permission, specific instruction as to how, and under a watchful eye.

You need to expose your dog to new places that provide happy experiences and variant odors. Socialization with livestock, who are penned at first, and with your dog on lead, is important for her. In Britain, the Search and Rescue Dog Association (SARDA) requires a "stock test."[2] The test places the dog in the middle of a flock of about 60 sheep that the dog must ignore as they run past her. The test also places the dog and handler on opposite sides of a flock of roaming sheep. When the handler gives a recall, the dog must respond and ignore the flock as she works her way between them and back to her handler; the dog must also continue to ignore the sheep when getting her favorite toy or ball from the middle of the herd. Livestock training means the difference between outraged farmers or ranchers—some have shot dogs for spooking, chasing, and possibly hurting their stock—and a team that can successfully search around, near, and among such distractions.

Touch

Getting your dog used to having all parts of her body touched is critical for injury assessment, first-aid, and grooming. Feel her paws and in between her toes; look in and touch her mouth, tongue, and teeth; gently handle her eye area, ears, and other parts of her body. You may need to assess your dog in the field, so it is essential that she is accustomed to you touching her in all areas.

Fear Periods

Fear periods have been defined as times in puppyhood when a bad experience could scar a puppy's psyche for the rest of her life. It has since been determined that although puppies do go through periods when they are more fearful, the time those periods occur varies with each pup. Counter-conditioning and desensitizing for any incident is necessary, as is the handler's proper response to a dog's fear. You should first learn exactly what object or area your dog fears. Don't just guess what it could be or assume you know. Experts say not to baby or soothe the dog because the dog views this as rewarding her for fearful behavior, and it gives her the idea that being scared is okay. Instead, be matter-of-fact and distract your puppy with an activity rather than focusing on the fear. Once her attention turns toward the distraction, praise her.

Obedience Training

Obedience training is imperative to minimize the risk of injury to or death of your dog. How much obedience is necessary is a somewhat debated issue. Some believe absolute obedience is always necessary, regardless of the situation. However, many handlers, including some law-enforcement K9 instructors with many years on the street, believe some aspects of K9 obedience are not needed. Handlers comment, for example, that obedience exercises like the "long wait" are not relevant to their type of searches. They say they would never have their dogs stay in a position in the field while they are out of site for any period. They say they have seen K9s put in that position at busy disaster scenes, potentially causing safety issues. Some handlers say too much obedience training will lead to a dog's total dependence on the handler. They think the dog will be more focused on the handler and social side of behavior and lose the desire to do anything on her own. SAR/R dogs must work independently while their handlers maintain appropriate control. Some trainers believe that handler dependence can result if rigid obedience training begins before the handler and dog have created a strong bond or before the dog develops commitment to the specific target odor. Even so, the well-trained dog may exhibit "intelligent disobedience." Intelligent disobedience can be described via two examples. First, the dog has commitment to the target odor and will not leave it when the handler, not believing it is a valid alert, calls her off. Second, the dog refuses to go forward into brush or another area when directed, thereby warning the handler of something she has noticed—this "disobedience" can be vital to avoiding tragedy. The dog may sense danger—a snake, a sheer drop, or another hazard—so she disobeys. This behavior is akin to that of a seeing-eye dog that is given the command to move forward but does not step off a curb because a vehicle is approaching.

Remember that always giving obedience commands in the same order—sit, down, stay, come, and so on—can pattern train a dog. An excited dog will anticipate and usually act out the next command or the entire routine when you have only said, "Sit." For that reason, varying the behavior commands will encourage your dog to focus on the command itself. Even those basic commands can become too rigorous for the dog if they are given with intensity and over the course of exhaustive training periods.

K9 Agility and Non-nose Work

Agility basics for SAR/R involve training the dog to go over, under, through, in, up, and down obstacles. The SAR/R dog must also know how to crawl, walk across a long narrow surface, or maybe climb a ladder. K9s require non-nose work, such as physical and emotional training that incorporates the different types of areas and obstructions the team will encounter on a search.

Object heights and difficulties properly adjusted for your puppy will challenge her but not injure her growing joints and bones. If a puppy is pushed too hard, she may end up with hip dysplasia, sprains, and other physical ailments.

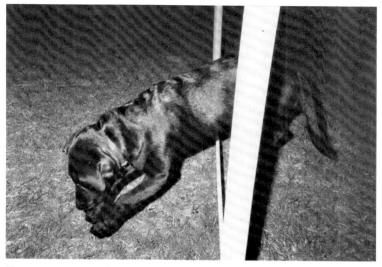

Figure 10.1 A ten-week-old puppy can easily learn the command "Over" when you present her with a low bar.

Figure 10.2 The wooden spool here helps the puppy gain confidence and experience crawling over obstacles.

The following represent only a portion of K9 non-nose work:

- swimming;
- rappelling;

- traveling in the back of an off-road vehicle with other dogs and handlers;
- flying in fixed-wing aircraft;
- riding in a variety of vehicles, including boats;
- riding on ski lifts; and
- going through long tunnels.

SAR/R dogs must also be accustomed to boarding helicopters, with and without rotors in motion. Engine and rotor noise levels in military helicopters may bother some dogs, likely because of the loudness, pitch, or frequency of the noise. Major Janice Baker notes that dogs do not like cotton plugs in their ears, but folding their ears down and placing a balaclava over their heads without obstructing their vision has been shown to calm them.[3]

Cardiovascular and Health Conditioning

"What is right is often forgotten by what is convenient." – Bodie Thoene, Warsaw Requiem

Out-of-shape dogs and handlers cannot perform well, usually have to take more frequent rest breaks, and have difficulty clearing their search areas due to obstacles. They do not make for a stable resource. Some TEAMs send handlers home, or restrict their field activities, until their physical condition improves. Cardiovascular conditioning requires the heart rate to be increased and maintained at a high level for a sustained period. Prior to increasing your physical exercise, consult a doctor. Dogs need a checkup too, as they work harder in the field than their handlers.

Although ball throwing and fetching until the dog gets tired will keep her higher heart rate sustained, use caution so the dog does not become exhausted or injured in the process. You may like this easy method of exercising your dog—but you also need exercise! Increasing your stamina by hiking, running, and walking outside of SAR/R training will help keep things fun and interesting, and will afford mental stimulation for both your dog and you. Swimming or water treadmills are resistance training and help dogs build strong muscles in the hindquarters and chest. Walking a dog through chest-high water can be more of a workout for the dog than swimming. All these activities give the extra benefit of building your relationship with and understanding of your dog.

Crate Training

Crate training is needed for SAR/R dogs so you can safely keep your dog in your vehicle if you are doing other tasks during training or on searches. (Crating your dog in your vehicle also keeps muddy paws and wet or skunk-sprayed fur and hair off car seats.) Both wire and plastic crates have problems if you and your dog are in a traffic accident, but a crate is still the safest place for your dog when you are traveling. Although some companies label their products "crash tested," there are no industry or government safety standards for crates at this writing. Pet products are an unregulated industry. Despite newer-model cars now having "crumple zones" and crate manufacturers evolving their style, material, and construction, I recommend checking the Center for Pet Safety for information and updates on crate safety.[4]

Regardless of type, the crate should be secured inside your vehicle to prevent it from rolling or flipping. Another safety point to consider is having your dog on a leash that extends partway out the crate door. In event of an accident, the leash will make it easier to get hold of your dog so she does not escape, or easier to catch her if she does. The crate should be large enough for the dog to stand up and turn around. Many rescue or shelter dogs have never experienced being in a crate. They have only known kennels that have room to walk around, so they may be more resistant—puppies can become terrified. The main thing to remember is the crate should be viewed as a safe and pleasant place for the dog—not a form of punishment. It is important to make sure the dog does not feel trapped and frustrated. Training is best done in small steps, beginning with the dog spending short periods in the crate. Mishaps inside the crate may be avoided if you give your dog a chance to relieve herself outside before you put her in the crate.

Where you keep your dog before going into the field to work is usually up to you. One study that showed that K9s kept in their crates—providing they are able to move and shift positions—display less stress than dogs required to maintain a "stay." Other observations have concluded that allowing the dog a short period to relieve herself and acclimate to the area before being confined in her crate may increase her level of excitement and motivation as she hears other dogs and activities around her. Staging areas on searches may not be close to where vehicles are parked, so your K9 may have to be with you as you wait to be fielded. Some handlers have their dogs sit or stand with them, or they spend that time playing with their dogs, feeling that activity helps release pent-up energy. However, keep in mind that having playtime before the dog works—especially if her reward is a form of play—amounts to rewarding the dog before she has done anything.

Kenneling

The practice of keeping a dog in a kennel when not working or training is a very old one that appears to have originated with hunting and field dogs. The dogs were kenneled to prevent them from getting spoiled or developing bad habits. The majority of those dogs had little obedience training and so were not suited for staying in a home. Although people believed the dogs would be more focused on working if kenneled, studies from the University of Bristol's Anthrozoology Institute reveal otherwise. Examining videotapes of 30 police-trained German shepherd dogs in their kennels after having finished working, the university researchers discovered the dogs showed telltale signs of severe distress and became repetitive in their actions: pacing, circling, and so on—activities commonly associated with mental illness.[5] Ethologists (animal behaviorists) contacted in the United States agreed with those findings with the exception of hounds that hunt in packs. Those pack hounds rely on the pack master and each other and are generally in numbers too large to be kept inside a home. However, they still need human interaction. One suggestion is that when someone has several dogs and cannot have them all indoors, the dogs should be rotated every few days so each can spend time inside the house with the family. Although this is not ideal, this strategy would provide a degree of socialization, interaction, and relationship with the handler.

Ethologists further state that even well-trained dogs develop behavior problems as a result of being kenneled or crated all the time and not receiving enough, or the proper, interplay with humans. They suggest that, in most instances, kenneling a dog that is a working partner detracts from the partnership. Some kenneled dogs lose their fun and/or spontaneity. Behaviorist William Campbell termed this problem "kennelosis." Even though a considerable number of agencies kennel their dogs when they are not working, more and more law-enforcement K9 handlers are keeping their partners inside their homes. A properly trained working dog knows when to be the pet and when to work. In fact, retired working dogs who have become their handlers' family pets still get excited when they see objects or actions that indicate the handlers are going to work.

"We find comfort among those who agree with us—growth among those who don't." – Frank Clark, American screenwriter

11

Understanding Training Methods

There are many schools of thought on training. The traditional method, used most in years past, was founded on the belief that all dogs, like wolves, are pack animals and the owners should establish themselves as leaders of the pack through dominance. This method includes the owner eating before the dog, going through doorways first, performing the alpha roll to show the dog that the owner is master—all things alpha wolves in a pack would do. This training by force and intimidation was sometimes heavy-handed, bordering on abuse. Other, more modern forms of training include lure training, coercive training, motivational training, balanced training, and observational learning.

The Modern Method

> *"'Positive reinforcement' is always, by definition, decided by the receiver, not by the 'giver.'" – Patricia McConnell in her blog, The Other End of the Leash*

The modern method, described by science as "operant conditioning," was first studied by Edward L. Thorndike, then developed by B. F. Skinner with experiments performed in and outside laboratories relating to the way animals learn and how their behavior can be influenced. Wild animal trainers needed ways of controlling animals that could not be handled or punished, and dog trainers soon adopted those strategies. In the 1970s some exotic animal trainers called this method "affection training." Operant conditioning makes use of positive and negative reinforcement: positive (something desirable is given), is used to maintain or increase a desired behavior; negative (something desirable is taken away), is used to eliminate or reduce a behavior. Positive reinforcement usually involves a "marker" like a using a clicker or a consistent word or sound that means a reward is coming for that behavior. Timing is critical when using this method! A dog's behavior is powerfully influenced by the immediate reward or correction.

Positive reinforcement can be done in two ways: giving a command such as "sit" and clicking immediately when the dog sits, and then rewarding the dog; or watching for the desired behavior to occur naturally and clicking at the instant it happens, while stating the command and rewarding. For more complex behaviors, clicking and rewarding is done in steps. You can add different elements to a behavior by introducing an additional command and clicking or using verbal approval when the dog responds. For example, slowing down a dog for a particular type of search, or controlling a dog that works too fast, can be done by adding the word "slow" to the command of "search," or whatever word you use. Then employ the marker when the dog obeys the "slow" command.

Some animal rescue groups argue that only positive reinforcement should be used, and any form of discipline constitutes cruelty. They refer to dolphin trainers who were able to develop desired results in this manner. However, the dolphins were contained in a small area and a whistle was used as the

Figure 11.1 John Shaffer luring puppy True through a tunnel. (Photo by John Hnath)

marker. That may work with dolphins, but with other species in basically unrestricted spaces, boundaries must be set, and bad behavior corrected properly. (Remember, to avoid confusion, behaviors should be allowed always or never. For example, don't expect your dog to learn that it's okay to jump on you when you are wearing old clothes but wrong to jump on you when you are dressed up. The dog doesn't know the difference between old and fancy clothes.)

Lure Training

In lure training, you lure the dog with a treat or toy to ensure he complies with the issued command and then you reward him immediately when he performs the desired behavior—such as luring a puppy to go through a tunnel. A clicker is not needed, since it does not add any information.

Coercive versus Motivational and Compulsive Training

Years ago, many law-enforcement K9 trainers used coercive training methods—sometimes harsh—to force the dog to comply, but they now adopt a combination of motivational training (also called reward-based training) and compulsive training. That combination is also used by some SAR/R dog handlers. Compulsive training involves either physically correcting the dog—like a hard jerk on the leash—or physically forcing the dog to comply with the command. This type of training has received negative comments because some trainers have carried it out too harshly. When thinking of how law-enforcement K9s must behave and what they are subjected to while working, it may be understood why this method is incorporated with motivational training. The combination provides a positive aspect to "making" the dog obey, rather than simply the application of brute force. While many SAR/R dog instructors have adopted some form of operant conditioning, alternative methods are still being used.

Mimicry or Observational Learning

The type of training method used may be determined by the situation, the dog's individual character, or the complexity and nature of the behavior at stake. For example, some trainers employ mimicry, also called observational learning, to teach certain behaviors. This strategy has the dog imitating his handler sometimes as long as 10 minutes after the action happened. Jozsef Topál, an ethologist at the Hungarian Academy of Sciences in Budapest, adapted a training method called Do as I Do.[1] He first tells the dog to stay and then commands, "Do as I do," and performs a simple activity such as barking or jumping in place. He next says, "Do it!" and the dog responds, matching the activity. There is no more than a five-second delay between the dog watching the action and repeating it. Claudia Fugazza and Ádám Miklósi, also from Hungary, studied deferred imitation by extending the time from 40 seconds to 10 minutes between the action of the owner and the command. Even after distractions during the wait time and when someone other than the owner, who did not know what had previously been demonstrated, gave the command, "Do it," the dog performed the correct action.[2]

Mimicry has been used a great deal in SAR/R training, specifically for a particular alert, such as scratching, paw-touch, or barking.

A delightful video on mimicry and training is "The Amazing Skidboot," easily found on YouTube. David Hartwig of Quinlan, Texas, is a farrier, not a dog trainer, but he watched and understood how his dog behaved and responded in training. While using one-word commands works best for most dogs, this method did not seem to impress Skidboot, who seemed to like conversation. As seen in this video and others, Hartwig says things like, "Now, back away," "Now, turn away," rather than simply "back" or "turn." His long narratives include the impressive "Now I'm going to tell you when you can touch that ball, and you'd better not do it until I say three," followed by Hartwig proceeding to say a variety of numbers, as Skidboot stands poised, until he finally says "three."

Mimicry and clicker training can be combined, as can a form of mimicry that involves rivalry with the handler. With rivalry, the behavior is performed by the handler who gets the click and the reward while the dog watches.

Many times, the training method used comes down to the instructor's personality or the TEAM's directive instead of what is best for the dog's temperament. The crux of the matter is, with all the acceptable variations in training, handlers and instructors alike should not frustrate a dog with a method he has a problem with or does not understand. Persisting with a frustrating training method is a disservice to the dog and the TEAM.

> *"When it is obvious that the goals cannot be reached, don't adjust the goals, adjust the action steps."* – *Confucius,* The Philosophy of Confucius

Devices and Collars

As well as different types of dog collars, there are Haltis, Gentle Leaders, head halters, and special harnesses to keep a dog from pulling while on lead. Numerous dog owners have praised these devices. However, a great number of dog trainers believe a dog should learn by correction—not distraction. That does not mean strong physical punishment but correcting the unwanted behavior and then rewarding the right behavior. Head halters offer distraction rather than correction because the dog's head is forced to turn in the direction it is pulled. The special harness provides distraction by pressure when the dog strains on the leash. Many trainers believe that all these devices can suppress the dog's behavior rather than rectify the problem, while other trainers believe they do correct the behavior. Again, it comes down to what works for the particular dog.

When it comes to collar types, K9 trainers have their own preferences, which are sometimes decided by the behavior they are trying to correct or teach. There are flat and rolled nylon or leather collars; Martingale collars, which come with a fabric flat tab or loop instead of a chain; and choke-chain and prong collars. As is the case with many training devices, there is criticism about using prong collars and choke-chain collars. Choke chains are supposed to sit high on the dog's neck, just behind the ears—not around the dog's throat.

Prong collars may look cruel, but some trainers say they are not if fitted and used correctly—as with any collar. They have flat tips—not sharp points. A dog that wears a prong collar and pulls while on a leash will feel the pinch in the loose skin around his neck. When he stops pulling, the tension is released and the pinching, which was spread out to each of the prong tips, stops. The dog has just corrected himself. If you use a prong collar, you should reward your dog as soon as he ceases pulling.

HOW A PRONG COLLAR SAVED A K9'S LIFE

In the aftermath of a flash flood, a human remains detection (HRD) K9 team was called to search for deceased victims. Large debris piles lined the banks of the still-turbulent river. Because the piles were unstable, the handler used a long lead and a prong collar rather than no lead or a harness that could easily be caught up in the ruins of trees, brush, and other objects. While the K9 searched a large pile of debris at the edge of the riverbank, the slippery soil caused the dog to slide and drop over four feet down into the fast-moving water. The handler used the lead to help pull the K9 up the sheer, mud-slick bank to safety. The K9 did not sustain any cuts, punctures, or injury to her throat and was not choked. After being thoroughly checked, she went back to work with no ill effects. A flat collar would possibly have slipped off over her head, allowing the dog to be carried away down the swift river. A choke-chain collar would have caused damage to this large-breed K9, which needed a great deal of assistance to reach safety.

Prong collars should be used only when necessary—not kept on the dog all the time.

THE E-COLLAR OR REMOTE TRAINING COLLAR

I mention this type of collar last due to the extreme controversy surrounding its use—even more than that of the prong collar. Since this method exists, I will address it. Ignoring it does not prevent any pain that can be inflicted if it is not used properly or make the practice go away. For some supporters of the e-collar, the term "shock collar" seems to exacerbate its bad reputation. It suggests a wrong application and bolsters images of dogs in convulsive spasms and extreme pain. Proponents believe it is the abuse of the collar by individuals that has created the criticism—the collar itself is an inanimate object. Of course, any apparatus mishandled or administered with malice can be negative.

The collars were first used in the 1960s to train hunting dogs and had a very high electrical current without a way to reduce the intensity. Soon they were being sold in pet stores for a variety of training purposes, and they were finally modified. The many modern e-collar versions offer controlled ranges of electrical stimuli or signals—some with a tingling sensation or vibration setting as an alternative to electrical stimulation. Others will sound a beep before producing the electric stimulus to signal the dog and also allow the instructor to give a verbal command—"leave it," "no," "down," and so forth—to disrupt the unwanted behavior. Timing is critical in its use!

If you opt to use an e-collar, you should *first* research how to use it properly, and get guidance from a qualified person. Using the collar is not simply about putting the collar on the dog and pushing a button.

SAR/R dog handlers who advocate for e-collars say they are not to be used as a punishment, but rather as a deterrent to train negative or unsafe behavior out of a dog. They theorize the dog will associate the uncomfortable or irritating stimuli with the unwanted behavior. For example, e-collars are often used in snake-aversion training, with handlers believing the dog will attribute the electric shock to the snake's smell and sound. But, that may not always happen, since no one knows exactly what the dog will be associating with the shock. The shock may cause a dog to attack the snake rather than avoid it; one dog trained this way became terrified of oscillating sprinklers because of their rattlesnake-like sound. Dogs respond differently to snakes—some are very cautious or reluctant while others are eager to inspect, smell, attack, or chase.

In snake-avoidance training it does not matter how knowledgeable the instructor is about snakes—it matters how educated he or she is about dogs, timing, and use of the e-collar. Dogs may also get "collar smart" and behave correctly simply because they are wearing the collar but revert to other actions when not.

At this writing there are many information sites and even e-collar chats on the Internet. It is important for handlers to understand the use of each type of collar for training purposes and working in the field.

SNAKE AVOIDANCE ALTERNATIVES TO E-COLLARS

In her book *Snake Avoidance Without Shock*, Jamie Robinson gives detailed instructions for what she calls "structured game training." Her approach combines play with purpose, cooperation, and goals. "If you really want a dog to stay away from something," she writes, "you have to make it the dog's choice, not just a conditioned response. The most important part of teaching snake avoidance does not involve humans. The dog must learn what to do when confronted with the sight, sound, and/or smell of a snake even when the human is missing. An estimated 85 percent of all snake bites to pets happen in their own backyard."[3]

There is considerable information on the Internet about snake-avoidance training in the forms of articles, books, workshops, training programs, and webinars. Make sure you verify the avoidance trainer's qualifications and methods before attending a class or applying the techniques. Some SAR/R handlers remain fearful that force-free snake-aversion training will not be enough to ensure their dog's safety, since they may be dealing with life-and-death matters in remote locations. Neither method provides a guarantee, so it is important to do research and make the choice you feel most comfortable with.

12

Training Sessions

"You know what you say—but you don't know what they hear." – Old adage

Training environments range from classroom to fieldwork to self-study and learning through observation, webinars, and reading posts on social media. Regardless where the training takes place, it is the source of the training information that is important.

Classroom Training

Classroom training promotes note-taking and is a comfortable setting for focused learning. It allows all TEAM members to receive information at the same time, along with the ability to ask questions, as a group, for clarity. Classroom training should cover a variety of subjects, including updates on training practices, legal issues, and other pertinent topics if they are not discussed at business meetings or elsewhere.

Education regarding lost and missing persons behavior is an indispensable element in SAR/R and ought to be a requisite for every TEAM, whether in a classroom or required self-study. There are many books on this subject, some of which are designed for easy use in the field.

Some TEAMs periodically issue written tests in their class-room sessions. Those tests can cover whatever subjects are believed necessary to reinforce. Examples of questions include the following: What are signs of heat exhaustion in a dog? What is proper crime-scene preservation? What are search urgency factors?

Fieldwork

Fieldwork involves individual, hands-on training that allows handlers and K9s to apply what has been learned and gain new knowledge through trial and error. To become a mission-ready (operational), credible K9 team, training should be implemented in individual increments—work on one behavior until the dog is consistent and reliable before introducing another action. Each step is a building block. As training progresses and a new element is added, the problem should be shorter or not as difficult to allow more focus on the new component. For example, if an air scent team has never worked a night search or a moving victim situation and is trying to work out a problem that includes both, it might be unclear with which circumstance the K9 team is having difficulty. Or, for trailing, it would be contrary to the principle of "one step at a time" to substantially increase both the age of a trail and its number of turns.

When training a *specific behavior*, the length of each session should not be overdone. Numerous short, five- to 15-minute rep-etitions of the desired behavior work better than a long period of performing the exercise repeatedly. Dogs can not only get bored, but they can also get full if treats are used as rewards. The dog should be excited about training and be left wanting more.

Some handlers feel insecure and want to make a good show-ing to their TEAM members by constantly performing the same behaviors and level of difficulty their K9s do well at. That is not training or advancing. Instead, take advantage of fieldwork sessions where you will have the readily available advice and assistance of the instructor or other qualified TEAMmates. Teams learn better and retain the difference between right and wrong by making mistakes and learning from them. If a team never makes a mistake, the pair are only practicing what they know—not what they need to know. The handler, in fact, the entire TEAM, needs to be open-minded and not oversensitive about corrections or criticism. Criticism is inevitable, but it should be constructive and supportive.

"The trouble with most of us is that we would rather be ruined by praise than saved by criticism." – Norman Vincent Peale

Considerations for Training

"A goal without a plan is just a wish." – Antoine de Saint-Exupéry

Training provides the time for you not only to work on problem-solving skills but also to develop and maintain endurance. As training progresses, problem setups should vary in difficulty and length. If a dog always makes a find within 20 minutes, she will establish an inner clock. After 20 minutes, she may lose motivation to continue or false alert because the time has passed the point when she usually makes a find and gets her reward.

Setbacks in training can happen, often because the dog gets bored by the ease of the problems or because you advance the level of ability too often or too quickly. This also leads to lack of confidence in the handler. It is a good idea for even certified, proven dog teams to routinely take a few steps backward in training to sharpen skills.

If the instructor considers the K9 team's level of training, everyone avoids frustration, or overconfidence because of luck rather than learning. If the instructor designs an objective for each field-work problem, training sessions will be more productive, rather than just playing "hide and seek." The problems should be set strategically to accomplish a goal.

Issues may arise if the person playing the part of the victim decides to do his or her own thing—not as instructed—and the K9 team is not experienced. Everyone's time is valuable, so having written lesson plans or training action plans helps sessions move along efficiently and be well-documented.

Questions instructors should consider when planning their sessions include:

- What is the purpose of the setup?
- What behavior is the focus?
- Is the problem consistent with what was established in the previous training session? Does the new session include a correction, reinforcement, new element, scent travel, or increased difficulty?

The K9 trainer who estimates how the scent may travel when setting up a problem and compares that to the scent conditions when the K9 team is working adds important information to the exercise. The wind may have shifted, and the problem and scent movement are different from what the trainer anticipated. If those changes are not taken into consideration, wrong assessment of how the dog is working and incorrect feedback may be given to the handler as the team is searching.

Planning and setting up training situations takes thought and time. Asking TEAM members what they learned at the end of each training session—what they accomplished or need to work on—will correct any misunderstandings arising from the lesson and assist the K9 instructor in planning future training problems. This is especially true with a new handler in the group, to help ensure he or she did not misinterpret what was taught.

13

Training Areas

It is important that training exercises are conducted in all types of areas and include the variables a TEAM may be called to search. This includes improbable locations in your territory—searches can occur in the strangest of places. Always using the same areas may cause dogs to search by memory first—checking out all the places training aids or subjects have previously been hidden, rather than searching for odor from the onset. Fortunate TEAMs have access to vast acreage, diverse urban settings, or even sites constructed for disaster-type training. Others have to seek training locations to avoid using the same ones over and over. Regardless of which circumstance applies, it is incumbent upon the TEAM to get permission from the proper individual and to respect the land, structures, and privilege of their use. Furnishing a TEAM "release of liability" document to the property owner often helps get approval.

It is wise to notify local law enforcement of the date, times, and location where the TEAM will be training. This also informs or reminds them of the TEAM's resources. Providing a flyer or note for anyone living or working in proximity to the training area is also advisable and will decrease the chance of concerns or problems. Being confronted by an armed property owner or having the police respond with flashing lights at a night training session is not only frightening for residents in the area but is also disruptive to the training. Welcome taking advantage of opportunities as they come, even if it means changing a scheduled training location. You may, for example, become aware of scout training at a particular location, or receive consent to train at a burned structure, one being demolished, or at a construction site.

Buildings

Studying and training for building searches are part of SAR/R; these kinds of searches often occur, especially in human remains detection.

Heat, or lack thereof, can have an effect on the odor concentration and movement in a building. This does not mean only mechanical heat but also that caused by direct sunlight flowing into the room where the source is located. Scent can fill a room, or several rooms, causing difficulty pinpointing its origin. Airflow patterns and scent pools in structures are caused by ventilation systems, drafts, wind, and even human activity, and are different from those outside. Air pressure differences created by these forces move airborne pollutants from areas of higher pressure to areas of lower pressure through any available openings in building walls, ceilings, floors, doors, windows, and heating ventilation and air conditioning (HVAC) systems. One room could be said to be "exhaling" while others close by could be "inhaling." In addition to requesting mechanical ventilation and fans be turned off, it is advised to close exterior doors to alleviate additional airflow before searching. Prior to testing airflow patterns with an ignitable device like a smoke bomb, all combustion appliances should be checked for leakage to avoid explosions.

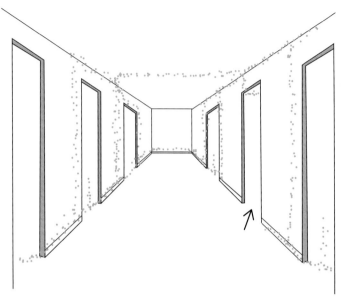

Figure 13.1 The source was in the room indicated by the arrow. Scent rose straight up to the ceiling, traveled across the ceiling and then out the door to the hall ceiling, at which point it dropped down and moved into rooms across the hall and into rooms on either side of the room containing the source. The doorway to the room with the source was void of scent, as was the hallway near that door.

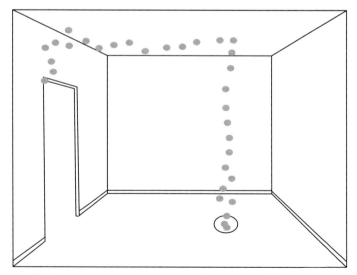

Figure 13.2 Scent emanating from a source inside the room, which rose and then moved along the ceiling before descending to exit through the top of the door.

Traveling to Locations

"Great organizations demand a high level of commitment by the people involved." – Bill Gates, as interviewed by David Rensin, July 1994

Traveling to areas beyond the TEAM's normal radius introduces unfamiliar places to teams and can replicate driving time to a search location. Being in the habit of driving 20 minutes or an hour to a destination can produce a set time of emotions. When the trip to an actual search is then three or four hours, frustration can build, and anxiety and fatigue can affect your behavior. This also applies to the dog's comfort and stress level in traveling longer distances before going into the field to work. Some TEAMs admit they would travel farther away for training, but a few of their members do not want a longer drive. In this situation, questions to ask include the following: Is the TEAM condoning this behavior without just cause for fear of losing members? Is it a political issue, going only where certain members want to train? Is this practice contributing to TEAM dissatisfaction and loss of camaraderie?

Some benefits of strange training locations for the dogs are different smells, sounds, and objects, and tempting segments, such as a lake or pond. Handlers will be challenged by negotiating unfamiliar terrain, devising different search strategies, contending with problem surroundings, and training their dogs to ignore new distractions. Dogs in early stages of training may be more interested in exploring and not behave as they would in a known training area. Giving them a few minutes to relieve themselves and check out new odors is helpful before the exercise begins.

14

Field Training

"The essence of training is to allow error without consequences." – Orson Scott Card, Ender's Game

Field training should be conducted with the same effort and enthusiasm as would be present on a real search. And, from the very beginning of dog training, every session—even obedience—should be documented. Without training in harsh weather and varied terrain and structures, a team will never be fully prepared. The pair's competency will be limited to the conditions in which they have trained. Different environments, noise influence, and stressors can be problematic for both dog and handler. Learning to search in inclement weather—which occurs in many actual searches—is an important part of training. Curtailing training because it is too hot or cold, too dark or windy, or whatever excuse, is not fulfilling the commitment the TEAM has made. Just be sure to use common sense and make safety a priority.

Wind and Scent

Training in adverse or unpleasant circumstances affords teams the practical use of what they learned about scent theory and weather conditions.

According to Lt. Weldon Wood of the Charles County, Maryland, Sheriff's Department, an experiment conducted in the south of England found that "At ground surface the temperature was 111°F, at one inch above; it was 94°F; at twelve inches it was 80°F and at forty inches it was 85 °F."[1] When hot air rises and passes through cooler layers, it causes updrafts. This can keep the scent-laden rafts airborne for a substantial length of time, while a crosswind can carry them great distances before dropping the scent down and then rising again, with the process repeated several times. This airflow pattern is called "looping" and is among other patterns that affect scent plumes that a handler must learn.

Wind direction cannot be judged by wetting a finger and holding it in the air. Holding out a piece of flagging tape will indicate the wind bearing at the level the tape is being held—not at the level of the dog's nose. Tying the tape below the knee will give you a somewhat better idea of what the wind is doing closer to the ground. Checking wind direction on a wireless weather device or relying on historical weather data on the Internet will only show prevailing winds. For instance, an iPhone weather app states the wind is from the southwest; however, it is evident that at your location the wind is coming from north–northwest, due to the terrain. This shows the importance of being aware of actual conditions— including wind speed, which may necessitate a change in search strategy. Changes in air movement or strategy should be noted mentally or physically by you or the flanker, rather than relying on recorded weather data. Determining wind speed in the field can be accomplished by using an anemometer or the Beaufort Scale. Developed in 1805 by Sir Francis Beaufort of Britain's Royal Navy, this scale is extremely helpful and can be easily committed to memory.[2]

Some handlers use colored smoke bombs for air-flow visualization to show how scent rafts will likely be carried and pooled. But smoke bombs themselves produce heat. When the bomb is ignited, the burning mixture evaporates the colored substance inside. The material is forced out, where it condenses in the atmosphere and forms "smoke" composed of finely scattered particles. The smoke plume is usually narrow and thick at the point of emission, as pressure causes it to rise quickly. The strength and direction of the wind and temperature changes in the surrounding air determine how the smoke travels. After the bomb has expelled its contents, the colored particle cloud lingers airborne for a few minutes as it diffuses. This provides an overall picture of what may be happening to airborne scent rafts. However, it does not analyze what is happening at ground level—how the air eddies, weaves through vegetation, or forms areas of concentration regardless of wind. Therefore, the following experiment with dry ice was conducted.

Dry ice is not frozen water but frozen CO_2—at a temperature of $-109°F$ ($-78°C$). Adding a piece of dry ice to a container of warm water will create a fog that is heavier than air, moves slower than smoke-bomb particles, and rises only about 2 to 3 feet (0.6 to 0.9 m). The channeling and concentrations of the fog seem to provide a better image of air movement close to the ground.

Should you wish to use dry ice to check directions of air flow, remember: dry ice is a harmful substance and should be used only during training in well-ventilated areas. Dry ice experiments should not be conducted without reading and applying all safety procedures necessary, which include the following: containers/bags must be able to vent; do not use in confined spaces; many objects will crack due to the extremely low temperature. Touching dry ice or its container is injurious—as little as four seconds of contact can result in frostbite or frost nip!

Comparing the dry ice photos to a smoke bomb ignited at the identical spot less than one minute later shows the difference between the two. Even subtle air flow can be significant when searching for disarticulated human remains and trace evidence.

Figure 14.1 Dry ice added to water is transformed into gaseous carbon dioxide, which creates a thick fog.

Figure 14.2 As seconds go by, the fog spreads but remains at a low level, the way scent on the ground may travel.

Figure 14.3 The ignition of a smoke bomb forces colored particles straight up into the air.

Figure 14.4 The airborne particles show scent travel at that level but do not necessarily show what is happening on the ground.

Work Signals for the Dog

During field training, some handlers use a special collar or harness, or attach a bell to the dog's collar so the dog will associate that item with the work. The placement of the object is usually done when the dog exits the vehicle and is about to go into the field. The dog soon learns that it is a signal for what is going to happen.

With time, most dogs link the handler putting on hiking boots or a uniform to the work and become excited. The bell is also used on dogs that range out of sight so handlers can keep track of where the dogs are working.

Some handlers put search vests—called shabracks—on their dogs for training and searches. Shabracks help identify the dogs as working dogs, especially during hunting season, when searching farm or ranch land or areas with livestock, or when the dog is working in busy or congested locations. K9s also wear them for demonstrations and public events. Thought should be given as to why the dog should wear the vest in the field, however. Is it necessary? Will it make the dog hot or potentially get hung up in brush? Is the handler not considering the dog but just trying to draw attention to him or herself?

Training in Search Disciplines

GENERAL AIR SCENTING

In this discipline, the dog will find any human subject in her search area. Training in this discipline begins with the handler running off in beginner run-away problems, and is usually followed by TEAM members and then others playing the role of the "victim." The problems are short with great excitement, praise, and reward for the dog. This stimulates her desire and eagerness to search for a person and for the reward at the find. Note that the general air scent discipline is not commonly used in heavily populated environments because the dog will find anyone in the given area.

As the dog and handler progress through the levels of training, the role of the person simulating a victim becomes more involved in activity and duration. The "victim" may be told to hide in a dumpster, climb a tree, walk through a creek, or sit in dense brush for several hours. The training scenarios in searching for a lost person are almost unlimited, but safety is always important—the

AN "ALREADY TRAINED" DOG STILL NEEDS TRAINING

When a K9 vendor is contracted to supply a new law enforcement (LE) handler with a trained detection dog committed to a target odor, as a part of the sales contract the handler usually receives a few weeks or months of training in both classroom and fieldwork through a K9 academy course or by a private trainer. However, although that training is intense, it is not all the training needed—LE K9 instructors consider it amounts to only basic training. The handler and dog must continue to train in all aspects of the discipline, including the handler learning about his or her specific K9's behaviors in the field. The team should be pushed to progress in competency.

dog must traverse the area where the "victim" hides or is asked to hide, and all the hazards therein.

SCENT DISCRIMINATION

Scent discrimination means finding one scent over all others. The K9 sniffs an object worn or touched by the person to be found and searches for the matching scent. However, just presenting a dog with a scent article does not mean anything to them. The dog must be taught that the scent article holds the target odor they are to find.

AIR SCENT SPECIFIC

TEAMs differ on when to begin air scent specific training. Some believe this training should begin only after the dog has passed certification for general air scenting, whereas others start discrimination training as soon as the dog understands the game of searching. Either way, it is suggested that in the beginning stages, training should be conducted in areas where the dog has had success in searching. The "victim" should be someone the dog knows and the scent article a piece of that person's just-worn clothing, which is strong with the person's scent. A dog can be trained in both the general air scent discipline and to air scent discriminate. However, you should train in only one discipline at a time until you and your dog are proficient and operational.

THE REFIND

Air scent dogs and off-lead trailing dogs range a distance from their handlers and many times are not in view. The refind is a behavior mostly taught, but some dogs do it naturally—they are so excited they found the victim or target odor that they run back to their handlers and jump or bark to tell them. The handlers then prompt the dogs with a word or signal to take them back to the location. A dog's natural refind behavior is a wonderful indication of their enthusiasm. Trained refind techniques may mean the dog runs back to the handler and barks, sits, jumps up, grabs a toy or object such as a short rope tied to the handler's belt, or uses a bringsel. Some handlers do not want their K9 to do a refind and train the dog to stay with the victim or scent source until they arrive.

TRACKING

The disciplines of tracking and trailing are frequently confused, and many times the terms are used interchangeably. Tracking requires the dog to wear a well-fitting tracking harness and the handler to use a 30-foot (9-m) lead. However, some handlers use 40 feet (12 m) or longer if they are comfortable with and can control that length. The concept behind tracking is that the dog follows a subject's footprints step by step, searching not only for the specific human scent given by way of a scent article, but also for the entire scent picture, which includes crushed vegetation and disturbed earth. It should be noted that some freshly crushed vegetation can give off a very pungent odor. The step-by-step method requires the dog's nose to be down on the ground in each footprint. If the dog raises her head above a specific height from the track, commonly her head is forcibly pulled down by a lead that runs between the dog's legs to the collar. Training practices developed from this theory suggest that if the dog raises her head, she has lost the odor. That presumption has not been validated.

The hypothesis that tracking involves the dog searching for a combination of odors may be accurate while she is working on soft surfaces such as grass and earth. Dogs are introduced to a scent with a scent article, but when looking for it they find that scent is combined with the other odors of the crushed vegetation or disturbed earth. That combination is what is imprinted as the target odor. But, when tracking on concrete, gravel, and other hard surfaces such as tile or carpet, the combination of odors they are accustomed to are missing, so dogs have to be conditioned to discriminate and follow only a particular human scent. It has been suggested that hard surface or pavement tracking requires a tracking dog to have a very strong Prey Drive. However, a strong Hunt Drive is also needed, as discussed on page 41.

Some instructors propose that when training your dog for hard-surface tracking, the track layer should walk barefoot initially. Once the dog is doing well, the track layer should wear socks and then eventually shoes. Another method is to soak the track layer's strong-smelling shirt in water. Pour that water into a spray bottle and spray it on the pavement at the "point last seen" (PLS, also called the "last known place," LKP) and periodically spray the scent on the trail. The places and amount of spray would then be gradually reduced.

Another type of tracking is done without a scent article. Instead, the dog searches for the freshest track of any human scent. This is especially used by LE when searching for a fleeing subject and wanting to know exactly where the subject has gone in the event the person discarded anything that could be used as evidence. The person's increase in adrenaline and alarm pheromones are usually part of this scent picture.

Scent-discrimination training for tracking dogs is a long process, which must successfully supersede the dog's normal instinct to search for the freshest track—whether human or animal. Note that stating a dog can scent discriminate when she is not reliable and consistent is perilous. The dog can lead searchers on a wild-goose chase and waste valuable time that might cost the victim his or her life. If unreliable, the dog can also identify the wrong person in scent-association situations.

TRAILING

Trailing, called ground scenting in the UK, is a variation of tracking but also includes air scenting. As in tracking, a scent article is offered to the dog very close to the PLS. If that place has not been identified, the scent article is offered at areas of interest to determine if the person has been at those locations. If the dog finds the matching scent, she will follow only that scent wherever it is—on the ground or in the air. Depending on the age of the trail, the terrain, and the wind conditions, scent can be blown a great distance from where the person actually walked, and that place is where the dog will detect the person's odor trail.

In the early stages of training a dog to cast for a trail (sniff the ground around the PLS to find the matching scent) it helps if the trail layer scuffs his or her feet at the starting point. Furthermore, if the trail is scuffed periodically, it provides encouragement to the dog. If there is concern that strong odor from crushed weeds will initially overpower the human scent for the novice dog, a place with more dirt and less vegetation should be selected. Eventually, of course, the K9 team must learn to work through vegetation odors in order to be reliable.

The majority of handlers use a harness and work their trailing dogs on lead, though some choose to have their dogs search "free"—off lead. In some areas TEAMs consider off-lead trailing the same as air scent specific. If you use a lead, it must be attached to a harness—never to the dog's collar. Pressure and strain on the dog's neck and throat can result in injury! Many handlers believe there is a benefit to working on lead as it enables them to feel the movement of their K9, not just see it. That direct connection between dog and handler—the tension awareness of the slightest slowing down, hesitation, or speeding up when the dog is trying to work out a problem affords the handler insight into what is going on at the other end of the leash.

The question, "How does the dog know which way to go when she finds a scent trail?" has been asked by many unfamiliar with tracking and trailing. Answer: The dog knows the stronger scent is in the direction of travel—the same as how an animal follows prey.

TRACKING AND TRAILING WITH MARKED TRAILS

Marking a trail in training is simply a way to help the handler know the dog is on the right trail and where there are turns. If there is a problem, the marked trail allows the handler to take the dog back to where she went wrong and let her rework the problem. Marked trails are frequently employed in the early stages of training when turns, or other new elements such as streets or obstacles, are added. Wire stake flags and flagging tape are popular but can be detrimental if the handler constantly uses them to guide the dog rather than letting her search. When flags are no longer used, flag-dependent handlers may lose confidence and change how they work their dogs and question and/or correct their dogs' actions because of what *they* think. Increasing the distances between flags until omitting them altogether may help alleviate dependency. Tying pieces of flagging tape onto clothespins and clipping them on objects is another way to mark a trail. For hard surfaces or places where there is nothing to which the trail layer can affix a flag, one can tie tape onto small, metal washers and just drop them on the ground.

If markings are close to ground level a dog may use the tapes as visual clues or as additional scent articles, since they were touched by the trail layer "victim." Wearing gloves when tying flags does not keep the trail layer's scent from collecting on those items. Human scent, whether particulate or gaseous in nature, is airborne and can be moved from one surface to another with or without contact. A dog checking a flag is no different from a dog inspecting or alerting on an article the victim dropped.

A suggestion for using tape to only indicate turns is to tie it on the right side if a right turn is made or on the left for a left turn. Highly wooded or brushy areas might cause some confusion in terms of right or left turns, however, so possibly tying one tape strip for a right turn and two strips for a left turn, or vice-versa, will help.

Removing all tape and flags at the end of training is a common courtesy, shows respect for the area, and avoids confusion at later training sessions in the same place or if other TEAMs train at that same location. Just in case any tape is missed during clean-up, use a different color of tape each time you reuse an area. A few TEAMs report having used toilet tissue rather than flagging tape, and state that tissue is biodegradable. While true, it becomes windblown and is litter if not collected at the end of each practice. Other substances people use to mark trails or turns are squirts of powder on tree trunks, the ground, or stationary objects, or surveyor's chalk powder. But high winds may disrupt powder and the longevity of surveyor's chalk will result in confusion at subsequent trainings. Stick chalk and colored stickers may be good choices in urban areas.

> *"The greatest obstacle to progress is not the absence of knowledge, but the illusion of knowledge." – Daniel Boorstin,* The Discoverers

Training Two Dogs at Once

At times TEAMs will face the issue of a handler wanting to train two dogs at the same time, either in the same discipline or in different ones. The success of this endeavor depends on, first, the

handler's knowledge of the scent disciplines and level of experience, and second, the time the handler can allot to training. If
either one is lacking, the results likely will be less than satisfactory
when the goal in SAR/R is proficiency in the highest degree. The
instructor should consider those facts before agreeing to set up
field training problems.

WORKING TWO DOGS AT A TIME

One handler working two dogs individually is common in many locations. But
what about one handler working two dogs *at the same time*? Some handlers
believe this scenario can be effective for air scent dogs in certain situations,
but others disapprove—especially for HRD work. The dispute is not about
whether two dogs can work together, or whether an agency would oppose,
but about the handler undertaking too much. The dogs may have different
working styles, and in HRD it would be difficult to maintain situation awareness and make sure the entire area is searched and no clues missed, while having to watch *both* dogs not only for their locations but for the subtle changes
in body language that so often happen in HRD work. One handler working
two dogs at the same time would also give a defense attorney more issues to
question while trying to discredit the K9 team's competence.

15

The Scent Article

Handlers usually prefer to collect their own scent articles to ensure they are collected properly and to be sure they are not handled by anyone on scene. The ideal scent article is uncontaminated. It is anything with which only the missing person has been in physical contact. Some scent articles are easy to transport into the field: a worn piece of clothing, socks, shoes, wallet, or ball cap. But the item does not have to be portable. A dog can be scented off whatever stationary object the person has touched—a bed, a car-door handle, gate, bicycle, even the subject's footprint. However, while it is important to train a scent-discriminating dog to acquire odor from a variety of different, and at times strange, items, it is more important to focus on the fundamentals of decision making and problem solving at complex points or locations.

Obtaining an uncontaminated article can be difficult. Many times, in an effort to help, family members or friends have handled things or converged upon the last place the victim was seen, which adds their scents to the mixture. Although this type of contaminated article is often useless, a method called the "Missing Member" may allow you to use it. The dog is offered the tainted scent article and then sniffs each person who touched it or has been at the scene. The dog must then differentiate between their scents and the remaining odor—that of the missing person. While difficult and not completely reliable, the "Missing Member" method is sometimes necessary; otherwise, a tracking dog may just search for the freshest trail.

Collecting Scent Articles and Scent-Collection Methods

Scent articles should always be picked up or handled with surgical-type gloves or with an unused, unscented plastic bag—never bare hands. Without touching the inside of the bag, a hand should be placed at the bottom of the bag and forced upward to provide a barrier over the hand to pick up the article and pull it into the bag. The untouched article is now secured so it can be transported to the field. Paper bags are too porous to protect a scent article from contamination and should not be used. In the instance an article cannot be picked up due to its evidentiary value, a sterile 4 × 4-inch (10 × 10-cm) gauze pad placed on the item will absorb its odor within a few minutes. The pad should then be picked up and contained by the method described.

Another technique involves use of the STU-100, which employs dynamic airflow to move human scent from the surface of the evidence to a sterile gauze pad. This is a safe method for capturing scent without touching the evidence. Multiple scent pads can be easily and quickly collected from objects, clothing, and even bodies. The pads can then be placed in special scent evidence bags or jars and stored for a great length of time in a scent bank. Vacuuming human scent uses the same principle as breathing, which creates a vacuum that draws odor into nasal passages. Although the STU-100 has been controversial in several court proceedings, it is still being used by the FBI and other law-enforcement agencies, and along with corroborated evidence, has prevailed in court decisions.

A review of defense expert witness testimonies and the subsequent appellate court decisions underscores the misunderstanding of human-scent evidence.[1] In 2000, a defense expert testified, "We don't know what human scent is."[2] Yet that same expert surmised in later testimony that the method used to clean scent from the STU-100, "does not remove all of the odors reliably by any means."[3] How would he know, if he doesn't know what human scent is? These types of "expert opinions"—this one expressed by someone who had never seen the STU-100 before—cast unfavorable and incorrect perceptions on a tool the FBI deems useful. In 2004, the expert further stated, "It's going to collect a sample that has an unknown degree of contamination."[4] An expert witness's statements, although contradictory and uncorroborated, may still be admissible and persuasive testimony.

Because human scent is easily transferred, there will always be some slight degree of blended odors, regardless of how the item was collected. The air itself holds contaminants, so to think any object will hold only one scent is unrealistic. In the end, a positive trail or identification resulting from even the purest scent article only shows a relationship to that article and must be verified and corroborated through other investigative means.

Presenting a Scent Article

One method suggested when beginning scent-specific training is for the person playing the role of victim to remove a piece of clothing or ball cap and give it to the gloved handler while the dog watches. That "victim" and another person acting as a decoy both walk or run off a short distance and hide several yards apart. At that point the dog is offered the scent article by the handler, and the search command is given. Another method is to have the "victim" provide the handler with a bagged, uncontaminated article of his or her clothing. The "victim" is then the only person to run and hide. As training progresses, the K9 team should no longer see the "victim" walk away.

Some handlers will just hold the scent article an inch or so in front of the dog's nose while others wave it for the dog to sniff, drop it on the ground, or offer it to the dog from an open Ziploc-type bag. There are handlers who force the plastic bag over the dog's entire nose "giving them the scent," believing the dog will get more scent that way. That method—as well as jamming the article in the dog's face—has been determined unnecessary by many instructors. It appears this is more for the handler's assurance than for the dog.

"Preconceived notions are the locks on the door to wisdom." –
Merry Browne, The Price of Prejudice

16

Training Scenarios for Live-Victim Searches

The "Victim" in Training

Finding people willing to sit out in the woods for hours, hide under a house or in bizarre places may become difficult after a while. After exhausting the supply of friends, relatives, and neighbors to play the role, Scout troops, schools, or local organizations can be contacted and may accommodate the need for fresh "victims" as well as new training locations. Law enforcement officers and firefighters may have an interest in assisting or even joining the TEAM. Note that non-TEAM members attending training sessions, or volunteering to assist, should each sign a TEAM "hold-harmless" waiver as well as one for the property owner. If a participant is not of legal age, a parent must sign the waiver. Keep in mind that if the "victim" is giving the reward, an overly excited dog may be eager to get her toy or treat and nip the "victim's" hand.

Many willing subjects do not understand the importance of their position playing "victim." Some, even Scouts and those one would never expect, get impulsive and do things contrary to instructions. The actor may think it is a shrewd maneuver to climb fences, cross through, or encroach on adjoining property. Without explicit permission, those actions, besides being dangerous, are illegal and can result in serious consequences. Because of such experiences, I wrote the following article, "Search and Rescue Dog Training: The Role of the Victim," which has been used by many organizations. Training scenarios should be creative but realistic. And real life can be incredibly strange, as is evidenced in newspapers, TV shows, and non-fiction books that offer a host of ideas. All the activities in the following article stem from actual experiences.

SEARCH AND RESCUE DOG TRAINING: THE ROLE OF THE "VICTIM"
VI HUMMEL SHAFFER, K-9 SPECIALTY DETECTION

The "victim" plays a very important role in search and rescue dog training. The "victim" can be an asset or create problems. Problems created by the volunteer "victim" can result in serious setbacks in beginning- or intermediate-level dogs.

The "victim's" role in training is to help create situations that occur with a lost or missing person—not to confuse or trick the dog. Remember, this is a training session to help the dog and handler work out a variety of problems with scent, wind, terrain, lost/missing-person behavior, and other issues. Each planned problem has a specific reason behind it.

Instructions

Follow the instructions given to you by the training instructor. If someone is personally taking you into the field, listen to what he or she tells you to do. If the instructions are different than what the instructor told you, notify the instructor. If you are told to go to a specific place or walk a certain number of yards in a particular direction—go there! If you are a "trail layer" and supposed to walk a certain pattern for the dog to follow, do as you are told. If the instructions are not clear, ask for clarification! *Do not be creative, circle back, go somewhere else, or do something different.* Do exactly what you were told to do for your safety and the success of the training problem. Any person who repeatedly does not follow instructions will no longer be allowed to participate.

Look for unsafe areas or objects in your hiding place when you first arrive at the spot. If you see something unsafe and the person who took you is still there, tell him or her what you see so your location can change. If your guide has already left, radio base camp for advice. Do not leave your spot unless there is a safety issue, in which case, move to the closest similar spot. If you are behind a bush, go behind another similar bush; if in a tree, go to the closest similar tree and then notify base camp about where you went and approximately how far away it is from your original location. Once you are in place, *stay in place. Do not wander around*—unless you are told to do so!

When the Dog Finds You

In air scent problems, the dog usually works "free"—meaning off lead—and will reach you before the handler will. In tracking or trailing problems, most dogs work on a long lead, so the handler is usually within 30 feet (9 m) of the dog. It is important for you to respond (or not respond) to the dog *as you are told.*

FOR AIR SCENT DOGS

You will be told what to do when the dog first finds you, or you will be told to *not do anything but stay in place.* Do not grab the dog when he finds you; and do not tell the dog what to do or try to get him to sit down or stay with you unless you are told to do so. *Only the handler should give the dog commands!* The only exception to this is if you see the dog in danger. If the dog is wearing a bell, *do not* try to be funny and hold the bell to see if the handler can still find you. The dog may be trained to remain with you or to leave to get his handler. If the dog leaves, stay where you are until he brings his handler all the way up to you. Do not come out of your hiding spot when you see the handler approaching.

FOR BOTH AIR SCENT AND TRACKING/TRAILING DOGS

The dog may need to work on "unconscious victim" problems, or he may need a "happy victim." Sometimes you will be told not to move or make a sound and other times you will be told to react in a different way. If the dog passes you by or is searching the area close to you—do not make any noise or grunt, cough, move, etc.

You may be told not to praise the dog at all, or you may be asked to praise or reward the dog only when he brings his handler *all the way* up to you. You might also be told to *wait* to do anything until the handler has rewarded the dog first.

If you are given a food treat as a reward to give the dog at the end, you must make sure you do not drop any part of it on the way to your location—and you should not rub it on any objects to play a joke on the dog. When you are allowed to praise the dog, give a lot of praise! Make a big fuss how good the dog is. After all, if this was an actual search, the dog may have just saved your life.

Ask the handler or training instructor if you have not been given any instructions about what to do.

Radio Communications

If you are given a radio to use and are not familiar with one—ask. Turn the volume to low once you are in your hiding place and never play with the radio by keying the mic or fooling around. Your radio is for vital communications only. Radio base camp if no one is taking you to your location, or if you are laying a trail and you've arrive at your designated spot: tell them you are in place.

IN AIR SCENT OR OFF-LEAD DOG TRAINING

Radio base camp *when the dog first finds you* even before the handler appears. Say: "We have a find." If you are told to be quiet and not move, *radio only when the dog cannot hear you*. When the dog brings the handler to you, *radio base again* and say: "We have a refind." The marked difference in time between the find and refind helps the handler know if the dog is immediately returning to lead him or her back to you or if the dog got sidetracked by something.

IN TRACKING/TRAILING DOGS OR DOGS ON LEAD

In this scenario, it will only be necessary to let base camp know when the dog has found you the *first* time. The handler will be with the dog and there will not be a refind. If the search is taking a long time, base camp may radio you to see if you are okay. If so, and the dog is in the area but has not found you yet—do not speak. Instead, key the mic twice (give two clicks on the radio) to indicate the dog is close but *no find* yet. [Your TEAM may have another quiet method for this notification—there is no standard.] If base camp radios as the dog is running up to you and looking at you—tell them: "We have a find." If you are supposed to be unresponsive, ask the instructor or handler what you should do.

If You Are One of Several "Victims"

If the dog is expected to find more than one person in the area, that is called a multiple-victim search. If you are the first "victim" found and the dog has brought the handler to you, *stay where you are!* The handler may tell you to stay there while they continue to search, or say it is okay for you to go with them and be an observer for the second "victim." If you are an observer, *you must stay with* the handler or flanker. Once they start moving, you must keep up and not lag, wander off, or get in the dog's way. Only necessary conversation should be made. This is a training session, not a social event. *If you see the second "victim," do not say anything and do not stop in front of the "victim" even if the dog and handler pass by.* The wind may be moving in such a way that the dog has not detected that "victim's" exact location, and the handler is letting the dog work out the problem. Just quietly follow wherever the handler and flanker go, even if it's off a marked trail. Remember: this is a training problem for the dog and handler—let them do their job.

There may come a time when you are allowed to be creative in a search problem. But the base camp must know exactly where you are—in any case, *never do anything to scare the dog or put the dog, handler, or yourself in a danger.*

There are many dos and don'ts in these instructions for the valuable part you play. But, you must remember that this is not a game or a joke. We train constantly to help save lives. Be proud that your role as "victim" is a *great* contribution and is very much appreciated. Thank you.

Victim Responses

"Victims" should periodically be asked, by the trainer, to respond in different ways when the dog finds them to expose the K9 team to an assortment of encounters. Some example scenarios have the "victim":

- wearing a big hat;
- holding implements or tools;
- concealed under brush, leaves, or a tarp;
- from different ethnic groups and ages;
- in a vehicle, building, cave, or long culvert, or up in a tree;
- unresponsive;
- crying;
- laughing;
- screaming;
- acting frightened;
- running from the dog;
- moving from the original location when the dog goes back to the handler to do a refind; and
- having a dog with him/her.

Distractions in Training

Sometimes training scenarios should include distractions that the dog must work around, such as encountering people other than the victim in the search area. Other times, a human remains training aid or other type of interference should be placed in the search area for variation of the scene.

All SAR dogs should be exposed to human decomposition. Some dogs have an aversion to the odor and run from it. Others are fearful and cower or become immobilized and will not continue searching. Those dogs should not be thought inadequate—it is their genetic makeup to behave that way. The handler must know the dog's behavior and train to counter-condition unwanted conduct. Dogs rolling on, consuming, urinating on, or defecating on bodies or remains can destroy evidence. Law enforcement consider such actions inexcusable and, should they occur, there is a good possibility the agency will not request that TEAM again.

"Your level of success is predetermined by your level of effort." – *Anonymous*

The K9's Alert for Live Victims

While there are benefits and drawbacks to all alerts, two types of alert have the greatest chance of frightening a victim: the bark alert and the jump up/on alert.

CONSIDERATIONS FOR THE BARK ALERT

The bark alert is a standard in live victim disaster searches. Most victims hearing a barking dog close by feel relief: the barking dog is a sign they have been found. However, a barking dog may terrify a victim or cause the victim to react in a defensive way, such as a lost hunter who aims his gun at the barking K9. In addition, if the search area has loud noises such as thunder, heavy rain, aircraft, machinery, equipment, or vehicles, it may be difficult to hear the dog barking. Some handlers say noise isn't a problem, because if their dogs are gone longer than usual, the handlers go looking for them, or the dogs come back to them for a refind. In addition, the disaster dog generally works in a contained area and does not range far off, so it is closely observed by the handler and SAR technician. Even if noise prevents the handler from hearing an alert, he or she can observe the dog's behavior. However, some breeds of dog start

barking the second they hit the odor of the person they are looking for and continue barking, or baying, for long distances. Such
behavior may reduce the effectiveness of a bark alert.

CONSIDERATIONS FOR THE JUMP UP/ON ALERT

While a dog jumping on a criminal may be fine, jumping on small
or frail victims in SAR may injure or frighten them. With all types
of alerts for live victims, handlers should decide how close they
want their dogs to get to missing persons when they make the find.
A fearful or deranged person could harm the dog or him or herself
when trying to get away. In addition, the dog may become protective of the handler when faced with threatening victim behavior.
If the victim is frightened of the dog but does not, or is unable
to, speak, the handler should carefully observe the victim's body
language and not wait for verbal communication to move the dog
away.

Beyond the Find

"Prepare and prevent, don't repair and repent." – Anonymous

A crisis can occur if a K9 team is not trained in first aid. Unfortunately, there are still TEAMs that provide only K9 search assistance, believing medical assistance at base camp, the command
post, or administered by an accompanying TEAM member is
sufficient. However, a search area's base camp and the command
post may be in different locations, depending on the size of the
search area/s. All teams should know what to do when a victim
is found. The period between the find and when the agency, or
medical or SAR technician, arrives to treat an injured person or
control a panicked, demented, or suicidal subject is crucial. Yet
many live-victim training scenarios use the following sequence:
dog finds victim, dog is rewarded, job done. That type of training
is fine until the K9 team is operational. After that, more complex

training is necessary if the handler does not already have that training.

It comes down to the well-being of the victim and the safety of the K9 team. Knowing how to respond in particular situations will better equip a team—if not in knowing exactly what to do, then at least in knowing what *not* to do. A handler cannot rely on only the flanker or field technician, who may get injured or need assistance. Training in all subjects that could be used in the field is indispensable. You do not know what you may need and when you might need it.

Create a wide variety of training scenarios to better prepare teams for what may happen on an actual search—they maximize the effectiveness of the training. Scenarios should be challenging, involve all aspects in K9 search, and require training that goes beyond the find.

Problem Setups

"We don't rise to the level of our expectations...we fall to the level of our training." – *Archilochus,* On Fighting Against Soldiers from Naxos

Training exercises should be conducted at various times of day or night, in different weather, and in as wide a variety of locations as you can find. To become confident in your dog's ability to perform and avoid being distressed on actual searches, ensure your training includes difficult situations and problems, some of which are described in this chapter. You never know what you and your dog are capable of unless you try—and failure is not necessarily a limitation. A change in training techniques may be the answer to achieving success.

Trailing Setup Ideas
- Split trails and cross trails—should be well-marked in the beginning so the handler can learn to read the dog's

reaction at those points and work out any problems (e.g., the dog loses the scent or begins to follow the wrong trail).

- Contaminated Point Last Scene (PLS) start.
- Contaminated trail.
- A trail crossing an intersection.
- A trail leading to a street where the "victim" has been taken away by a vehicle.
- Vehicle trails and bicycle trails.
- Drop trails.
- Trailing into a store, business, or house.
- Variable surface trailing in one problem: grass, concrete, sand, water, gravel, and so on.
- A wandering trail.
- A trail that goes up and over obstacles—boulders, downed trees, fences.
- A running trail with distance between each footfall.
- A person (not the "victim") sitting at a location on the trail.
- Periodic negative trails (the person matching the scent article is not hiding in that area).

AGED TRAILS AND VEHICLE TRAILS

Training on aged trails is crucial since most law enforcement requests for assistance occur hours or days after the person goes missing. While some handlers attest to their dog's proficiency in working two-day old trails, or two-day old vehicle trails, such claims are a subject of controversy.

THE IMPORTANCE OF NEGATIVE TRAILS

You should learn to read your dog's behavior in all the situations listed above—especially on negative trails. After the dog casts, she may go back to the scent article, sniff it, and then cast again before letting you know a matching scent is not there. Many handlers believe it is better to let the dog determine how she wants to indicate "no scent," as long as she is consistent, instead of training another type of behavior. After a "negative trail" scenario, the team can be taken to another area a short distance away where the "victim" is hiding—just as it happens many times in reality. Using the same scent article, the dog is able to locate the trail and find the matching subject, ending the search happily. Another suggestion has been to remain at the same location but present the dog with a different scent article—this one from the person who is actually in the area—and have the dog cast again.

Do not train with negative areas until the dog is competent in searching positive areas. Overtraining negative areas can cause major problems, with the dog indicating "no scent" after casting only for a short time in an area where there might be scent. Allow your dog to cast for the target odor far enough beyond the PLS to determine there is not any matching scent in that area. Some handlers mistakenly think training negative areas takes up too much time, even though speculative areas are the majority of searches.

Air Scent Discriminating Setup Ideas*
- A group of people, including the "victim," standing around the final destination waiting for the dog to identify the right individual.
- The "victim" casually walks toward and passes the K9 team while they are searching.
- The "victim" and another person walk together toward the K9 team.
- The "victim" walks in a creek or jumps into a pool or pond, or possibly enters a building before continuing to walk a short distance.

- The "victim" walks a distance and then enters and sits in a parked car.

* Can also be used for tracking/trailing dogs

"It's fine to celebrate success, but it is more important to heed the lessons of failure." – Bill Gates, Helping Kids Overcome Fear and Failure

17

Training Is Training, and Testing Is Testing

Blind Problems

A "blind" problem is a situation a team must work out. The handler does not know where the subject or source is located. This scenario is a good way to evaluate a team's level of training. Periodic blind problems are an important part of training; they are usually administered chiefly to judge the handler's ability and knowledge of learned skills, since every problem is a blind one for a dog. Automatically advancing a team to more difficult situations without determining the team's competence in blind problems can result in false security or deficiency in performance. That being said, if training problems are always blind, then they are always a test. Until the handler can read the dog well and the dog appears skilled at whatever level he is at in training, there should be more known problems than blind ones.

Many TEAMs only set up blind problems, or too many of them, for training exercises. This can hamper a handler's hands-on learning of all aspects of what is necessary in search and detection. Even in training the handler is usually focused on one thing—making the find—which, naturally, is the goal. But the find should not be your only objective in training. Knowing where the "victim" is (in training) enables you to concentrate on and learn your dog's body language and breathing pattern when he is in scent and when he loses it. With the help of the instructor, you begin to recognize the possible meanings of those behaviors, and to appropriately encourage or correct your dog without micromanaging him. The instructor's feedback also helps you become more aware of how scent can disseminate or collect based on the terrain, vegetation, and obstacles and how to adjust search strategies appropriate to the conditions. Adjusting a search strategy is imperative to make sure your dog's nose is where he can locate any target odor if it is in that area. Also, the instructor will be able to point out the non-verbal communication you may unconsciously have with your dog as it happens, not after the fact.

The stress trailing and tracking handlers feel during blind problems, when they wonder if the dog is on scent, is increased for those who have become flag dependent and able to see the markers pointing to the correct trail. Without the flags in play, these handlers have to make the call, without visual assistance, to keep going in a direction or to go back to the last place the dog appeared to be in strong scent and start again at that spot. The instructor should continue to follow the training team, even if the pair is going in the wrong direction, and allow the handler to work out the blind problem. This is, after all, an evaluation. An instructor's body position, stopping while the K9 team moves ahead or questioning the handler's movements, can, of course, cue the handler that something is amiss. Some instructors, however, do stop tests to give handlers the opportunity to refocus if they are so very far off target that a find would take an immense amount of time and be by luck rather than accomplishment.

Some handlers question the fairness of some blind evaluations. The question of fairness can come up if the instructor uses the same test area with the same "victim" for *all* teams evaluated on one day. This means that as the day wears on, each subsequent team being tested is subjected to different environmental factors that could help or hinder them—more contamination, or the advantage of larger/ stronger scent cones than there were earlier in the day. Thus, the problem is not the same, yet the teams' abilities are rated as if it were. The level of difficulty for scent-specific K9s will go up as time goes by and the number of mixtures of odors for them to process and work through increases, and the trails become older and increasingly scent corrupted. If the last team being evaluated on this day does not do well, how can the instructor compare that result to the first team of the day's success? Were other added elements a factor that created more difficulty for that team in that stage of training? If the final team is successful, does that mean it is more competent than the first team that accomplished the problem? Questions of fairness in this context are important insights in an evaluation setup and can lead to more uniform and accurate assessments. The solution? Either different test areas could be set up for each team with problems of equal difficulty and length, or only one team should be evaluated per day. Naturally, there are variables in the different disciplines and for different levels of training; you could, for example, reuse a testing area to evaluate a team in a more advanced stage of training.

Double-Blind Tests

A double-blind test is a realistic scenario in which neither the handler nor anyone accompanying the handler knows the trail or where the "victim" or training aid is located. This kind of test gives you a modified sense of what it is like to be on a real search. Of course, nothing compares to the emotions and pressure of an actual search when someone's life is on the line. There are many views on double-blind tests and what they mean.

Viewpoints include:

- They are just a training tool to be used periodically.
- They should not be attempted until the team is ready to test for certification.

- They take too long for some teams, which wander all over the woods while others are waiting to test.
- Trailing double-blind tests have the lowest pass rate of all evaluations.
- They should be conducted to check for handler bias or inadvertent cuing.
- Evidence of them is necessary for legal testimony—providing more reliability.
- They should be conducted to see what the team has really learned.
- Since all dogs work differently, their actions may not be understood by the evaluator.
- They should be done to determine problems areas.
- They should not be done until problem areas have been resolved.
- They can check the handler's performance but not the dog's.
- The evaluator may not be qualified.
- They provide good lessons for evaluators, who at times can be too quick to critique a dog's actions when they know the trail.

Taking all these perspectives into consideration, double-blind tests that replicate real-world scenarios are the most precise method by which you can gauge a K9 team's abilities. These tests are still considered double blind if they include dropped articles, scuffed areas, footprints, broken branches, trampled vegetation, and areas of heavy scent concentration where the "victim" stayed or rested for a period. After all, those elements are all part of the "real world," though they do not always exist. You should recognize them as possible clues, and the dog should acknowledge, in some manner, items with the "victim's" scent. The objects only show the "victim" has been at that site—not where he or she went. These clues help reinforce that the dog is working the correct trail or area and may indicate the condition of the missing person or possibly a direction of travel. Evaluators should not second guess how a dog is working. Not until they review GPS data or do a comparison of the training "victim's" movements by map or video to his or her end location, along with wind at that time, coupled with the atmospheric conditions during the search, will they know where scent could possibly be. A tracking dog, however, should follow the exact track.

One More Time: One More Problem

During training you may become so excited about your dog's success in working out a difficult problem that you want "just one more" problem to solve. But there is danger in this. The next problem may not end so well. It is always best to conclude training with a positive experience for your dog.

PLATEAUS

"You must have long-range goals to keep you from being frustrated by short-range failures." – Charles Noble, "The Magic of Believing"

A dog might reach a plateau in training. At times it can seem insurmountable, cause frustration, and even enough discouragement that you want to quit. You may think too much about what *other* dogs have achieved. For some, those achievements are motivating but for others they are disheartening. Instructors must learn how to address these problems, be supportive, and be willing to try different methods to help handlers get past the plateau. Patience is necessary.

18

The Controversy over Cross-Training

One of the most disputed areas in SAR/R is whether a dog should be cross-trained or whether it should specialize in one discipline. Cross-training can refer to training a dog in SAR/R, protection sports, or other undertakings, such as drug detection. In SAR/R the controversy—voiced with passion by instructors and handlers alike—concerns cross-training in disciplines related to human scent—live or deceased. Such cross-training may include air scent for live victims and human remains detection (HRD); disaster search for both live and deceased victims; and other combinations of SAR/R disciplines. A summary of the diverse viewpoints on cross-training follow.

Viewpoints Supporting Cross-Training
- On many searches the team does not know if the victim will be alive or deceased, so dogs should be cross-trained in both.

- Long before there was specialty training, dogs were finding dead people with no problem. It was never considered a problem.

- A dog can be trained in different disciplines if the dog is willing and able, but the dog should be taught a different command and alert for each.

- Small TEAMs with only a few dogs need to cross-train. Some agencies lack funding for more dogs and handlers. The dual-purpose dog provides an acceptable tool with one handler, with the least amount of resources committed.
- Scent is scent. A properly selected, trained, and handled dog will find any odor she has been trained to locate, wherever it is.
- No one has been able to prove a cross-trained dog is completely unreliable when given a specific command to search for and alert on live versus cadaver.
- If a dog has all the foundation training and drive, she should not have a problem with other disciplines.
- If handlers do not cross-train cadaver dogs, they risk missing a live victim.
- It is less expensive for a volunteer to have a dual-purpose dog than to have two dogs.
- Wilderness SAR dogs have to be cross-trained in live and cadaver search.
- The TEAM works a lot of old cases and want all air scent dogs to know decomposition odor and have some recognizable type of response to it.

Viewpoints Against Cross-Training

- It takes a great deal of time to train and maintain reliability in just one discipline. Without spending equal time training in each discipline, the team will be deficient in one of them.
- Teams that cross-train in human remains simply to get more call-outs should realize if they do poorly in that discipline, their abilities, even for live-victim searches, may be denigrated and they may not be called again. The handler must be willing and able to undertake the great amount of additional education he or she will need to handle a cross-trained dog; otherwise, the team will not be fully competent.
- Cross-training means *total reliability and consistency* with two commands and two alerts, and no one has been able to

prove a live/cadaver cross-trained dog is *absolutely* reliable
and consistent when given a specific command.

- There is the possibility of both odors—live and deceased—
being present in the same area. The dog may alert on the
deceased person first and then stop searching due to the
activity that results from the find. This creates a delay, and
any delay in locating a live victim may cost a life.

- If a dog is *not proofed off* live-victim scent, she will still give
some indication—body language or otherwise—that a live
person is in the area. There is no need to cross-train.

- Credibility and being well-trained for the mission a team
is undertaking is always discussed in SAR/R. Even though
dogs are capable of much more than most handlers ever
compel them to do, handlers have to be honest with
themselves about their K9's reliability and consistency.

- Dogs specifically trained to find live victims only should be
proofed against indicating on human remains.

- A lot of good dogs are not good enough to be proficient in
multiple areas.

- Dogs cross-trained in cadaver and live victims may find and
alert on other searchers and personnel when searching for
cadavers. This might be disparaged by law enforcement or
forensic experts, casting doubt upon the qualifications of
the team.

- If live and deceased victims are in the same vicinity in a
disaster, can a handler ensure the dog will alert on the live
victim first and not waste critical, life-or-death minutes
because the decomposition odor is stronger?

- Volunteer handlers usually train only several hours a week.
Instead of using those valuable hours to progress, perfect,
and maintain their K9's search skills in one discipline, they
have to focus on a second discipline and may end up being
mediocre in both areas.

- Evaluating a cross-trained team in training or certification
is one thing, but a handler's or K9's stress on a long,

laborious, actual search can create confusion and result in problems—especially in large-scale detection work.

- Some handlers use the same command for live and cadaver work, but that does not mean the dog is cross-trained. What does that command mean to the dog—find *anything*? Does it waste time while the dog is working the scent of another searcher in their area when they are supposed to be searching for human decay?

- Live-victim dogs may have found deceased victims without specialty training, but does the dog just go to a scent that interests her or does she accidently come across some remains? Did she do the same with dead animals? Does she give any indication or alert if the handler is yards away when she makes the find?

- We use dogs to make our job easier not harder. There are enough unknowns in SAR without complicating the issues by injecting extra variables in the dog's ability to make a find and make a decision about which alert to give.

- Properly selecting and training a dog does not mean the dog will be perfect. Handlers must remember they are the other half of their team. They can ruin a dog or overtask her to the point of confusion. The handler is better off focusing on one discipline and gaining the knowledge about how to develop and implement the proper search strategies for that discipline alone.

- While the SAR dog should be exposed to human decomposition and may even give a specific natural indication, that does not make her proficient or constitute a cross-trained or dual-purpose dog.

- If a team is not cross-trained *properly and completely in all facets* of the disciplines, search strategies can be wrong, lives lost, crime scenes compromised, valuable evidence destroyed, dog's body language misread or ignored, testimony discredited, and court cases dismissed.

International Reddingshonden Groep

International Reddingshonden Groep, a disaster relief organizations in the Netherlands, operates with rescue dogs on a national and international scale. It came to the following conclusions about cross-training:

1.   [International Reddingshonden Groep] has a strong preference to train a SAR dog for a *specific task,* with its *specific scent* or scent complex, and not for a large number of tasks. This will avoid unnecessary confusion and problems.

2.   If a SAR dog is trained for more disciplines with a *possibility of confusion* then we have to pay *much attention* to this problem in the training of this dog.

3.   SAR dogs trained to search for *living* victims should be trained with living victims only. Furthermore, they should be tested regularly to ensure they do not give false alerts on objects carrying human scents or on dead victims.

4.   SAR dogs trained to search for *dead* victims should be trained on human tissue only. Also, these dogs should be tested to ensure they do not give false alerts on objects carrying human scents.[1]

A CASE AGAINST CROSS-TRAINED DOGS IN DISASTERS

Performance of scent-detection dogs might be negatively affected when they have been trained to discriminate between scents according to a handler-issued verbal cue, compared to dogs trained to only locate one scent. The performance of scent-detection dogs trained to locate only live scent (live-only dogs) was compared to that of scent-detection dogs trained to locate either live or cadaver scent depending on the handler's verbal cue (cross-trained dogs). Specifically, it was predicted that live-only dogs would be more successful than cross-trained dogs at locating live scent when cadaver scent was present.

In the study, twenty-three dogs (11 live-only and 12 cross-trained) were given handler commands to search for live scent in four search areas containing different combinations of scent: no scent, live scent, cadaver scent, and live/cadaver scent. Each dog ran each search area twice. Live-only dogs had significantly more correct responses than cross-trained dogs in the no scent, cadaver scent, and live/cadaver scent search areas. There was no significant performance difference between live-only and cross-trained dogs in the live-scent search area, confirming detection abilities of the cross-trained dogs when presented with only live scent. The ability of cross-trained dogs to correctly indicate the presence or absence of live scent according to a verbal cue was compromised when cadaver scent or no scent was present.

This strongly suggests that cross-trained dogs should not be deployed where cadaver scent is present and the desired target is live scent, for example, a disaster deployment of search dogs to locate surviving victims among possible non-survivors.[2] Note that this study should *not* be confused with another, also led by Lisa Lit, "Handler Beliefs Affect Scent Detection Dog Outcomes," which SWGDOG responded to by saying, "...a number of characteristics of the study presented . . . limit or invalidate the research conclusions."[3]

Considerations for Cross-Training

Cross-training requires much extra training. It not just teaching commitment to an odor but requires you and your K9 to have explicit education for the different types of areas you will be searching: buildings, deserts, fire scenes, mountains and high elevations, urban, vehicles, and wilderness; swamps and other bodies of water: flat or swift, lakes, ponds, rivers, or oceans. Each has its own challenges and may require different search strategies.

Another consideration is your dog's stimulus threshold. A stimulus threshold is the amount of stimulus needed to become perceptible to the dog's senses. Individual dogs have unique stimulus thresholds. If the human remains you are searching for do not have the amount of scent that can be detected by your dog's sensory capabilities, the target odor will be missed. A live victim's body continues to emit odor; thus that scent increases over time, providing a stronger scent cone. That is not the case in searching for human remains. While a decomposing body produces a strong smell detectable even to humans, old or buried remains do not. A "clean" bone—one void of any tissue, can have such a weak odor some dogs can miss it. In addition, decomposed remains are often highly contaminated by wildlife, which can make the faint human scent even more difficult for the dog to detect. Note that your dog's stimulus threshold can change, depending on her state of health, the weather, physical conditioning, aging, and other contingencies.

"Every job is a self-portrait of the person who does it. Autograph your work with excellence." – Unknown

19

TEAM Training Sessions

Joint TEAM Training

Joint training sessions provide opportunities to become familiar with another TEAM's resources, abilities, and training practices. Handlers mention that these sessions lead to a sense of camaraderie, as well as insights, assurances, clarification of mistaken beliefs, and understandings about how other TEAMs search. The TEAMs that do not want joint training sessions lead others to believe they fear coming together would reveal they are not as accomplished as they claim. Some may also suspect that joint training sessions are merely judging ventures and will not produce constructive results—a kind of "us against them" in competition for call-outs. It is helpful to think about joint sessions this way: you train with other TEAMs and observe their methods, character, and assets in a prearranged setting, or you face the unknown by being paired with them when someone's life is on the line.

"Real learning comes about when the competitive spirit has ceased."
– Jiddu Krishnamurti, Krishnamurti on Education

AROUND THE WORLD: HOW OFTEN TEAMS TRAIN

Before becoming an operational *cynotechnique* (dog and handler) in France, the team must train every day for at least one and a half years. After that, training is weekly. Following are the various training requirements of some K9 teams from around the world:

- At least one of three TEAM training sessions per week.
- A four-hour training session each week and one business meeting per month with optional training during the week.
- 300 to 500 hours per year.
- Weekly with alternating days.
- Twice a week and one business meeting per month.
- Every weekend with a dinner get together afterwards to discuss the training.
- Six to seven hours each week.
- A minimum of five field training hours per team each week.
- Twice a month with members training on their own several times a week.
- A minimum of 10 hours per week.

Standards vary widely, and only a few of the TEAMs I studied specified the number of training hours required. Some TEAMS just note the number of training *sessions*, which means actual training hours can vary greatly, depending on how many hours are in each session. In determining your own TEAM's training schedule, remember: training to the minimum requirement may produce a good TEAM; training above and beyond will produce a better a one.

How Often TEAMs Train

A TEAM's agency affiliation—local, state, national, or international—might dictate how often members train. Members of local or regional SAR/R units could be required to attend monthly training sessions, in addition to TEAM training. In some parts of the world, training two or three times a week may be compulsory for those specializing in disaster search. This type of training can require other types of SAR personnel to attend periodically.

Teams that train in addition to structured TEAM exercises usually progress and refine skills at a faster rate. They utilize TEAM training for feedback, working through problems and increasing proficiency levels. Individual training problems, observed by the K9 instructor, may be limited to only one per session due to the number of members participating. In spite of that, you can learn a tremendous amount by watching other teams work. Many times, you recognize your own flawed actions in the work of other handlers: talking too much, perhaps, or micromanaging the dog.

If a TEAM trains only once a month due to low member turnout, it is suggested the group review its training and deployment standards. TEAMs tired of poor excuses for not attending training sessions have cut members from their rosters. They realized they had a choice to make: a high number of members or TEAM quality.

Being able to plan around a specific time and day each week is beneficial for members and their families, but always training during mornings or afternoons excludes nocturnal experiences, which occur on actual searches and so should be part of training exercises.

"Attitude affects performance—a professional is a person who will do his best even when he doesn't particularly feel like it." – *Unknown*

Maintenance Training

Maintenance training is not optional. Some may believe once the team is operational—or because the pair has had many searches in succession—that the handler and K9 no longer have to train regularly. That is a dangerous fallacy. Certified, proven dogs still need to participate in TEAM exercises to refine or maintain skills, or fix problems. The team that does not continue to train begins to decline.

20

Seminars and Workshops

A conference is a formal meeting place for presentations and discussions and can last from hours to days. Workshops usually last two or three days while seminars can go on for five days to a week. Hosting a seminar or workshop is complex and requires a great deal of work. The instructor–K9 team ratio is important to ensure each team gets ample attention. Some instructors bring helpers to assist in fieldwork, which can help more teams participate. Although this provides personal attention, some handlers comment that they attend seminars to be under the watchful eye of a specific instructor—not an assistant.

The most common complaint by handlers about seminars and workshops, however, is the amount of downtime. Setting up challenging problems for experienced K9 teams, then rushing them through the exercises to comply with a strict timeframe, does not fulfill the reason teams have come to the seminar—to learn. The instructor must maintain a delicate balance between teams engaging in activity and hanging in downtime. Even if other activities are set up, those problems may be accomplished quickly. However, you can gain a wealth of information and ideas by watching other teams work. Of course, watching the other teams may not be an option, for example if the problem is being worked out in difficult or close quarters, would interfere with the K9 and handler, or if the problem is a blind one that you and your K9 have not yet completed.

Sometimes, long stretches of downtime can happen in advanced seminars if one of the participants has registered for a class that deals with material above his or her abilities. The extra time the instructor must give this person is unfair to other participants. Instructors speculate that handlers may do this because they believe they are qualified, because that seminar is less costly than another, or to exaggerate their qualifications by saying they attended a particular instructor's "advanced" class. To avoid this problem, instructors should have registrants meet certain prerequisites. But if prerequisites are based on only the handler's *opinion*, evaluations are necessary at the beginning of the seminar, which means some teams might be asked to leave the class and attend a different level. This may then exceed the limit of the number of teams in the class they belong and place a burden on that instructor. One possible way for instructors to proceed would be to ask registering handlers to state their SAR/R experience and how long they have been working with the dog they will bring, along with their class preferences. Their choice can be granted, or a different class suggested. Combining different levels of training in one class is usually frustrating for everyone involved. In those instances, no one receives sufficient instruction.

Another issue in workshops and seminars is the handler who brings multiple dogs. Certain seminars limit classes to one dog per handler. Some charge for an additional dog, and other instructors have been blindsided by this problem because it was not addressed in registration. One handler who brings two dogs is actually two teams. A maximum of six teams per class would have to be reduced to five paying teams. Failing to take this into account creates an oversized class and reduced registration fees for the host organization.

Another point to consider when organizing a seminar is whether or not observers will be allowed to attend without a charge and what guidelines they should have to follow. Will it be acceptable for them to offer advice to individual teams? Several instructors have described events where attending K9 handlers, with big egos, have been so ill-mannered they began to counsel other handlers about how to work their dogs *during the class.* Scholars have said a student cannot learn anything when they are trying to look like the smartest person in the room. Not only are they not learning, but they are taking a learning opportunity away from another student.

> *"It is impossible for a man to learn what he thinks he already knows." – Epictetus, in Arrian's* The Discourses, Book II

Comments and Suggestions

The following comments and suggestions come from handlers and instructors about workshops and seminars.

HOST ORGANIZATIONS

It is judicious for the host organization to verify claims and credentials of instructors before inviting them to teach. Handlers should also familiarize themselves with the instructors' qualifications—this includes instructors from the host organization. Has the instructor finished a dog through certification in the discipline she or he is teaching, or is that not necessary for the class? Comment sheets should be given to all participants at the end of the seminar. Handlers should be encouraged to complete the sheets and be specific if there were any problems.

Organizations that have been disappointed with a few "big name instructors" who are "more sizzle than steak" (or, as is said in Texas, "all hat but no cattle") have become more particular about who they ask to teach. Instructors have been rated anywhere from "awesome" all the way to "an instructor from hell!" The latter is often described as arrogant, rigid, and prone to berating handlers in front of others to the point of tears. Instructors like this lead to students becoming afraid to ask questions. The instructor's philosophy of "my way or the highway" and "you *will* follow only my instructions"—at times disregarding venue rules (e.g., training in prohibited locations or ignoring mandated quiet hours to carry on night training)—can alienate the facility managers and affect future use.

Hosts should ensure that all the proper equipment and personnel are ready for the seminar. Handlers say trailing classes usually provide dedicated trail runners. But, while attending air scent classes, some handlers have been asked to play "victim" because the host did not supply extra helpers. These volunteer "victims" unfairly miss out watching and hearing comments from the instructor because they are in hiding.

Finally, in terms of organizing seminars and workshops, numerous comments indicate that handlers favor venues that provide on-site lodging, or availability for camping—with or without electricity—rather than staying in a motel. The all-inclusive location offers more opportunity to ask questions of instructors, share information, and form friendships without losing time driving back and forth between classes and hotels. If all meals are cooked on the premises, the cost of the seminar would increase but overall may be less expensive than requiring handlers to traveling into town to purchase their own meals. Hosts may also plan for handlers to remain on-site by sending someone to pick up individual food orders.

"The more informed you are, the less arrogant and aggressive you are." – Nelson Mandela, O, The Oprah Magazine South Africa (2013)

HANDLERS AND INSTRUCTORS

A great number of handlers say they prefer seminars that are more directed at training than socialization. Experienced handlers seem to favor scenario-based training that includes search strategies and longer, more complex problems. But you have to bear in mind the balancing act that hosts and instructors must perform. They must correlate the degree of challenges, the size of the area or length of trail for each problem, and the amount of time the lead instructor, or instructors, can spend with each K9 team versus the number of paying teams needed to cover seminar costs. This also includes the extra expense if the instructor brings a helper.

Once the seminar is in full swing, and the balancing act has hopefully been successful, it is suggested that both students and instructors keep an open mind. People never learn anything from someone who always agrees with them. Handlers should be able to articulate and understand why they do things the way they do, so they can discern if a new approach will fit into, or conflict with, any other training concept being worked. Facing new elements and training techniques are a part of seminars. As long as the instructor is not suggesting anything you believe may be detrimental to the K9, you should be willing to try it and advise the instructor of any concerns. A minor adjustment may be all that is needed for your particular dog to make you feel comfortable. If the new idea still creates uneasiness, be wary and ask more questions. Instructors who talk you through the pros and cons of a new method will help you make your own decision about the method.

"If you always do what you've always done, you will always get what you've always gotten." – Jessie Potter, quoted in The Milwaukee Sentinel

Some new handlers are not interested in learning from older, more experienced handlers. What they want is to learn the "new" training tools, reward gimmicks, and latest ideas. Without having knowledge of proven methods to compare with the new approaches, however, these handlers and their dogs won't improve. Remember that many old ways of training are not bad, just like all the new ways are not good—or, not good for your dog.

Whether an instructor is teaching a new method or an old one, handlers must remember that asking questions is one thing, but debating an instructor in front of the group is something else. This comes back to the need for open mindedness. If your view differs from that of the instructor, ask questions respectfully, and later research what was said—the instructor's view may prove to be valid, or it may prove to be unsound. Students set in their outlook do not care what the instructor is saying. They do not listen to understand, they listen to reply—at times trying to chip away at the instructor's confidence. This can demoralize the entire class. Those handlers believe they already know everything—and in a way, they do: they know all they will ever know because they will never listen and learn. If, after a short exchange, the handler continues with a challenge, some educators try the following response: simply smile, say little more on the subject, nod with an occasional "Mmm," and then announce it is time to move on with the lesson.

The very best instructors may be teaching, but if attendees have to witness handlers arguing and bashing others, that negativity affects the entire seminar. Negativity is a strong force that will consume people if they let it. Gossip or rumors are also destructive. Those who want to believe something bad about another handler do not need much to convince them. That poisoned thinking is carried beyond the seminar. You should never repeat something if you are not willing to sign your name to it.

"Gossip dies when it hits a wise person's ears." – Unknown

Cadaver / human remains detection seminars require specific information be given to the attending handlers. That information, for proper training documentation, must identify each training aid used, its age, size, if it has been contaminated in any way, in addition to the location it was placed for each exercise and the length of time it was there.

Instructor Feedback

Instructor feedback during seminars commonly takes place while the K9 team is working the problem and/or when the exercise is completed, depending on the situation. Debriefing can be broad in content as the instructor comments and makes suggestions to the entire class. A lot of debriefings happen during meal times if eating arrangements and table space can accommodate the entire group. This is another benefit of all-inclusive locations where discussions can continue into the night. The feedback given is not always what handlers want to hear, and occasionally handlers may blame the instructor for a poor review. Compliments are wonderful, but are instructors who give only compliments doing their job? There is usually something about every team that needs improvement.

Even with limited time, a great deal can be learned at seminars and workshops. But it is important to not take those lessons out of context or attempt to apply every method or idea at once. Beginning and intermediate-level classes teach more than one element in the discipline. That does not mean you should continue your training from where the seminar left off—rather, you should continue from where that seminar training *began*. Advanced and complicated problems also need new difficulties added by degrees and not all at once so your K9 will not become frustrated.

21

Certifications

First, certifications are for K9 teams—*not* individual dogs.

A K9 SAR/R certification is conditional upon a handler and a specific K9 passing a test or tests imposed by a certifying organization. The team becomes a certified K9 team, by *that* organization, for a defined period. A TEAM may allow a handler to test with an additional SAR/R dog, and if that team successfully completes the certification process, that team would be certified for the discipline tested for—thus, one handler could be certified as part of two separate K9 teams. Some K9 teams purport to be certified in almost every discipline. But the big question is this: certified by whom and according to what standards?

> *"It's not the honors and not the titles and not the power that is of ultimate importance. It's what resides inside." – Fred Rogers, at a ceremony marking the 25th anniversary of* Mister Rogers' Neighborhood

In some occupations a certification signals mastery of a specific skill or discipline. In SAR/R, certification shows that a team has accomplished proficiency in the minimal operational test standards of an organization for a specific stage of work—in a controlled scenario and location, and under the conditions present at the time of the certification test. It does not necessarily mean the pinnacle of success and is not a guarantee of future performances or a reflection of past ones. On average, handlers and their K9s spend about two years training before being ready for certification. Still, certifying officials/evaluators have seen very good teams fail and poor teams pass.

Certifying evaluators should be competent and qualified in the discipline they are appraising—so, someone who has worked only air scent dogs is inadequate to judge a trailing team. In addition, it is helpful if evaluators have knowledge of what to expect from different dog breeds.

TEAMs do not unquestioningly consider a member and his or her dog operational or "mission ready" if the pair gains an outside certification—the TEAM may require additional testing and in-house certification too. That said, not all TEAMs have in-house certifications, but those that do most often incorporate elements intrinsic to their geographic location and types of searches. In-house certifications are a starting point and may even have stricter requirements than certifications gained elsewhere. Although some feel being judged in-house could be biased, others believe a TEAMmate would be harder on them than an outside evaluator. Still, some handlers have questioned, with raised eyebrows, the honesty and integrity of a TEAM that has a member who is a certifying official for a national organization and tests his or her own TEAM members for that certification—at times in private sessions.

Because of the limited information certification provides, a wide range of handlers believe certifications are meaningless. Training for a test rather than training for the mission places focus temporarily on specific points just to pass—missing the big picture. If those skills are not instilled in training, they can be forgotten or poorly executed when needed.

An agency does not always ask for certification papers. This can be due to the nature of the search. For example, the agency may want as many searchers out there as possible, have a good working relationship with the team, or receive a high recommendation for a team from another department. Or, perhaps checking certification papers is just not standard procedure for the agency. However, some handlers have remarked that when an incident commander is in charge, that commander is going to determine what dogs to deploy, and the commander will be more inclined to field average K9 teams that have a paper that says "National Certification" than teams with other certifications—even though they may be more qualified—but lack that "National" stamp.

K9 Team Certification and Proficiency Criteria

The following is a condensed version of the diverse requirements for certification, as well as contingencies some TEAMs have *before* testing a K9 team's operational status. Those contingencies can consist of checklists for handler, dog, and team.

GENERAL SKILLS TESTED

A handler may have to accomplish or become certified in any one, or all, of the following:

- land navigation with map and compass;
- navigating at night in unfamiliar surroundings;
- first aid or CPR;
- surviving in the field for 24 hours, using a day pack;
- translating field activity onto a base map;
- visual man tracking;
- GPS reading;
- hazardous materials awareness;
- crime-scene preservation;

- search strategies; and,
- participating as a flanker / field technician on a certain number of actual searches.

General dog skills include the following:

- being able to perform agility and obedience exercises;
- working effectively alongside other dog teams without undue distraction;
- working efficiently around noise and disruptions;
- working prolonged searches;
- not destroying human remains (HR) sources; and
- having reliable refind indications.

Certification may require the K9 team as a whole to:

- be proficient at night searches;
- locate a wandering victim within the search sector;
- locate concealed or unreachable victims;
- perform activities on snowshoes, skis, or via a variety of boats; and,
- work for four to six hours a day for two consecutive days.

LIMITED OR RESTRICTED CERTIFICATIONS

Limited certifications exist in several organizations for K9 teams that have been dedicated members for years. Those TEAMs see the value of a team that may be limited in its abilities due to age or infirmity but that can still work effectively in specific areas or situations.

TESTING ADMINISTRATION, CRITERIA, AND EVALUATION PRACTICES

To certify is to vouch for or confirm certain standards have been met by a K9 team. Evaluators are accountable for those endorsements, and they should not take that responsibility lightly.

Some certifications are evaluated pass/fail—a handler error in signifying an alert that is false, for example, would constitute an automatic fail for the team. Others are determined according to a percentage, with a passing grade ranging from 70 to 90 percent, with allowances for a false alert and one miss in locating the target odor. Since testing is a strategic plan in a contained area, some believe percentage-based results can be problematic because of too much leeway in the results. What important area(s) did the team fail in but were still able to achieve the minimum passing score? Other organizations give teams four evaluations and average the totals for a final judgment. If any one of the four evaluations is lower than a fixed number, the K9 team does not pass.

Tests can be set up to evaluate only the dog's ability or tests may include handler know-how, such as search strategy, being able to read the dog, and other criteria. Although, on occasion, evaluating handler skills has been called "subjective interpretation about the team's quality of performance," it is essential in the making of a good K9 team; after all, the handler is the other half of the team. A number of handlers believe evaluators engage in misconduct if they talk to handlers while they are being tested—or ask them questions that help them work out the problem—other than giving a two-minute notification (if that is allowed).

In certification evaluations, the size of the search areas for specific tests may vary based on the organization's standard, as does the delay time the "victim" / training material was in place; the age and length of a trail; the duration of testing time; or the weight of the backpack, if required. In addition, restrictions may be placed on who can play "victim" for live-victim testing. Some testing criteria prohibit any person known to the dog being used. Organizations might also have levels of certification based on difficulty.

AIR SCENTING
Most air scenting tests take place in areas ranging from 20 to 160 acres (8 to 65 ha), some with an unknown number of "victims." Some tests

include multiple phases, negative areas, or human remains in the live-victim search area. Advanced testing may have three "victims" in a 2-square-mile (3.2 km²) radius or include working at altitude changes.

TRAILING

Trailing tests are set in urban or wilderness locations, or both. Many handlers say that the evaluator must know where the trail is to accurately determine if the dog is working. The ages of trails in testing are normally from two to 24 hours old, although advanced testing can have 48-hour-old trails. Some TEAMs require teams to complete two-night searches with a find—one with a trail that is 72 hours old and the other with a 96-hour-old trail. Certifying in such old trails can add to the problem K9 teams already face in not being called immediately for searches. Such certifications lead to the misconception that 48- and 72-hour-old urban trails are typical, and that *all* dogs are reliable working trails that old. Because of these mistaken ideas, law enforcement may believe it can use other methods first before calling in K9 teams.

CADAVER AND HUMAN REMAINS DETECTION

A considerable number of TEAMs test separately for cadaver and human remains detection (HRD). The differences between the two tests are not only the size of the testing areas but also the strength/concentration of the testing materials. Whereas 20 acres (8 ha) might be a realistic size to search for a full body or very strong source, it would be excessive for weak, buried remains in a wooded area or rugged terrain. A test's allowed time and area size may also depend on how the test is presented: "Here's your search area," versus providing a search scenario, which is when the instructor/evaluator gives the handler some information and a timeframe about the "case." Providing a scenario allows the handler to decide how to section large acreage for priority segments to form his or her search strategy and create a clue mind-set (being vigilant of objects, signs, or areas that might pertain to the case)—all part of real searches. Tests have been designed for specific types of searches, such as old, disarticulated remains; combinations of buried and scattered bones; or surface and elevated sources. These are conducted on an average area of 2 acres (0.8 ha).

Cadaver and HRD certification tests also specify the type of human remains testing materials to be used. Almost all tests prohibit the use of imitation scents (Sigma Pseudo scents are discussed on page 193). The dogs may also have to show they can work both on and off lead. Some tests incorporate buildings, wilderness/outdoors, and vehicle searches. Most tests have blank containers, animal remains, distractions (including people), and negative holes dug in the search areas. Actual searches are unpredictable, of course, and it is difficult to address everything in one test.

Non-certified K9 teams are sometimes deployed on actual searches, and some have found the victim. However, strong comments have been made on SAR/R discussion lists that these "finds" do not mean those K9 teams are automatically certified. A find may show an uncertified team has a good working dog or that the dog was in the right place at the right time—but that is all.

THE DURATION OF TESTS

Though nearly all certification tests are completed in one day, some organizations' tests last for two or three days, with several evaluators and two or more different problems each day. Though still not covering all that is necessary, this method may produce a more comprehensive representation of abilities. Those tests, coupled with a consensus of the evaluators as a review panel, give more confidence in the certification system.

Certification Tests versus Training Records

Testing criteria should be realistic and challenging. Some handlers have questioned where to draw the line in terms of how many different types of certification tests (e.g., live-victim/10 acre test;

live-victim night search test, live-victim/100 acre test) TEAMs should have. The answer, although simple, comes back to not the number of certifications, but the value of them versus what your training records indicate about continued competency and varied experience. Training should expose the K9 team to as many different possibilities as they may face on actual searches. Whether all, or some, are included as a part of the certification process is the choice of the organization conducting the tests. Either way, everything should be well-documented in training logs, casework, and other forms of authentication. That includes errors and problems and what was done to rectify them. It is those records that show the K9 team's true abilities, reliability, and consistency. Every team stands on its own merit.

Retesting and Recertification

There is no across-the-board, recognized timespan observed before permitting retesting if a K9 team fails a certification process. An organization may allow retesting the next day, or it may require a wait of 30 or 60 days. Some TEAMs do not allow retesting for six months or more and require teams to participate in remedial training during that period. It seems that a six-month or longer delay may indicate that K9 teams are being tested before they are ready.

Recertification test timespans also vary. Many are annual; some are every two years. INSARG (International Search and Rescue Group) requires recertification every three years, and teams with dogs 10 years and older must recertify every year. Questions have arisen about the wait period for certified teams failing recertification tests. Answers include:

- They should be allowed to retest immediately.
- If the organization requires a 30- or 60-day waiting period, the K9 team should be allowed to go to a different organization to recertify sooner.

- If the team has done excellent and consistent work during its original certification period, it should still be fielded on searches as long as another recertification test is forthcoming in the near future.

The structure and content of recertification tests are particular to each TEAM or certifying agency. Some are the same as the initial tests; some are different or more advanced than the original tests; and some are just small-area tests. The purpose is to ensure the K9 team is still competent.

General or Certification Seminars?

General seminar classes are broad in scope and being walked through a test a day before taking it or training only for the test devalues its purpose. Many veteran handlers believe a certificate of attendance or certificate of participation are more appropriate for such seminars than a certification of skill. Some handlers think certification testing should be made available only at certification events specifically designed for that purpose—not general seminars—to maintain the value and veracity of certifications.

Outside Evaluators

Even though most evaluators ask for only their expenses and volunteer their time and expertise, someone must pay for even limited expenses. That is why hosting TEAMs charge an attendance fee. Since volunteer SAR/R handlers are told up front that there are a variety of financial obligations, this should not come as a surprise. It is a matter of choice that each of us makes. At times, organizations—most of which have a tax-exempt standing—absorb or offset costs for their members, using donations and grant money. Independent handlers rarely, if ever, file for nonprofit status. They do not have the time or human resources to deal with mandatory government paperwork or to conduct fundraising events—thus they do not receive any outside funding. Everything they do is out-of-pocket, which requires an extremely tight budget.

Test Anxiety

Even excellent handlers with great K9s can experience test anxiety. In all fairness, tested K9 teams should not be in the same gathering area as untested ones. However, if tested teams are in the vicinity, it is only common courtesy for them to keep quiet and not brag about their results or how quickly they accomplished the problems. That kind of behavior only adds to untested handlers' tension.

Part IV

Cadaver and Human Remains Detection

Prelude to Human Remains Detection

Dr. William M. Bass, DABFA[1]

In most forensic cases, law enforcement usually asks two questions: who is it and how long has the person been dead? These are difficult questions involving many fields of science as well as climate, temperature, clothing, DNA, entomology (insects), sunlight, recent rain fall, and multiple other factors, as you will read in this book.

I am not a dog handler or trainer, but early in my career I learned that the type of research that I was doing in forensic anthropology, such as the length of time since death, was also important in training dogs to locate human remains in different stages of decomposition.

Four months after I arrived at the University of Tennessee in Knoxville, in June 1971, I requested land to place dead bodies on to study the changes that occur after death. I was not only a faculty member in Anthropology but was also State Forensic Anthropologist for the Tennessee Medical Examiners System.

Realizing the great need for training cadaver dogs, I began to invite dog handlers to share the learning experiences that my students and I were observing. For years, between the late 1970s and early 2000s, we offered dog handlers the opportunity to train their dogs on active decay and skeletonized cases. Much of what the dogs, the handlers, and I learned is discussed in depth in this book. Congratulations on selecting a book that will be of great value to dog handlers and law enforcement.

22

What is Cadaver / Human Remains Detection?

Before forensic television shows became popular, the discipline of cadaver / human remains detection (HRD) did not receive much special attention by handlers—searching for live victims was the focus. Now it seems to be the fastest growing area in K9 detection work. Some newcomers may believe it is "cool" to consider themselves in this realm without realizing all it entails, what will be expected of them, and possibly the emotional consequences of its gruesome nature.

Common questions include, "What is the difference between a cadaver dog and an HRD dog?" and "When does a cadaver become human remains?" The answer to the first is that the terms are subjective. To certain handlers, the label is just a name—for others, the title applied is based upon the advanced degrees of training the K9 team has accomplished and in which they have become proficient. For the second question, a cadaver does not "become" human remains—they are one and the same. The different terminology is used because when most people think of a cadaver, they visualize a full body, whereas "human remains" suggests parts and scattered remains. Searching for human remains is not just about the dog working in an area trying to find a target scent, but also about the odor threshold of the dog (the amount of odor the particular dog needs to detect the scent), the handler's ability to gather specific information to formulate the proper search strategy, and the handler's knowledge about topics such as forensic taphonomy and soil types and their effects on buried bodies (discussed later in this chapter).

It is important to understand that these dogs are trained to find the odor/scent of human decomposition, which varies in strength due to the level of decomposition or how the body was disposed or concealed.

Handlers sometimes suggest that cadaver search work is easy, commenting that urgency is not an issue because the person is already dead and "not going anywhere"; that if a dog cannot handle the rigors of live-victim search, she can be trained for cadaver search; and that cadaver search is not difficult because "scent is scent." The first statement would not sit well with law enforcement (LE) officers who work homicide cases tirelessly to find the victim and evidence that will conclude with the killer being found and successfully prosecuted—possibly preventing more victims. They feel urgency. There may be an urgent request for a qualified team when a search warrant, with a narrow window of time, has been issued. LE may immediately need a K9 team because they were able to schedule all their forensic personnel for a specific time and now want a K9 team too. In reply to the second comment, areas searched for a deceased person are no different than those teams must search for a live person. In fact, they can be more difficult to navigate when trying to detect old, disarticulated remains in thick brush and vegetation, swamps, and a myriad of other places where a *full body* might be visible and more easily accessible.

The final comment by those who think cadaver search is not difficult may be because most dogs will likely go to a strong odor of decomposition regardless of what it is. But that does not make them "cadaver dogs." Cadaver/HRD has many elements besides a dog trained to alert on that target odor and the handler knowing crime-scene preservation. Search strategies are different, and much can be missed if an area is not searched properly. Dogs that alert on dead animals or give false alerts not only waste time but possibly resources and money. The handler may be asked, "Based on what your dog did, should we tear up this driveway or foundation?"

Information on homicide searches is not as attainable as it is for a missing person. Confidentiality is a worry for investigators. Teams must realize whatever information they receive from or overhear in the presence of LE—even if it seems inconsequential—may impact the case if disclosed to the public. Handler testimony in court may also be required, which again can affect the case outcome.

"No Greater honor will ever be bestowed on you as a Police Officer or a more profound duty imposed on you than when you are entrusted with the investigation of the death of a human being . . . . It is a heavy responsibility . . . ." – From The Homicide Investigators of Texas Creed

Then, there are the family and friends of the victim to consider. When a person is missing for many days, whether as a result of innocent or criminal circumstances, some presume he or she is no longer alive, but the family holds on to threads of hope. Their wait is excruciating and the pain of not knowing can be crippling. When a victim is recovered, the words "the family has closure" have been used. But the victim's recovery may not be enough to subdue the family's nightmare. They may need to see the killer or person responsible face justice and be convicted before they can even attempt to move forward. Therein lies the significance of evidence, evidence found, missed, unrecognized, or compromised by those searching.

DOES CLOSURE REALLY EXIST?

There is no time limit on grief. Families have been torn apart, divorces and mental breakdowns have ensued, and suicides have resulted when people cannot live without their beloved. Confirmation that the beloved is deceased is a horrible ending to a family's wait for answers—the only solace it gives is a point of contact as opposed to the unknown. A point of contact is something that connects individuals physically or emotionally. A physical point of contact could be the burial site or the cremation urn. An emotional one might be a place on the shoreline in the vicinity where an airliner went down into the ocean. Flowers may be placed on the shore or wreaths cast into the waters. That shoreline is the point of contact—a place the family can commune with their loved one, a place where they can feel connected.

What Is a Cadaver Dog?

The definition of "cadaver dog" has become broad and inconsistent. When law enforcement officers hear that term, they are inclined to think the related K9 team is capable in the entire scope of this discipline. However, this title *does not* fit all dogs working in this discipline.

As with other disciplines, HRD training is done in steps and levels, with each building upon the previous to reach a goal. Not until a K9 team has successfully tested and passed all levels is the pair qualified as "mission ready" and able to participate in actual searches. However, in cadaver search / human remains detection, there are stages of attainment after which a K9 team may be considered competent for a particular type of search. The level you attain depends on how far you (usually cross-training the K9) want to take your education and training and how much time you have while continuing to train in another discipline. Because of this, many handlers have redefined and renamed the "cadaver search dog." To them, the term "cadaver dog" no longer encompasses all types of human decomposition search work. New names added include the following: human remains detection dog (HRD—the second-most used title after "cadaver dog"), death investigation dog, death detection dog, decomposition dog, body detection dog, victim recovery dog, and forensic human remains detection K9. There are also historical human remains detection dogs.

Searching for a live person is a top priority, but that does not diminish the importance or possible immediacy of having proficient K9 teams search for deceased victims.

Levels of Training

At this writing, there are no standardized levels for this discipline that include the handler's knowledge as well as the dog's detection ability and scent threshold. However, opinions put forth about levels include the following:

Level One: May include basic search where the K9 team is qualified to search for a lost person, presumably deceased, and the K9 has a consistent alert.
Level Two: May include shallow burials, proofing off animal remains, and slightly more complicated searches.
Advanced Levels: Might include deep burials, fire scenes, disarticulated remains, all stages of decomposition, recognition of remains, and difficult situations.

"Forensic HRD" requires consistent and competent K9 teams to search for and detect the target odor in all types of areas and circumstances. This includes all types of searches mentioned above plus crime-scene search, searches for evidence and trace evidence, and cold cases. A "cold case" is defined as an unsolved case—homicide or missing person—without an active investigation due to long-term lack of information or clues. I should note that some law enforcement K9 handlers don't believe the word "forensic" should be applied to the work of K9s. But the word "forensic," according Merriam-Webster Dictionary, is "relating to or dealing with the application of scientific knowledge to legal problems." Because of their additional forensic studies and substantial K9 training in finding trace evidence with the odor of human decomposition, many handlers feel justified in calling themselves "forensic HRD teams."

Another version of levels of training in this discipline includes the following levels:

Basic Cadaver: The ability to detect a deceased victim on the land—surface or hanging—such as expired missing persons and suicides. This is normally for dogs with "live-victim search" as their primary search discipline.

Intermediate Cadaver: The ability to detect recent deaths and shallow burials, including proofing the dog against alerting on animal remains and rotting food. The handler must study human decomposition to attain this level.

Advanced Cadaver: Defined as the ability to detect victims in old cases, deep burials, and disarticulated remains, and includes the study of predator habits, soil influences, understanding the taphonomic process (how the environment and wildlife can disassemble and alter human remains), and other issues, including fire scenes and water search. (Water search involves specific training. A team may be highly trained in water search while being trained in only the basics of land cadaver search or vice versa.)

Forensic Cadaver Search: As mentioned, some teams use the word "forensic" to describe their ability, proficiency, and qualifications concerning human decomposition and related subjects to conduct *all the above-mentioned types* of searches in all types of scenarios and environments. These include vehicle searches, building searches, and crime-scene detection in addition to trace-evidence detection. The handler must know how to proceed or direct the K9 in searching the scene from the spot of her alert to being able to pinpoint the source. In other words, in most cases, the handler should be able to say, "It's right here"—indicating the immediate spot of the target odor or *within a few of inches*—rather than, "It's somewhere over here." The handler must have training not only in gravesite recognition and appraisal of a possible grave regarding plant growth and distribution, but also in insect activity as it relates to decomposition.

Although there are more opinions regarding what each level of training should entail, these two examples illustrate the demands placed on the handler and not just the dog when searching for the odor of human decay.

Specializing in Human Remains Detection

At the time of this writing, it seems more handlers are now stating that K9 HRD is such a specialty that a dog should not be cross-trained. (Here again is that controversial subject. For the pros and cons of cross-training, see chapter 18.) In some parts of the world, "cadaver dogs" are *proofed off* live-victim scent.

It has been established that cross-trained dogs can find deceased victims. It has also been established that dogs like to investigate things that have strong odors. Even untrained dogs have found human remains, and in many cases, they have carried them home. Be that as it may, it is crucial that dogs be used in situations appropriate to their training level, and that handlers are able to support their testimony about their dogs' training and behavior with accurate training logs. That does not mean a K9 trained in only basic cadaver work could not make a find in a complicated situation because of the search circumstances. If so, it would be ludicrous to not consider that a legitimate find. However, exaggerating qualifications to intentionally field a dog not trained for the task is dishonest and can impede an entire investigation.

Some LE agencies have been reluctant to use civilian cadaver dog teams because they are unsure about the teams' trustworthiness. Many TEAMs have worked hard to build positive and honorable relationships with the agencies. But, in 2002, distrust

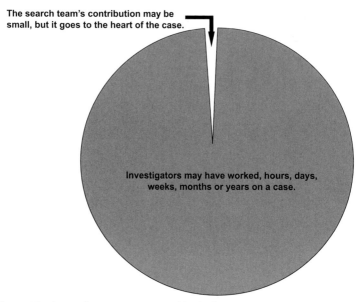

The search team's contribution may be small, but it goes to the heart of the case.

Investigators may have worked, hours, days, weeks, months or years on a case.

Figure 22.1 Law enforcement is pressured by the families, their superiors, the media, city or county officials, and, at times, state officials to find the victim and/or evidence and resolve the case.

had grown because of the highly publicized international case of "world-renowned" K9 handler Sandra Marie Anderson, who was found to be planting bones and evidence at search scenes. Her actions went as far as "finding" blood on a hacksaw blade in a homicide case. Later DNA analysis determined the blood was her own. Court documents showed she had even testified against that defendant on the witness stand. In her apparent quest for fame, she not only brought about more pain for victims' families but also forced the FBI to review over 50 cases they believed might be tainted by her involvement. Faced with a 10 count indictment in which she could have received 65 years in prison, she finally confessed in a plea bargain and spent 21 months in federal prison. The website "Forensic Solutions LLC; Forensic Fraud Archive" has 39 articles on this abhorrent case.[1] There have been other fraudulent handlers before and since, but not to the magnitude of the crimes perpetrated by Anderson.

Handlers must strive to build a TEAM committed to knowledge, dedication, and honesty to erase the stigma caused by fraudsters. Agencies that have had bad experiences with a team may develop a prejudice against using any SAR/R teams in the future. As it has been said before, what one TEAM does affects all TEAMs.

Handlers who assert they cross-train their dogs in several disciplines with different commands and alerts for each must be honest with themselves. Regardless of how much confidence you have in your dog's ability to perform, there is no such thing as a perfect dog. There are complex factors and unpredictable variables in detecting human remains in most searches. Homicide investigators want the best resources to help them with each case. They must feel confident an area has been searched to the best of the ability of a highly trained HRD K9 team, because that may determine the investigative direction.

An analogy: If you needed delicate brain surgery and had the choice between a doctor who said he was an orthopedic surgeon, an oncologist, a brain surgeon and a proctologist—or one who specialized in only brain surgery—which one would you chose?

23

Odor of Death

Dogs react to smell—it is part of their communications system. Studies found that putrescine, one of the chemicals produced by decaying animal tissue, can cause increased vigilance or retreat in humans, similar to the fight-or-flight response in animals.[1] This can be the major factor in dogs that have an aversion to decomposition odor.

At the time of death, a person's unique scent undergoes an almost immediate alteration. Due to autolysis—the breaking down of cells or tissues by their own enzymes (also called self-digestion)—the odor becomes more generic. In 2004 Dr. Arpad Vass and his team compiled their Decompositional Odor Analysis Database, which consists of 478 chemical compounds that are released by decomposing humans.[2] However, by 2012 Vass found additional chemical compounds that increased the number to 500, which he discusses in his video "CommonScents."[3] Of those now 500 compounds, 30 were identified as key markers in human decomposition.

Dr. Vass's team was able to break down the chemical compounds into classes, and subsequent studies distinguished a pattern of odor based on the stages of decomposition.

Since individuals have different levels of natural chemicals in their bodies, it is understandable why more particularized components could not be identified. Different illnesses can bring about different odors. Urinary tract infections can produce a fruity-like body smell, while diabetics may have a sweet odor. People who suffer from the metabolic disorder trimethylaminuria, known as "fish odor syndrome," have a smell resembling rotting fish. Medications, poisons, narcotics, alcohol, and other chemicals, depending on their volatility, can also be a part of the odors that accompany decomposition. Insulin may produce an acetone-like smell and someone poisoned with arsenic can have the odor of almonds.

Understanding cadaveric decomposition chemistry and exactly what chemical, or combination of chemicals, dogs identify as the odor of human decay is ongoing. Regardless, once a K9 is properly trained and committed to only the odor of human decay, additional chemical compounds should not impede her work. In several training sessions at the Forensic Anthropological Facility in Knoxville, Tennessee—also known as "The Body Farm"—all the cadaver dogs participating identified the target odor and alerted on bodies that had undergone chemotherapy and other medical treatments, drug and alcohol overdoses, and even embalming.

One to Two Parts Per Trillion

The claim that the amount of odor a dog can detect is one to two parts per trillion, which I made in chapter 7, The Dog's Nose, needs to be clarified here in the context of human decomposition. Human decomposition odor is often so limited it is possible that the dog may not identify it. The dog may exhibit intense sniffing in the odor's presence but not alert because the full scent picture is not present. This is where your knowledge of your dog's body language and behavior comes into play. Detection and identification are two different things. In some cases, a dog will be able to both detect and recognize the minute odor, but in other instances she may not.

In 2016 I communicated with research scientist Brent A. Craven regarding fluid dynamics in canine olfaction. In our email correspondence, he stated:

> When most studies talk of detection in terms of one or two parts per trillion they are referring to levels for a specific chemical. There are not many studies that report canine detection levels for different chemicals. The one to two parts per trillion value comes from a particular study we cited in our research.[4] But, importantly, I believe that these levels will depend on the specific chemical (e.g., if the chemical is highly soluble or not, which affects odorant deposition in the nose). So, the dog might be able to detect some compounds associated with decomposing human remains at very low concentrations (1–2 parts per trillion), but likely not all the chemicals at such low levels.[5]

24

Training Materials or Scent Sources

"Training aid," "scent source," and "training materials" are the words I use throughout for the training tool that is, or contains, human decomposition or its odor.

Because you decide to train in K9 HRD does not mean you are entitled to be given materials. Some handlers have demanded that doctors provide them with human tissue, teeth, and other specimens, mistakenly believing they have that right. It is illegal in the United States to sell transplant organs such as kidneys, hearts, tendons, and so on, and the organ transplant industry is regulated by the government. However, at this writing, there is only one federal law regarding the sale of body parts and cadavers for other purposes. That law restricts the sale or possession of remains of Native Americans and their funerary objects to protect their burial sites. Laws concerning the sale and possession of human remains by others for vital research, medicine, and education are created at the state level, and thus they differ widely across the country. Each state has its own criteria for what it identifies as a legal organ or body part. Although training dogs to locate deceased individuals is a worthy cause, there are those who believe the sale of human remains is beyond the specifics of what is or is not legal but is primarily a matter of respect, ethics, spiritual beliefs, and the dignity of the deceased. That may be one of the reasons some handlers' requests for training aids have been refused. Because some states and countries forbid the possession or even use of body parts for training purposes, handlers must learn *all* the legalities where they live and train—some of which have changed in recent years. A few states have enacted laws allowing handlers to acquire human sources for training if those handlers meet specific qualifications.

Handlers must be sensitive when discussing training materials. Different cultures think and feel differently about death, the soul, and the afterlife. Regardless of culture, some people believe that authentic remains should not be used for training and are repulsed by the thought, so it is best to be subtle in conversation. Some instructors suggest explaining that you use a chemical reproduction of decomposing human tissue, such as Sigma Pseudo Scent, which will be discussed later in this chapter. To avoid telling a lie, make a point of actually using a chemical reproduction in at least a training or two. Even if using actual remains is legal, you never know the reaction you will get or what problems use of those materials may cause. But you will likely encounter much curiosity about what you are using to train your dog to find a "cadaver," so think ahead to plan what your explanation will be. Being discreet without lying may be best, mentioning sources usually viewed as acceptable, such as teeth, blood on bandages, or soil from under a body.

Bear in mind that if you can legally acquire human sources, it may take time for you to prove credibility to legitimate contacts. Even if the "part" belongs to you as the requesting person, such as something you have had removed in surgery, it may have to be sent to a pathology lab, so acquisition will be denied. Human remains and blood are considered biohazardous materials— disease-producing substances including viruses, bacteria, toxins, and other microorganisms that can pose serious threats to health.

"To be persuasive we must be believable; to be believable we must be credible; to be credible we must be truthful." – Edward R. Murrow, when he was director of United States Information Agency, in testimony before a 1963 Congressional Committee

Natural Training Aids

Although training aids will be buried, hung, concealed, and put in strange places, they should be treated responsibly and with appreciation for the purpose they serve. Handlers may mentally distance themselves from what they are actually holding or using when training their K9s. However, when a find is made on an actual HRD search, it can put things in perspective and remind them that their training materials are a part of someone's loved one. A donated body or body part is the most generous gift a person can give and should be treated in the manner for which it was intended. The use of bones for Halloween decorations, parts of a scarecrow or snowman, or other unseemly displays is disgraceful and definitely unprofessional (and sadly, yes, this has actually happened!)

Around 2004 and again in 2013, the subject of selling human remains began to be scrutinized more than in years past. Many professionals and other members of society believe that body and body-part commercialization is commensurate with the actions of grave/body robbers of the 19th century and violates the dignity of dead. Furthermore, they believe it is inconsistent with the custom of respect generally given to deceased human beings. In several states, use of human remains in training may constitute the "abuse of a corpse," which is a criminal offense. If you locate a point of supply where you can obtain all types of HRD training aids, proceed with caution. What may appear as a treasure trove can be, and has been, remains that were stolen, purchased illegally, or misappropriated from crime scenes. Not only is that wrong on all counts, in court a defense attorney would further attempt to discredit you as lacking ethics or a moral compass.

Almost anyone can be taken in by frauds—like the unsuspecting medical researchers who rented heads, arms, and legs that were later found to be riddled with diseases. A person was indicted for running an illegal cadaver business, along with charges for dismembering bodies without consent.[1] Several states and countries ban the possession, sale, and transport of human remains. India and China, which were major suppliers, now prohibit exportation. This has increased the supply coming from elsewhere and by unknown means. Handlers should find out the origin of the remains and how they were obtained to avoid legal and health problems. If bones are described as "pathological," it means that person had a disease, but this is not always known to the seller. Bones offered for sale from well-known companies will be cleaned in some manner to remove the soft tissue. If any tissue remains after the initial process, the bone may be nature-cleaned using demisted beetles, or by other methods to remove what is left. (The natural progression of tissue decomposition can take considerable time and is not lucrative for those in the business of selling human remains.) Once cleaned, the bones are usually fully degreased and whitened with products.

In 2002 one of the popular sellers of bone was questioned about health and safety issues related to the product they sold. They were asked what measures were taken to prevent the spread of any type of infectious disease with questions such as, "Were the bones preserved with formaldehyde or other chemicals and had they been sterilized in an autoclave machine or another type of sterilizing method?" The company's reply was vague: "All our bones have been cleaned to a degree that allows them to be imported. They have not had any preservative added; some may have been sterilized in an autoclave . . . " and that "reports are that all the bones, even the most processed, still have whatever it is dogs need to recognize human material." They did not say exactly how they cleaned the bones.[2] The concern here is not what happens if a K9

Figure 24.1 The slight sheen on this mammoth's tooth indicates a sealant has been applied.

trained with a processed bone finds skeletal remains on a search—a find is a find. The concern is one of infectious disease control.

Another issue is that cleaned bones may have sealant coatings such as plastic, shellac, lacquer, white glue, or polyurethane applied. Those coatings add chemicals to the scent picture, and if a dog is imprinted on *only* those bones, the chemicals become part of the target odor. If the chemical composition is known, it is wise to proof the dog off those chemicals. Caution should also be taken in using artificial composite bones rather than the real thing. If you are the recipient of a bone, you should verify that it is human.

HUMAN FLESH
Human flesh includes skin, tissue, muscle, and fat—an excellent source but hard to obtain.

TEETH
Teeth extracted due to decay already produce a stronger odor than healthy teeth. Many dentists will not give teeth or will insist on

cleaning them first. According to the Centers for Disease Control and Prevention (CDC), "Extracted teeth may be returned to the patients upon request and are not subject to the provisions of the OSHA Bloodborne Pathogens Standard."[3] If teeth are rinsed clean they are still a good training aid since the pulp chamber contains nerves, blood vessels, and connective tissue.

BONE

Bone is an excellent source, but untreated ones can be difficult to acquire. Human bones and body parts can be legally purchased on the Internet; however, some major sites no longer allow those types of sales. Due to a lack of oversight, there have been sellers whose practices have broken the law.

BLOOD

Blood is probably the easiest source to acquire—from bandages, clothing, and so on, especially those having scabs and other tissue. However, other types of training aids are preferred. Blood—professionally drawn—from the handler, or a friend or relative, is another way of getting this training material. Some handlers have stated that fresh blood is okay to use as a scent article, since it will retain that person's specific scent for an undetermined period. Others disagree and think it is not the blood retaining the odor, but the rafts shed onto it by the person. Therefore, to be safe, perhaps let your own blood, or that of someone close to the dog, age for at least two weeks before using it as an HRD training aid.

Some handlers ask if blood decomposes or just dries out. Blood decomposes. Small amounts of blood can become dry and flaky at first, while a large amount will get thick, coagulate, and then crusty as it decays. Consider a drop of blood on pavement versus the scab on a large wound.

Automobiles involved in serious accidents or crimes can be sources for blood or tissue training aids. Personal protection should always be used in the collection of items. If a vehicle has been released by law enforcement (LE) and the family, or discarded/abandoned by its owner, a wrecking or impound yard may allow cutting pieces of upholstery or taking items that have blood or body fluids on them. Any person granting that permission must have the authority to do so, though, and you should record his or her name before proceeding. It may also be necessary to provide that person with personal or TEAM information for his or her own records. While collecting your sample, if you find anything of sentimental or monetary value in the vehicle that may have been overlooked, document it and turn it over to the appropriate department. It is also important to watch for slivers of glass and sharp metal edges. Note that when working with trauma blood, such as that collected right after an accident, your dog may react differently than he would to drawn blood. Accidents create fear and fear causes chemical changes in a person's body—among them the release of adrenaline. Because a dog has an innate response to stress and fear pheromones, he may at first indicate that blood by being very cautious or even by cringing.

SOIL

Soil collected from under a body is another source of training materials because decomposition may mean that body fluids, fatty acids, and decay have soaked into the ground. There are times when skeletal remains are found but there is no decomposition visible in the soil beneath it. This can happen when the body has been moved by the killer or by predators from where it decomposed. As revolting as it sounds, there are killers who have moved a decaying body for fear it would be discovered where they first put it. Fatty acids and body fluids may be in the soil at the original location, and finding that site may also provide evidence and have great impact on the investigation.

Figure 24.2 The black areas in this photo are erroneously called "body burn" by some handlers. The black areas are volatile fatty acids in the soil. An almost complete outline of how the body was lying as it decomposed is revealed. (Photo courtesy of Lt. Roger Seals, Hunt County Sheriff's Department, Texas)

If you ask LE for permission to collect affected soil, do so discreetly and only after the scene is released. Authorization must come from the investigator in charge. Take precautions when collecting the dirt and put entrenching tools in large bags or containers before placing them back in your vehicle. Prior to storage, clean the tools with a bleach/water mixture to kill bacteria. This also prevents soil and other elements from being transported to another search scene.

ADIPOCERE

Adipocere can be found on bodies or in soil beneath a body. It is commonly called "grave wax" and can be white, brown, grayish, or black. This waxy substance is a result of fat tissue (adipose) beneath the skin that has saponified—meaning turned into

Figure 24.3 Adipocere can be clearly seen on portions of these remains.

soap-like matter. Adipocere develops on parts of a body that have been subjected to water for a length of time. Heavyset people, however, have a great deal of adipose tissue and can produce adipocere without being subjected to water. Drowned victims can be completely covered in adipocere.

PLACENTA

The placenta is a complex organ. After giving birth, a new mother may bury her placenta or prepare it in a variety of ways and consume it for its helpful nutritional content. In some cultures, the placenta has spiritual meaning and must be dealt with according to rituals. Doctors, hospitals, and midwives all have their own views about making a placenta available to others. Legal issues may also be involved.

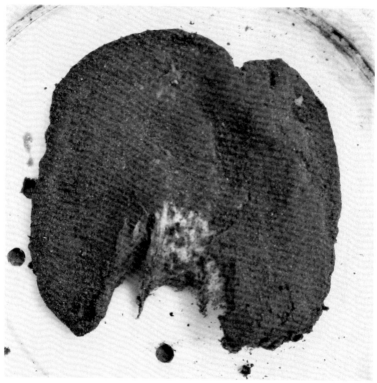

Figure 24.4 A fresh placenta may look only like a mass of blood encased in a layer of tissue, but it is actually a complexly structured organ. A 15-year-old placenta subjected to both freezing and ambient temperatures takes on a very different appearance. Fibrous membranes can be seen where a piece has been cut out.

BURNED TISSUE

Burned tissue can sometimes be found in the area where a victim is discovered. Even if not identifiable, clothing and fragments mixed with debris under where the body was should contain burned human odor. As with removing soil from a scene, permission is necessary before taking any substances.

"CADAVER BRICKS"

These "bricks" are a combination of human decay and concrete. A full description of and a list of misconceptions related to their making is addressed in the next chapter.

Figure 24.5 This photo shows pieces of the shoe the victim was wearing (A) and a zipper from his pants (B). Other remnants are scattered throughout the debris.

Trading Training Materials

Using only one source in training or continued use of just a few sources is not a good idea. It provides the same familiar scent picture to your dog, repeatedly. Borrowing from or exchanging training materials with other TEAMs—even if it is blood for blood, or bone for bone—provides your dog with different layers of odor, since the new-to-you source will have been exposed to elements your dog may not have investigated, both human and environmental.

Body or Body Part Donations

Once in a while, a person offers to donate his or her body or parts thereof to assist in training HRD dogs. It is an honor to be the recipient and should be regarded as such. However, this endeavor is not easy, simple, or inexpensive. The first step is to determine if it is legal in the state or states where the donor and recipient live—should they live in different states. You must discover this in the form of firsthand knowledge, not hearsay. Signed, witnessed, and otherwise detailed documentation of the "last wishes" should include the donor, his or her lawyer, next-of-kin or caregiver, and the attending doctor. The agreement may also outline what part or parts of the body are included in the donation—fat, limbs, organs, and so on—and the disposition of the remainder of the departed and at whose expense. This document should stipulate the recipient of the body to be notified immediately upon death to ensure the remains are not transported somewhere else. Thought must also be given to the following:

- Who will transport the donor body?
- Who will "harvest" the remains legally?
- What will it cost for those services?
- Where and how will the remains be stored until distributed?
- How large and what part of the body will each source be?
- Will the parts be in compliance with what is legal to possess as training materials?
- Who will ensure recipients have training for handling biohazardous matter?

Researching body donation websites in your area can provide additional information on this complicated process.

PUTRESCINE AND CADAVERINE

Putrescine and cadaverine are natural chemical compounds produced by decomposition of all animal tissues. But they represent only a fraction of the target odor, and the stand-alone chemicals are *not* recommended by many instructors. They are toxic, so inhalation and absorption through the skin should be avoided. In addition, they have an intense impact on the environment and will remain in the area you train in for a long period.

DOCUMENTATION

A paper trail must be created for every human source you receive. Defense attorneys may try to cast doubt of credibility based on how training aids are received or stored. Documentation should include what it is, its size, where it came from, and its stage or age of decomposition when received. As you use the training material, its state of decomposition changes, so uses and training time must also be tracked. Soil from under a body decomposed for six months is a six-month-old source. If you keep it for a year and a half at ambient temperatures, it becomes a two-year-old source. The same applies to sources that are frozen. A fresh source with little or no tissue destruction that is frozen, then thawed and buried for one week, has progressed in decomposition. Adding the time a source is thawed and used to your documentation will provide a more accurate age of the training material.

Imitation Scents

Other manufacturers may be working on creating artificial HR odor training aids or may be successful in doing so in the future. However, Sigma Pseudo Corpse Scents formulas I and II that replicate the odors of human decomposition have been the imitation scents used to this point and are the ones discussed below. There is also Distressed Victim Pseudo Scent and Drowned Victim Pseudo Scent. These chemical reproductions have been around for many years and are still being used, although their efficacy is subject to debate, and you need to be aware of specific restrictions in their use. For example, Drowned Victim scent has limited working time (30–45 minutes per Sigma) but its duration depends on the water temperature. In addition, Sigma Pseudo scents should only be used at depths of 12 feet (3.7 m) or less.

Pseudo scents are interesting and perplexing because it has not been determined exactly what a dog is identifying as human decomposition in the scents. To say there are contrary opinions about using Pseudo scents is putting it mildly. Some of the widely contrasting views follow:

- Dogs trained with Pseudo scents will not alert on actual human remains.
- Dogs trained with Pseudo scents have no problem alerting on actual remains.
- Some dogs trained only with Pseudo scent were able to certify on cadaver.
- Dogs trained on the real thing will not alert on Pseudo scents.
- Dogs have been trained on both and there are no problems.
- Pseudo scents are worthless as a decomposition odor.
- Pseudo scents in water draw alligators to the area.
- It is better to use Pseudo scents in water than have alligators or aquatic life take the human source.
- Dogs trained on Pseudo scents have trouble working a full body or large body part.
- Dogs should be trained on actual remains before using Pseudo scents or they may have issues with strong smelling human sources.
- There are harmful chemicals in Pseudo scents.
- Training with Pseudo scents properly did not produce any health problems for the dogs.
- The odor of Pseudo scents weakens with time. Setting up delayed problems will not generate strong scent pools for dogs to work through, as human sources will.
- Pseudo scents are convenient to use and more easily acquired than human sources.
- Pseudo scents are expensive.

All the conflicting views make you wonder how they were derived. Were those opinions based on all dogs, some dogs—and always, sometimes, or never? Were they informed opinions or were they hearsay? Were the dogs introduced and trained correctly with the imitation odor? Whether a TEAM or handler uses either imitation scent or a human source, or both, the goal should always be a well-trained dog that is consistent and reliable at finding human remains.

Size of Training Aids

The National Incident Management System (NIMS) and Federal Emergency Management Agency (FEMA) standards, plus the standards of a few other organizations, stipulate that training aids of less than 15 grams (0.5 oz) of human remains are appropriate for training cadaver dogs and for Land Cadaver Types I, II, III, and IV (Non-Disaster Operations) certification tests.

However, many instructors believe these small sizes are unrealistic and only work for dogs with low odor thresholds. Odor concentration also makes a difference—15 grams of fresh adipocere is stronger than 15 grams of dry bone. Some handlers say that using such small amounts will create problems in real-world searches, even though requirements have been met and the team deemed operational. When the dog then encounters a massive area of odor from a full, decomposing body, he may get caught up in the scent and "fringe"—a term used to characterize the dog alerting on the first smell of the target odor he detects rather than continuing to the victim's or source's actual location. Handlers who want to train for only basic cadaver work need to expose their dogs to strong decomposition to avoid that problem. For those training for forensic HRD, minute sources are necessary or there is the chance evidence may be missed.

Other handlers question whether source sizes should be measured in weight. In the real world, a handler looking at a training aid or portion of remains does not think, "Gee, that looks like it's about 300 grams." Instead, the handler thinks about its dimensions—4 × 6 inches (10 × 15 cm), say, depending on the type of aid, or 2 cups (0.5 L), or the strength of its odor. Another question is whether handlers need to actually weigh sources in order to comply with standards, or whether common sense can be used.

Other organizations have different standards for the size of training and materials:

- The North American Police Work Dog Association (NAPWDA): determines testing sources by age and elements;
- The National Narcotic Detector Dog Association: stipulates only types but not sizes;
- The National Search Dog Alliance: specifies certifying training aids in size and substance; and
- The National Association for Search and Rescue (NASAR: states that "no less than 30 grams (1.1 oz)" is to be used for "Canine Human Remains Detection Land Type Other (Non-Disaster Operations)." That means 30 grams comply, but so do larger training aids for that type IV certification.

25

Handling and Storage
of Training Aids

Biohazardous material training is critical for all HRD handlers. In 2018, Aftermath, a biohazard remediation company, produced a pamphlet about blood and biohazards. In their brochure they stated that 1 in 26 people have Hepatitis B; 1 in 77 people are infected by Hepatitis C; and 1 out of every 258 people has HIV. These numbers confirm the need for personal protection when handling and storing training materials.

Handling

Training aids should always be handled while wearing *powder-free* disposable examination-type gloves. Gloves prevent skin from exposure to the biohazardous substances and deter the handler's body oils / direct scent from contacting the training aid or its container. Bacteria and residue will be left on glove exteriors after handling an aid. Do not touch eyes, mouth, or any open wounds, and properly remove and discard gloves after each use. Do not turn them inside-out and wear again to save on the cost—that defeats the purpose of personal protection. Using dishwashing-type rubber gloves instead is not recommended because:

- the gloves will repeatedly collect and transfer bacteria and residual odors to other sources;
- skin contact with biohazardous matter from continued handling will be almost unavoidable;
- oils from some decomposition materials will, in time, break down and melt latex, turning it gooey; and
- washing the gloves will not get all the oils out of the nooks and crannies in the gloves' texture.

Storage

Because decomposition is corrosive to metal, human decay should not come in direct contact with metal containers when being stored. Many handlers use clean plastic containers and food freezer bags—devoid of any odors. Others believe only glass containers—heavy glass canning-type jars, thick glass jelly jars, etc.—should be used. Handling and placement of glass containers should be done carefully, and do not place them somewhere where they can be knocked over and broken. The broken pieces could cut and infect your dog or you when you pick up the glass, and they can contaminate the spot where the training source fell. The containers used, either plastic or glass, may have two fitting lids: one with holes to vent and allow the odor to escape from the source within, and a solid lid for storage purposes. If double lids are not used, the vented-led container can be placed in a clean plastic freezer-type bag to either freeze or store in a larger receptacle.

A variety of sizes of plastic pipes are also popular for holding sources. The two types of pipe used are white pipe (made of PVC, poly-vinyl chloride) and black pipe (ABS, acrylonitrile-butadiene-styrene, a thermoplastic resin). Many handlers favor the less-visible black ABS for training. Holes drilled in the pipe will allow scent to escape while the pipe ends are capped. A lid can be permanently affixed to one end while the other screws or snaps on tightly to allow placement of the source inside. ABS and PVC each require different glues for affixing sections or caps. Training materials can remain in these pipes for storage; however, each pipe should also be placed in a clean plastic bag to prevent its contents from getting on other containers. Placing soil in a knee-high nylon stocking before putting it in the pipe keeps the soil in place. A knee-high nylon stocking (or cut portion of pantyhose) placed over the top of other types of containers will keep your dog from being in direct contact with the source and helps keep dirt and insects out when the containers are buried. A solid lid will still snap or screw on over the nylon.

Many kinds of containers can be used as long as they are free of odor from previous contents—even new containers must be washed to make sure they do not contain manufacturing odors. Double bagging containers have helped keep freezers and totes somewhat dirt free. Fluids may accumulate in a container from the moisture of a defrosting source, and as it further decomposes. Collecting the fluids accumulated in the container with gauze or in a vial provides you with another training aid.

Storing Dry Bones

Dry bones, containing marrow but no other tissue, can be stored in cardboard boxes, or they can be frozen. It is not necessary to freeze those without marrow. A few handlers have expressed concern that dry bones could be cross-scented from different people if they are stored together. Others say that because human decomposition odor is basically generic, and skeletal remains of more than one person have been found in the same burial site, storing bones together is not a problem. However, if there is a vast difference in the ages of the bones, such as three years versus 30 years, it is best to store them separately to retain the different concentrations of odor.

Freezing Sources

Bacteria will continue to grow if training aids are kept at temperatures at or above 40°F (4.4°C). Freezing training aids will retard bacterial growth and thus the stage of decomposition. Aids can be frozen indefinitely. While a human body decomposes from the inside out, regenerated decomposition from a thawed source will create new decomposition from the outside in. The bacteria that were killed by freezing will not resume growth. Thus, much of the bacteria on the exterior will be environmental bacteria that will not have bearing on the target odor. Sources placed close to the sides or bottom of a freezer—the coldest parts—may get freezer-burn, which is a form of dehydration. A few drops of water will rejuvenate the growth of those microorganisms not killed by freezing. Remember that a source labeled "two-day decomposition," thawed and used for several days in a row, has decomposed further. Changing the label to approximate the new postmortem time will give a more accurate age of the source. TEAMs with only a few training materials can increase their aids by portioning a larger source and storing each part separately by different methods.

If you are using one freezer for both food items and training aids, take *extreme* caution when storing aids.

Labeling Training Materials

Identify and date each source on the plastic bag that holds the container—not on the container itself. Felt-tip pens and indelible markers have strong odors and a mark on the container becomes part of the target odor when you are imprinting a dog on an odor. If marking "hot" scratch boxes / containers—the ones holding the source—a marking should also be made on the "negative" ones (which do not hold the source) so they all have the same base scent. Some say this is excessive because the ink odor may be volatile and dissipate over time. But others have agreed they do not want their dogs to be cued to the hot container because of the

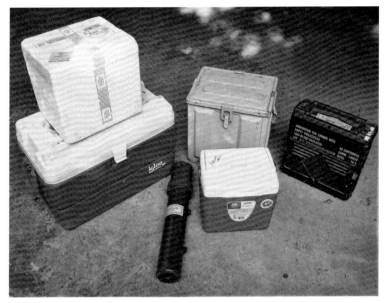

Figure 25.1 A few of the types of carriers used by handlers to transport scent materials.

additional odor of marker. To avoid residual odor contamination, all sources and hot containers should be kept in a totally different location from the negative and unused ones.

Transporting Training Aids

Different personal carriers are used to transport scent materials to training locations. Many use small coolers or military ammunition cans. Metal ammo containers are fine for transporting and storing as an exterior container because they do not come in direct contact with the source.

26

Training Materials Myths and Misconceptions

"Education should prepare our minds to use its own powers of reason and conception rather than fill it with the accumulated misconceptions of the past." – Bryant H. McGill

Various training materials myths and misconceptions have circulated for many years. This chapter will address the most prevalent and provide explanations as to why these beliefs are incorrect.

Pigs

It has long been a misunderstanding among handlers that pigs provide good training materials for the odor of human decay. For years pigs have been used to study *the decomposition process* because of their similarity to humans in terms of depth of skin; level of hairlessness; percentages of fat, tissue, and bone; and location of internal organs and diet—not because they have the same chemical compounds and odor as humans. New studies conducted by researchers at the University of Tennessee's Forensic Anthropological Center found human decomposition is much more variable, and pigs decompose at a faster rate.[1] Even though pig skin and pig valves are used in human transplants—a type of xenotransplantation—entire organs are not. Tissue from a pig's small intestine has been used as a guide to assist in regenerating human tissue to form a permanent repair, not as a replacement for human tissue.

Human Hair

The exterior cuticle of hair is composed of scales that overlap and protect the hair from normal bacterial invasion that leads to decay. The following explanation is detailed because many handlers incorrectly believe that hair alone is a suitable training aid.

The primary component of hair fiber is keratin. Keratins are proteins, long chains (polymers) of amino acids. In terms of raw

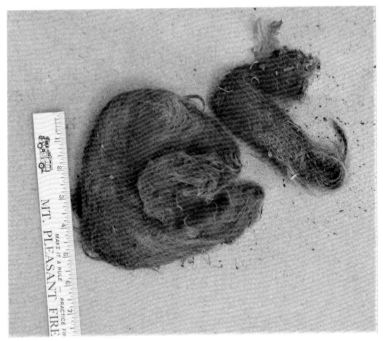

Figure 26.1 The hair may be a flat mass or have a rolled appearance, as is shown in this photo, due to taphonomic influences (movement affected by water, wind, soil, or scavengers).

elements, on average, hair is composed of 50.65 percent carbon, 20.85 percent oxygen, 17.14 percent nitrogen, 6.36 percent hydrogen, and 5.0 percent sulfur. Hair also contains trace amounts of arsenic, magnesium, iron, chromium, and other metals and minerals. Those chemical compounds in no way compare to those in human decomposition that produce the target odor for dogs. As Dr. William Bass stated so simply, "For decomposition to occur you need enzymes from inside the body."[2]

However, hair mats are different. A "hair mat" or "hair mass" is scalp hair that was attached to a decaying body; it contains the enzymes and residuals of tissue. Usually from the fifth through the eighth day of the decomposition process, hair sloughs off the head of a deceased person, forming a mass of matted hair that collects beneath the skull.

Fingernails

Like hair, fingernails are also composed of keratin and are resistant to most organisms and to decomposition. If tissue is affixed to the nail, then it is the tissue that decays and provides the odor, *not* the fingernails. Hair and fingernails are seen on corpses hundreds of years old, and they have not decomposed—and they do not grow after the person has died; rather, it is the shrinkage of the skin that makes it appear they have. Training with cut hair and/or fingernails mixed with decomposition fluids is simply training on the fluid. Similarly, if you mix hair/fingernails with blood, you are training your dog on blood. Fingernails, or hair from a salon or barber shop, contain human scent (not decomposition) from one or more people and are just another part of the scent picture—adding fingernails or hair is the same as adding a piece of fabric or a shoe. This is just a mixture of odors and should not be used to imprint dogs on human decomposition scent.

Frozen Training Materials

A comment was made that training aids should be thoroughly thawed before using. This is true if the desire is for the full, active, bacterial odor of the material. But even frozen solid training aids still furnish decomposition scent. The odor is weakened due to the inhibition of bacterial growth, but a frozen source is still a good training aid.

"Cadaver Bricks"

In an attempt to train for a body buried in or under a concrete slab, handlers have made what are referred to as "cadaver bricks." The problem with most of these is they are not realistic. Body fluids / bloody objects / water combinations sometimes called "soup" have been used in mixing the concrete, or in some cases just cement. Cement is just a binder—a substance that sets, hardens, and binds materials together. It is used in the production of mortar in masonry and concrete. Concrete is a combination of cement and an aggregate—a mixture of rock/minerals—such as gravel to form a strong building material. Likely, a killer would use concrete—not only cement—to conceal a body. Realistically, a killer would not mix blood and decomposition fluids in with the concrete so that type of "cadaver brick" is not authentic to human remains buried under a slab.

To replicate a source for odor being detected through concrete, it is suggested you follow the process below.

1. Request two or three cups of concrete from a construction site or anyone pouring it and place it in a clean receptacle. That is easier than mixing it yourself. No need for a long explanation—just say it is for a "project."

2. Have a clean plastic jar and a piece of human tissue, muscle, or small piece of bone with tissue ready.

3. Pour a couple of inches of the concrete into the clean plastic jar.

4. Next, immediately place the piece of tissue, bone, or muscle in the middle of it and pour the rest of the concrete over the top, ensuring the object is covered on all sides. Do not mix or shake.

5. Let it "cure"—which is the setting of concrete through chemical reaction—a minimum of 30 days.

6. Cut away the plastic to reveal the formed brick.

7. Store the brick in a plastic container or bag, and always wear gloves when handling. It can be, but does not need to be, frozen or refrigerated.

Figure 26.2 This cadaver brick measures 4.25 inches (10.8 cm) tall and contains one piece of skin/fat/muscle approximately 1 × 2 inches (2.5 × 5 cm) in size. Discoloration of the concrete is due to 14 years of use as a training aid.

"He who learns but does not think, is lost! He who thinks but does not learn is in great danger." – Confucius

Can Training Aids "Go Bad"?

Training aids do not "go bad"—even when contaminated. Regardless of how a training aid is stored, it continues to remain useful to some degree. The aid will, of course, come to a different stage of decomposition and condition than when acquired, but it continues to contain the odor of human decay (as is evident in historical remains being found by K9s). This includes using human training materials that have been contaminated by animal urine and other substances that occur in the environment. Those sources should be labeled as "Contaminated by [whatever circumstance caused contamination]."

MOLDY SOURCES

Human remains suffer the same fate as anything organic. Mold spores are living organisms (fungi) that occur naturally and are literally everywhere. According to the Centers for Disease Control and Prevention (CDC), the number of species of fungi "range from tens of thousands to perhaps three hundred thousand or more" and can be many different colors.[3] Mold grows best in warm, damp, and humid conditions. Outdoors it can be found in shady, damp places, but some can survive harsh environmental conditions, such as dry areas that do not support normal mold growth. Mold produces gases called microbial volatile organic compounds (MVOC). Some of those compounds are toxic and those toxins, as well as the actual mold spores, can, with increased levels or long exposure, cause a wide range of medical problems—difficulty breathing, sinus infections, bronchitis, and other health issues. It has been reported that some MVOCs have a musty odor, but many are odorless. However, the term "odorless" may only be in relation to a human's olfactory capabilities, as dogs have been trained to distinguish between certain mold species and Stachybotrys spores.

Because of these additions to the odor, you should not use moldy sources when imprinting your dog on human remains as the target scent. If you want to remove mold from your training aids, fresh air and direct sunlight is perhaps the only remedy. It will kill the spores but may also dry out the source and the mold will probably return if the source is again exposed to warm, humid conditions. While non-moldy training aids are preferred, moldy remains are a realistic source and while investigating a moldy source, your dog will only be inhaling for a few minutes, if not seconds.

Blood

There is a difference of opinion—not so much a misunderstanding—about the use of blood as a training aid. At one point, blood as a source was the subject of a major discussion on social media. Comments were both for and against:

- Blood is everywhere in the environment, so I don't train on blood.
- Forensic teams can find blood—you do not need a dog to do that.
- It doesn't make any sense to work a dog in an area that has already been processed by a crime-scene team.
- Blood found could have come from a person with a bloody nose or who cut himself shaving—not the victim.
- It is the dog's job to tell law enforcement that blood exists.
- An HRD team never knows what it will be called on to find or what it may come across, so the pair had better be ready.
- Training with blood can help identify a hidden weapon, blood on clothes, a crime scene, or the possible direction of travel by an injured victim or killer.

Experience dictates K9s should be trained on all the chemical compounds that make up the human body. It does not matter whose blood it is—the dog making the find will have done her

Figure 26.3 The K9 detected blood under paint.

Figure 26.4 A bloody knife found in the bottom layer of a cinder-block wall where the K9 alerted (arrow).

job and may have advanced the investigation. Three cases come to mind relative to detecting blood. First, a dog detected a victim's blood under a layer of paint in a homicide investigation. Second, a dog alerted on the base of a cinder-block wall. When the wall was disassembled, a bloody knife was found in the bottom portion.

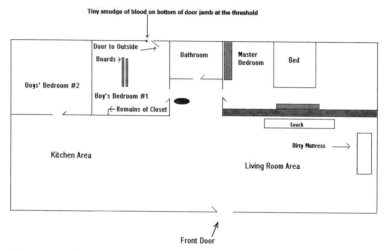

Figure 26.5 Blood can be in odd places as here—a tiny smudge on the bottom of the door jamb between the door and the threshold. This was the victim's blood, and its presence helped confirm the murder location and where he had been dragged out of the house.

Third is a case in which investigators trying to determine where a murder took place received written permission to search the suspect's house. Luminol, a chemical that exhibits a chemiluminescence in a bluish glow when in contact with blood, was sprayed to check for bloody areas. The results of luminol were invalidated because of interference due to the wood floors being washed with bleach. Several days later, permission was again granted to search the house, and law enforcement searched it once more to no avail. Then, approximately six weeks later, an evidentiary search warrant was issued and an HRD dog was requested to assist. The sheriff commented on the results, stating that the dog "was able to locate blood evidence at the crime scene that would not have been otherwise detected and which in fact had been overlooked on two previous crime scene searches both by my department and the Texas Department of Public Safety."[4]

Note that luminol is usually used in a much more controlled manner than the unrestrained and easy spraying seen on TV crime shows.

FACTS ABOUT CHEMILUMINESCENT ORGANIC COMPOUNDS

Many handlers question whether it is safe to work detection dogs in areas where luminol or other such substances have been applied. Because handlers have differences of opinion on this concern, I consulted Dr. David C. Dorman, professor of toxicology at the University of Carolina State's College of Veterinary Medicine, and Dr. Dennis J. Blodgett, professor of toxicology at Maryland Regional College of Veterinary Medicine, for their insights while researching this section.[5] Some of their information has been combined, since both doctors had basically the same answers.

LUMINOL

Luminol powder in concentrated form is an irritant. It causes pain and discomfort—the same as the pain that results from inhaling or sticking salt up your nose. The powder will irritate if handled without gloves, or if eaten or inhaled by the dog. Luminol reacts to several chemicals and hemoglobin—an oxygen-carrying protein in blood—and it also reacts to certain metals. The reaction is visible for a short period, until it dries.

LEUCOCRYSTAL VIOLET (LCV)

Leucocrystal Violet (leuco meaning no color) is a reduced form of crystal violet. Leucocrystal Violet is colorless, but when mixed with hydrogen peroxide, it reacts to specific materials, including the hemoglobin in blood, which turns the blood impression to a purple-violet color. Its coloration lasts longer than luminol.

LEUCOMALACHITE GREEN (LMG)

Leucomalachite Green had been abandoned for use in recent years because of the strong carcinogenic properties of two of its components: benzidine and o-toluidine. However, LMG is once again

Figure 26.6 Leucocrystal Violet initially turns bright purple in the presence of blood, but the whole sprayed area may stain purple if exposed to bright sunlight, as shown in this photo.

being used, but without o-toluidine and with tetramethylbenzdine replacing benzidine. It is now one of most commonly used reagents for presumptive blood tests.

CAN DOGS ABSORB THESE CHEMICALS THROUGH THEIR PADS, AND IS THAT DANGEROUS?

In answer to this question, Dr. David Dorman said:

> The molecular weight of Leucocrystal Violet and luminol are in a range where some absorption might occur. But when used in a solution with peroxide, they become more reactive and take on a configuration that, in essence, blocks absorption—this property has been looked at with fruits, vegetables, animal tissues, etc., where the chemiluminescent stain remains on the surface. Based on the chemistry and how the product is used, I would predict very low absorption from that site. Another protective feature to consider is that the surface area of the skin [foot pads] is small and contact time should be

minimal [60 minutes or less] so these also suggest minimal toxicological risk from dermal [skin] exposure.

Dr. Dennis Blodgett's reply to the question was:

I'm aware of some dermal absorption data for herbicides in dogs exposed to recently sprayed yards. Because the pads on the feet are so thick (i.e., keratinized), very little herbicide is absorbed through their pads. I suspect the same would be true for these chemiluminescent organic compounds. However, not much is known about the toxicity of luminol (and luminol-based products) and Leucocrystal Violet in dogs or other animals. The compounds (luminol and Leucocrystal Violet) have little to no toxicology data available—this reflects their use patterns where they are a specialty reagent (a substance used to produce a chemical reaction to detect other substances such as blood). Leucocrystal Violet has been found and examined in fish tissue, where the fish were originally treated with crystal violet for control of certain fish parasites—in general, fish handled it well.

Dr. Dorman added, "The material safety data sheets (MSDS) for these forensic chemicals don't provide much useful data and have generic statements that irritation may occur—thus they list using gloves, particle masks, etc. as precautions." Regarding inhalation, he said, "I would agree this is a low risk, especially since the materials used aren't very volatile and they are applied wet, which decreases the risk for aerosolization. I would keep the dogs away when the spray is being applied at a crime scene."

Note that while skin is an effective barrier for many chemicals, people can suffer from irritation if they have direct contact with the substance.

Precautions for Working Your Dog in Tested Areas
- Do not come in contact with powder forms.
- Keep dogs away when spray is being applied to a crime scene to prevent inhalation.

- Do not work dogs on wet, sprayed surfaces.

- Use soap (Dawn or a mild detergent) and water to decontaminate your dog's feet, legs, and face immediately after the search is done. Make sure to wash between her toes. Do not give her a chance to lick at a body part that has been exposed.

- If irritation of the skin or eyes occurred, the skin should be washed with soap and water, and the eyes should be flushed for up to 10 minutes with water. Every exposure to these compounds should be monitored afterward for potential irritation.

- Use common sense. If you are very concerned, use dog boots during a search and clean the boots afterward.

27

Introducing Odor, Imprinting, and Search Commands

Cadaver detection and HRD training progresses in stages. A serious handler does not rush the dog but studies step-by-step books and videos and follows the guidance of a good, hands-on instructor.

Standard Methods

There are several standard ways of introducing your dog to the odor of human decomposition and imprinting that scent. Each way culminates with praise and a reward your dog absolutely loves each time they are at the target odor. Rewards and rewarding will be discussed again later in this chapter.

Begin with your dog on lead but *do not* give any type of "search command"—that step comes much later in training. In introduction and imprinting exercises, one or two containers are "hot"—containing the HR training aid—and others contain distracting materials or are empty. Walk the on-lead dog close to the containers. Some handlers tell their dogs to sniff each one, but others do not say anything—they just walk. Do not acknowledge your dog in any way when he checks the negative containers, but

Figure 27.1 Some instructors have found that these PVC pipes work better if they are half their height so the dog works with his head closer to the ground. Other short plastic or PVC pipes, and scent tubes with heavyweight non-tipping bases are also sold.

when he sniffs the "hot" ones, even briefly, immediately praise and reward him, as close to the source as possible. This repetitive training is essential for the dog to develop commitment to the odor of HR.

Remember, a "standard way" of doing something does not mean there is not an equally good or better way, but standard methods should be included in training. Standard ways of introducing and imprinting HR odor may include:

- cinder blocks placed in a straight line, a circle, or another configuration, with one block containing the odor and the others empty;
- a long line of PVC pipes or small movable containers;
- the daisy wheel—a flat, circular, rotating apparatus that has small containers permanently affixed to either four "arms" or a continuous flat circle; one container holds the training material and the others are empty, as with cinder blocks; and
- in-ground PVC pipes, with one or several containing training materials placed in a circle and one pipe in the center where the K9 is to start. The K9 is led from the

Figure 27.2 Scent boxes are made in a variety of ways. These are simple wood frames topped with pieces of pegboard.

center pipe to one of the pipes and then around to the other pipes, checking each one for the target odor. Repeat this process several times—each time starting in the center but beginning with a different pipe in the circle. This is to keep the dog from being location-wise of the "hot" pipe(s). As the dog advances in training, he can be required to move faster in "speed drills."

More Sophisticated Methods

More sophisticated methods for odor imprinting include different types of scent walls—when the dog alerts on the correct opening in the wall, a helper drops the ball reward down the hole to the dog.

Figure 27.3 Right before the alert.

Figure 27.4 The back of the scent wall, where a helper works. The K9 is directed by the handler to check each of the relatively close openings and must alert on the correct hole. The dog's focus is on finding the target odor, and so the dog is usually not influenced by the helper's movements. However, the wall is high enough for the helper to crouch or bend over behind it if his or her presence appears to cause a distraction.

Figure 27.5 This photo shows movable "Dutch Boxes" hanging on a wall. Every box has a pipe or tube on top, a Plexiglas insert in the bottom half, and a special place to put the target odor. A ball is placed in the top tube of the "hot" box so that when the dog alerts on the correct box, a string is pulled that raises the Plexiglas and releases the ball, which drops and rolls out to the dog as reward. In this setup, the handler pulls the string at the direction of the instructor. Some setups use only half a wall, and a helper or the instructor behind it pulls the string.

Figure 27.6 A mechanism on the wooden box on the right wall projects a ball when the dog alerts on the right container. Here, True is ready to catch the tennis ball coming toward him.

NOT STANDARD BUT EFFECTIVE

In addition to the standard ways of introducing and imprinting HR odor, following is another method that has worked well and is fun for the dog:

1. Place several training aids in different locations in a large yard or area. One may be under a garden hose reel, another under a bush, a third in a corner, and so on.

2. The dog is taken for a walk on lead—you should be close, though, so you can reward immediately. Note: The dog is *not* searching, just simply taking a walk. (A lead made of parachute cord with a tiny clip will hardly be felt by a puppy not yet leash trained.) The handler should *not* lead the dog to the odor but walk only close enough for him to detect the smell and want to investigate.

3. At the very moment the dog goes to the source, praise and reward him. Going to the source is all that is required for the dog to receive a reward. This is also the time when a name can be given to the source—a name that will *eventually* be the search command. For example, when the dog goes to the training material, you should excitedly say, "Seek . . . good boy! Good boy, Seek!" (or whatever word you want to use) and reward the dog with a toy or treat. The walk then continues with the reward and same name repeated when the dog goes to each source. Giving a name to the training materials can also be done when using the standard methods of training.

This method is based on the same principle of a dog learning what his ball is—the repetition of its name and association with the object/odor. Here the dog is learning that smell has a name just like "ball" and along with that smell comes a reward. It is a simple process to both imprint the dog on the odor and teach the command that will be used *after they progress*. During the imprinting period, a command to search should never be given—the dog is nowhere near the searching stage. Do not expect or try to make your dog perform any behavior when he reaches the source.

Imprinting drills must typically be repeated hundreds of times for the dog to build commitment to the target odor. Switching out imprinting methods is a good way to avoid boredom for both dog and handler. Tennis balls and towels scented with (not soaked in) human decomposition odor have also been used. But it will be necessary to proof the dog off the scent of tennis balls if you use them in this method. There is a story of a narcotics detection dog trained with, but not proofed off, tennis balls. As the tale goes, while searching around high-school gym lockers, the K9 became extremely excited and alerted on one locker. This caused great anticipation—possibly a "mother lode" of drugs was inside. The concerned principal and other personnel were called to the location. However, when the locker was opened, it was discovered to be filled with nothing but tennis balls.

Rewards and Rewarding

Rewards should be something the dog absolutely loves—not something the handler wants to use. When choosing, also remember that the reward should be something replaceable if lost.

Try a wide variety of toys, objects, or food treats—even some rather strange—to find your dog's special reward. Some handlers think food should never be a reward in HRD work because it will entice the K9 to eat remains. However, many veteran handlers have successfully used food and say it is all in the training.

Food

Food rewards should be items that will not spoil in heat, crumble into tiny particles, leak, or have an overpowering smell. Rewards should be given *one piece at a time*—not a handful—to avoid fragments being dropped at the target odor. Dropping food is negligent and inexcusable, and food should never be placed on the ground.

Food reward SAR/R K9s do not have their basic food withheld as in disciplines such as accelerant detection. In those cases, the dogs are put through so many training repetitions, and receive so many rewards each day, they would be overfed if their rewards did not count as part of their daily food intake.

A benefit of food rewards is they can be given discreetly, even if others are watching. The difference between giving this type of reward and a toy is discussed next.

Toys

As I mentioned earlier, mechanized devices that provide or project the dog's reward when they alert on the correct item or container are available in the marketplace. The idea behind such devices is to eliminate the handler from the equation and have the dog associate the reward with only the target odor. This "handler elimination" method has been modified by some who throw their dog's toy close to the training materials when they make the find. Some handlers put the reward next to the source so their dog will find it along with the target odor, although many instructors believe the dog is smart and perceptive enough to know where the reward actually comes from.

Neither of these methods should be done with food. Throwing food will contaminate the area and can increase the propensity for a K9 to eat the training materials. Placing food next to the source will not only bring about those same results but will be training the dog to find food items.

On actual searches, tug or play toy rewards must be administered out of view and hearing range of family and media. Just seeing a K9 happily exiting the search area with a toy in his mouth can cause an unwelcome onrush of media to both the handler and law enforcement officers. This is where a subtle food reward has the advantage.

Variable Rewarding

A reward in different amounts of play or food is called "variable rewarding" or "variable reinforcement." Changing the length of playtime or the amount of reward is said to motivate the dog to perform the desired task in anticipation of a big prize. Sometimes the dog receives considerable play or treats, other times the reward is minimal, and occasionally the dog receives only praise. Handlers unfamiliar with this method, or when it should be employed in the stages of training, should get the assistance of a competent instructor for implementation to be successful.

Whatever reward you choose, it should be given *only* for HRD training and work—that is what keeps it special.

Verbal Search Commands

The next building block of a good training foundation is incorporating a search command—or using the name you gave the source during imprinting. Some handlers say that no command is necessary; they believe their use of a special collar, harness, or the attachment of a bell is sufficient when fielding their dogs. Others believe that those handlers do say something when the dog is released, but don't view their words (e.g., "okay" or "go") as commands. Most handlers, however, give a verbal search command with or without putting a specific piece of equipment on their dogs.

Commands commonly used are "search," "seek," "sook," and "find." Careful consideration should be given to the word chosen. The search command "Ne Poo" (pronounced nay-poo), was first used by Bill Tolhurst and adopted by many handlers because it is non-descript.[1] (According to Bill it is an "American Indian" word (no tribe named) for "dead.") Although law enforcement officers may keep the media or family members away from a search area, there is the possibility they are within earshot. The use of "bones," "ghost," and "find Fred," are also popular among handlers, but these can cause unease. "Bones" or "ghost" can be distressing if the family does not know the person is presumed dead. The command "find Fred" caused a delicate situation to arise for one team when a family friend, overhearing the command, said, "Excuse me, but his name is George." That handler later changed the command to "find your friend," which was close enough in sound to not confuse the dog.

It is recommended that cement blocks or scent boxes be used when combining the verbal command with the odor in training. The dog should still be worked on lead and should *not* be expected to search an area, regardless of how small, before making the connection between the command and target odor. The focus at this stage should be only on the association of the command with the source, and your dog immediately rewarded as close to the source as possible.

28

The Alert

There are two types of alerts: passive (sit, down, and bark) and aggressive, or "active" (scratch, dig, and touch). Some instructors consider the bark an aggressive alert, while others believe an aggressive alert is any action that might bring the K9 into contact with the source she is identifying. An age-old debate on alerts has not determined that one is better than another, as long as the alert is controlled. Most instructors think the alert should be the handler's choice. In other instances, or countries, a national or international organization determines the alert. Further to the two categories of alerts, there are natural alerts, which the dog does on its own, and trained alerts, which should be taught or reinforced at the target odor *independent of searching*.

Trained Alerts

A trained alert—frequently chosen relative to the type of search the K9 team will be working, or how far the dog will have to work from her handler—is accomplished by cuing or guiding the dog to perform a desired behavior. Trying to train an alert your dog does not want to perform will cause frustration, can repress enthusiasm, and will not be reliable. Instead, for efficiency and dependability, choose an alert that is suitable to your K9.

It is recommended that you teach a trained alert only after odor imprinting and the dog's commitment have been firmly established. The trained alert should be taught at the target source so your dog *establishes association between the behavior (alert) and that specific odor*. However, a few handlers have trained their dogs' alerts before imprinting by withholding a reward until the K9 complies with a desired behavior. These handlers hypothesize that when the dog is being imprinted on the target scent, she will execute the trained alert if her reward is again withheld. This process combines those two separate steps—imprinting odor and expecting the dog to perform a taught behavior/alert. Some believe this method is inadvisable and can come back to "bite" the handler in a court of law. The concern here is that the dog is not making the connection between her alert, the training materials, and her reward. Instead, she is focused only on what she was previously taught to do to get the reward. Training an alert does not mean constantly repeating the command. It is about giving the directive, waiting quietly for the dog to comply—initially guiding the dog into position if necessary—and instantly rewarding. Withholding the reward for a natural alert is different.

Natural Alerts

The natural alert is a K9's personal declaration—how she decides to tell her handler she has found the source—not an imposed action. Common natural alerts include barking, bowing, digging, lying down, jumping, giving a piercing stare, pointing, scratching, sitting, and touching. Carefully watch what your dog does each time she reaches the training aid in the imprinting phase. After numerous repetitions to solidify the connection between the scent and the reward, the K9 will anticipate her toy or treat at the target odor. If you delay giving the reward for a few seconds, your dog,

Figure 28.1 Spirit's natural alert: a gentle touch.

out of eagerness or frustration, may perform a natural alert at the source. Whatever she does is her way of saying, "Hey, here it is! Where's my reward?"

When trying to discover your dog's natural alert, it is not a good idea to wait too long to reward your dog if she does not

Figure 28.2 True's natural alert. The source is buried under the rock. The alert replicates a play bow, and True performs this posture only when he finds the source of the target odor.

respond in some fashion. Do not prompt an action by asking, "Do you have something?" or anything of that nature. That most likely will turn into a verbal cue for the alert. (That problem will be discussed further in this book.) Instead, reward her, but repeat the delay process in a few subsequent exercises to see if she will perform some natural behavior. If not, consider teaching a trained alert instead. Many handlers believe a natural alert is more reliable than a trained one, since a stressed or tired dog, or one in a precarious situation, may revert to her natural alert, even though she has been trained otherwise.

Digging or scratching is used by some in law enforcement (LE) for narcotics detection. Although this action could be a dog's natural alert, the dig or scratch needs to be drastically modified to a touch or gentle paw for other disciplines. While some LE agencies want only passive alerts, others do not have a preference, as long as there is no destruction or severe disturbance to the remains or scene. In situations where animals have damaged and scattered body parts or tangible items, for example, the handler must attempt to preserve the area as the K9 found it.

As mentioned previously, urinating or defecating are not acceptable natural alerts! *Some dogs may exhibit this terrible behavior before giving their alert.* Careful correction is necessary so the dog knows which of the actions she is displaying is the wrong one. One way to correct this problem is to use a specific word or sound, such as "fooey," "ack," "wrong," or "unh, unh," and attempt to stop the dog in the "process" then immediately prompt the desired alert. Repeated corrections, *not scolding or punishment*, will be needed before the dog breaks this bad habit.

Reliable, Respectable, Simple, and Readable

Whatever type of alert, trained or natural, it must be consistent, reliable, respectable, and readable, meaning you should be able to explain the difference between the K9's alert and her normal behavior. For instance: the dog is trained for a sit alert—but the dog sits at other times too—the same for the bark or the down. To distinguish the sit alert from any other sit, does your dog make eye contact with you when sitting? Does she stare at the source? When alerting with a bark, does she bark a certain number of times? How do you articulate the difference?

Two things happen before the K9's physical or vocal alert:

1. There is a change in the dog's body language and the way she moves as she goes toward the odor.
2. The dog's breathing and normal sniffing pattern changes when she detects the target odor.

You must be able to read your dog's subtle changes in sniffing, behavior, or body carriage. But keep in mind there are situations where your dog may not detect the odor until she is right next to the source. That is where body language and breathing changes can happen so quickly that you may or may not notice it right before your dog alerts.

Even if your dog has a reliable alert, the target odor can be in a location where she cannot get close enough or is unable to execute her alert and may resort to different or unusual actions. This might also happen with K9s trained to lie down with the target odor between their paws. In tough spots like this, the handler must be able to recognize there is significance to the dog's abnormal behavior. An adjustment in search strategy may enable the dog to get closer to the odor's origin.

PROBLEMS WITH THE DOWN ALERT IN HRD

The scene of a deceased person can be fouled by blood and liquefied remains. Also, in disaster situations, many scenes are polluted by a variety of toxins and can have fragmented remains throughout, requiring multiple alerts to pinpoint each one. So the popular down alert in HRD produces the question: Does the handler really want his or her K9 to lie down in blood and toxins, and on body-fluid soaked ground and surroundings?

The K9's proficiency in alerting at the source is determined by her handler and training. Allowing an alert to become lax is a problem. For example, the dog performs a down alert at the training aid but as her handler approaches, she gets up and moves toward the handler and is rewarded wherever she happens to be standing. Rewarding feet away from the source will not develop a reliable dog and can promote "fringing" instead of going to the highest concentration of odor. The reward should come *while the dog is in her alert position* and as close to the source as possible.

Handlers often have discussions about the K9 remaining totally focused on the source. Some handlers believe if the dog looks at her handler, she must be more interested in the reward than the target odor. In addition, these people think the break in the dog's concentration on the object can inhibit the handler from pinpointing its exact location. Other handlers believe that since they are the other half of their team, the K9 *should* look to them. This does not mean the dog should look to her handler for approval or a cue to alert, but rather to make a visual connection with her partner because she has found the target odor.

Keeping an alert simple is not only the easiest way to train but is more reliable in the field with thought given to how far the dog works from her handler. Whether or not you decide to train for a refind—some handlers want their dogs to stay with the victim/source—is another consideration. A sit-alert dog that works off lead, ranges far from her handler, and stays with the target odor could require her handler to search for her if the brush is dense or terrain features obscure the dog's location. In such as case, a dog that has a digging alert could get out of hand if the handler is not close enough to the dog to stop the behavior. The entire process of training for a refind should be simple. One standard refind consists of the K9 finding the source of the target odor, returning to you and signaling in some fashion—a jump, bark, and so on—and then taking you back to the source and performing the alert. Whether you train for a refind or not, simple is best. Some handlers overwhelm their dogs with a variety of actions. For example, some require the dogs to find the target odor and alert, then perform a refind by coming back to the handler, at which point the dogs are to sit at the handlers' feet and bark or go through other multiple actions before taking the handlers to the source, where once again the K9s are supposed to alert and immediately touch or point to the victim/source. That many behaviors have been regarded as for "show" and called over the top in expectations, decreasing the dogs consistency and dependability.

However, adding one element to an alert can be beneficial, as discussed in the next section.

Figure 28.3 There are two small bones behind and under the thorn-covered vines. Without a "show me" and the dog's touch alert, it would have taken considerable time to find them. That is the reason a K9 is being used—to save time. Their nose versus a human's eyes is much faster.

Adding to an Alert

Adding to an alert can be described as training a second phase of the established alert. In this phase, you ask your K9 to touch the source with her paw or point her nose to show the precise location of the target odor. Tiny pieces of remains or evidence—such as a tooth or small bone—cannot be seen if they blend with vegetation or other matter, and so this addition to the alert can be essential in finding the source.

The phrases "Show me?" "Where?" or "Whatcha got?" that some handlers use have a couple of meanings. In a *refind*, you say, "Show me," when you want your dog to take you to the victim or target odor source. In *HRD after an alert*, "Show Me," "Where?" or "Whatcha got?" ("Touch" or "Point") means you want your dog to pinpoint the source but does not mean you are prompting an alert.

Another addition to an alert is for when the K9 finds elevated sources. The dog may naturally, or by training, jump up on the structure or tree before performing her established alert. Only after the dog is steadfast and consistent with her alert should a second phase alert be taught.

Question: If you haven't trained your dog to display a second-phase alert, where do you look for the target odor?

Answer: Probably at the last place the K9 had her nose before alerting.

Changing an Alert

If you decide to change your dog's alert, you should first think carefully about why you think it is necessary. If your dog has suddenly switched her alert—such as barking at the source instead doing a sit—you should not go along with it and reward her or think that this is your dog's new natural alert. The change may be due to stress, her emotions at that time, or the placement of the training aid, and it will not be a consistent alert. Remember, the dog should not be rewarded simply because she has located the source. You should wait for the K9 to execute her established alert, with encouragement if needed, before rewarding. Be careful. Changing your dog's alert, whether as part of your own plan or because your dog randomly alerted differently one or a few times, can cause confusion for both members of the team and will be unreliable.

The "Clear" Alert

The "clear" or "negative area" alert is the dog's affirmation that area does not contain the target odor and can be eliminated from consideration. This type of alert is used by trailing/tracking and some air scenting K9 teams to show they have not located a specific scent trail or the live victim's scent. Some HRD handlers have admitted the use of this alert. However, not detecting the odor of human remains is always from the dog's frame of reference. Can an HRD handler be positive the area is negative, or could it be the area has been deemed negative because of one or more of the following factors?

1. The weather was not conducive for the type of search needed, so the K9 did not detect odor. A change in temperature, humidity, or wind may produce different results.

2. Not enough information was available to employ the proper search strategy.

3. The wrong search strategy was used even though adequate information was provided.

4. Handler error. The K9 was not worked or directed in such a way that she was able to determine if odor was present in all portions of the search area.

5. The handler did not read the K9's body language and bypassed a spot instead of investigating it. The K9 is in this instance being used as a biological detector device and, as with any tool, if the operator cannot recognize or interpret the results obtained by the device, results will not be reliable.

An overconfident handler, one who says, "My dog *always* gives her full alert if HR are present!" can also contribute to incorrect negative-area alerts. First, how would the handler know nothing was missed? Although most handlers strive for, and train their K9s to be, as close to perfect as possible, bomb-proof alerts do not exist. There are too many factors in searching for human remains to make such a bold statement. For example, the dog can only react or respond to what she has been subjected to in the search area. Likewise, the dog can only respond if the available odor of the human remains surpasses her scent threshold. So the K9's lack of a positive alert does not necessarily mean the area is negative. The most factual thing a handler can say is, "My dog did not alert in this area." After searching and before an area can be considered negative, a debriefing of the probability of detection (POD) should be conducted to discuss any elements that might have precluded the dog from detecting the target odor. The handler should also assess the dog's performance and if anything hampered her abilities during that particular search.

If atmospheric or other conditions are adverse for detection, the handler may want to ask the agency if it will permit them to search that area again when conditions are better. This may mean more favorable wind or weather, thick vegetation reduced, large obstacles moved to gain access, and so on. Whether or not the agency agrees could be based on the validity of the information they have so far uncovered or received in their investigation, new intelligence, available human resources, or perhaps budget.

The alert is your dog's communication to you that she has found the target odor. It must be consistent and reliable, or it will always be questioned and thus ineffectual. However, you are the other half of the team and without interaction with you, who understands her alert, her conduct may not mean anything to anyone else. You are obliged to understand your dog, the nuances of her body language and when her responses are inconsistent with her normal behavior.

Proofing

"Proofing" is training a dog that his target odor is human remains only, regardless of similar biological or camouflaging smells. In the wild, dead animals and scents from wildlife contaminate human remains. In urban areas, there are a multitude of smells from trash, rotting food, exhaust, animals—and humans. Proofing training should begin in areas where no HR sources have previously been to prevent the chance of their residual scent. Proofing off the same type of empty containers, PVC pipes, clean examination gloves, and anything else used to hold or contain training materials is also

Figure 28.4 K9 Grace kept working around this pack rat nest and wanted to continue searching there. Although she did not alert, her body language and uncharacteristic behavior revealed she was not interested in the rabbit skull (arrow).

necessary because they add something to the scent picture. Many materials off-gas and their odor can be somewhat absorbed by the source. Biodegradable containers and wraps, some of which are chemically treated, will not just off-gas but will also commingle with the human source, since over time they can be destroyed by bacteria.

After your K9 learns to ignore everything but the target odor, periodically place non-target odors in training areas as distractions. However, the dog must learn that if a proofed-off scent is on or present at human remains, he should still alert. A dog trained solely with strong smelling training materials may not detect minute odors and just bypass the spot. Don't forget about odor thresholds. If another odor is overpowering, even forensic HRD K9s may delay before committing to an alert. Nevertheless, their body language should let handlers know something is causing hesitation.

For example, a forensic HRD dog named Grace was searching for the disarticulated remains of a victim missing for three years in an area abundant with pack-rat nests. Pack rats carry a variety of diseases; therefore, it is not good for a dog to inhale bacterium-filled nests for any length of time. Grace kept intensely working for several minutes around a particular nest where there was a visible rabbit skull within. But she didn't alert. Because of the disease factor, Grace (who wanting to continue sniffing), was moved aside and investigators were asked to dismantle the nest. Buried in the dirt, amidst twigs, cactus spines, and debris, not far from the rabbit skull shown in the picture, they found a couple of severely gnawed human bones.

Other real-life instances illustrate the importance of training with combinations of target odors and proofed-off scents. One handler talked about a search where the body was under a dead cow, and in another case, a dog had been buried on top of the victim.

"I used to look at my dog and think 'if you were a little smarter you could tell me what you were thinking,' and he'd look at me like he was saying, 'if you were a little smarter I wouldn't have to.'" – Fred Jungclaus

PROOFING MATERIALS

Keep clean containers, gloves, and tongs in your vehicle so they are available to collect roadkill. But, before you do that, learn which species are illegal to possess, since laws apply to even portions of some dead animals. At times it may be difficult to determine what the dead animal on the road is because the animal may be DOR, FOR, or POR—dead on the road, flat on the road, or part of the road. In some countries, it is against the law to collect any roadkill. And, for example, it is illegal to possess any part of a raptor—even talons or feathers. This includes vultures, which are often found dead on a roadside.[1] In the United States, handlers

Figure 28.5 There is one piece of mummified skin in this photo, and it is virtually indistinguishable from the litterfall. It is *not* at the top of the photo.

should contact their game warden, the United States Fish and Wildlife Service, or the Department of Natural Resources for information and inquire about obtaining legal sources from taxidermists. Be certain to diligently document proofing materials to show where and how they were legally acquired.

Even after a dog is proofed, he may still investigate an animal odor or article. Proofing is not a one-time training activity, but must be repeated periodically. Further, it is suggested that the words "Leave it!" while searching should be used only when you are 100 percent sure there is no HR odor in the vicinity. The dog should not immediately be corrected or pulled off the object, since you do not know what the dog actually smells. Some remains are not recognizable, and if you instantly give a correction, you may be telling your dog to leave the very thing he was taught to find!

However, if the dog appears preoccupied at that place, a "Get to work" command is in order. If the K9 keeps checking the odor but has not alerted, you may want to give the dog a little more time to evaluate the spot, approach it from a different direction, have another dog check it, or have someone investigate the site, as was done with the pack-rat nest discussed on page 237. The K9 is just one tool in the investigation.

Trusting Your Dog

"One must gauge one's trust carefully." – Jacqueline Carey, in
Kushiel's Chosen

"Trust your dog" is the mantra of SAR/R handlers and rightly so—but it appears to be used selectively, especially in the HRD discipline. If a handler trusts his or her K9, why wait for an alert on an unseen source to be confirmed before providing a reward for the dog's behavior? The reason for not rewarding until the alert is verified is customarily voiced thus: "If the dog is rewarded and nothing is found, the handler just rewarded for a false alert and will have to spend a lot of time correcting that problem."

There are three general opinions on the matter: reward immediately, acknowledge the dog's alert with *some* praise, and do not reward until the alert is confirmed. There are handlers who, after their dog alerts, pull their dog off the spot, flag the location, and

Figure 28.6 True refusing to leave the training material after his alert.

move away. Other handlers reason that giving a little praise when the dog alerts avoids confusion. If the dog does not receive any type of acknowledgment and is always immediately pulled away from the target odor after alerting, he may become perplexed and think he was wrong. If the handler rewards the dog only after confirmation, the reward is given at a distance from the source, so the dog may be confused about exactly what he is rewarded for. Immediately returning to the spot to give the reward after it is confirmed would invade the crime scene, and waiting for the scene to be released may take days. As you can see, the matter requires some serious consideration.

Another method has been successful for unseen sources. Give a little positive feedback when the dog alerts, such as saying, "Good," and then direct the K9 away from the spot as you repeat the search command. If it was a false alert, the dog will most likely disregard the place at which she just alerted, since you did not give strong acknowledgment of her behavior. However, if the target odor is there, the dog should either refuse to leave the spot after you say, "Good," or she should immediately return to the spot after hearing the search command again, to redeclare her original alert.

The answer to whether an alert that yields nothing is false or unconfirmed may never be known. Dogs have alerted on residual odor or trace evidence that may be all that is left to find—so they are not wrong. But handlers who make excuses or always claim "unconfirmed alert" rather than recognizing a false alert can cast doubt on the K9's training and the handlers' integrity. Instructors have taught that no alert is better than a false alert on a search. But false alerts can occur, and should be acknowledged as such, followed by intense training to rectify the problem.

"Consistency and accuracy instills believability." – Bernard Kelvin Clive

False Alerts: Causes and Suggestions

False alerts can happen for a variety of reasons, most of which can be attributed to the handler or instructor and training. Following are the chief reasons for false alerts, as well as suggestions for correction.

- The K9 was rushed through training stages before she was fully committed to the target odor. Training should go back to basic repetitions of imprinting with scent blocks, boxes, or walls.

- The K9 is not proofed off distracting or similar scents. Again, going back to basics of odor commitment and proofing off distracting or similar odors is a must.

- The K9 is frustrated and tired because the situation is beyond her level of training. Go back to less complicated search problems and gradually increase the difficulty.

- The handler hovers over the dog and talks her into an alert. Usually this happens because the handler believes something is there, or it is a confirmation check from a previous K9's alert and the handler wants to make sure his or her dog alerts too. The handler should be quiet, make sure that particular object or place is detail-searched, evaluated, probed if necessary, and let the K9 decide if she should alert. After all, the first K9 to investigate the area could have false alerted.

- The K9 is handler-dependent and reads the emotions of her anxious handler. As difficult as it may be, the handler should try to remain calm and, while watching his or her dog, should also analyze the area and wind conditions to make sure the dog will be able to detect the target odor if it is in the team's search area.

- The K9 is repeatedly taken back to a suspect spot and told to recheck it so many times she thinks she is supposed to alert. If you need to take your dog back to an area: approach the area from different directions to ascertain if HR can be detected; have another K9 team check that area; or convey reasoning for LE to visually search that particular place.

Another reason for false alerts is the handler inadvertently cuing the dog to alert. The next section discusses this common problem.

"Some people create their own storm and then get upset when it rains!" – Unknown

Cuing an Alert

While it is relevant to encourage a dog to perform her alert during the alert-training phase, constantly coaxing an alert afterward may cause your dog to look to you first for verification before performing the behavior. Most cues are given inadvertently and include the handler:

- repeatedly saying any variation of, "Whatcha got? Whatcha got?" "You got something? Where is it? Show me!" as the dog stands at the presumed site. Under these circumstances those words *are* cues;

- moving his or her hand or any facial movements—a smile, frown, and so on;
- slowing down or stopping at the target odor location;
- reaching for the dog's toy or treat in full view of the dog; and
- subconsciously leading the dog to the training aid.

BREAKING THE CUE

WORDS MISTAKEN AS CUES

A dog that thinks the words "show me" or "where is it?" constitute a *cue* to alert and not a *request* to show you she has found the source can generally be corrected by using those words at negative spots. The point here is to entice your dog to respond with an alert while providing the opportunity to correct her mistaken understanding of what those words mean.

Start with a negative object or pile of debris, somewhere there is no chance of your dog encountering residual HR odor. Have your dog search it, telling her to "check it," then excitedly say those "cue words" several times to see if she responds. One of two things will happen:

1. The dog does not alert. You should offer a few words of praise as she continues searching. Do not just stand at that spot as your dog proceeds to work. Doing so may cause her to think she missed something and return to that spot.
2. The dog alerts. You should give a firm, "Wrong! Get to work!" command and walk away from the spot.

Following either occurrence, searching should continue for several minutes before the dog is directed to an area where there *is* a training aid. *After the dog has alerted on the target odor* and is rewarded and lavishly praised, you need to repeat those specific words (i.e., "show me" or "where is it?"). The dog ought to return to the source and once more alert, which should generate a reward and more praise. In this method the K9 learns that words such as "show me" means a reward *only when human remains are present*. Repeating this process has been successful in dogs learning to ignore the voice inflections of those phrases *if the area is negative*. If the handler is mistaken in thinking a spot is negative because he or she doesn't see anything, but HR is actually present in some form, many dogs will ignore the "Get to work" command, give their handler a "look," and stay at the target odor.

MOVEMENTS UNDERSTOOD AS CUES

Dogs are incredibly perceptive of their handlers' movements. If your dog was obedience trained with hand signals, you may unintentionally position your hand for a sit or down command, which may also be your dog's alert. Facial expressions are also influential. If you routinely display the same delighted look when your K9 is at a source, your dog may take that as a cue too. As the Clever Hans Effect shows, dogs can be trained to respond to frowns, smiles, raised eyebrows, and even blinking. In addition, a study in Vienna showed dogs can follow their humans' gaze to objects a short distance away.[2] Prior to the alert, the handler should attempt to maintain an impassive expression. Body and facial cues are especially problematic for handlers who work very close to their dogs at all times. Turning or looking sideways while peering out of the corner of the eye as the K9 approaches the source may help you avoid those cues.

Even if you are mindful of your hands and expressions during the search, a slight reach for the reward may cue your dog. Keeping your hands clasped behind your body and the toy reward secured in your back belt should ensure you do not accidentally cue the dog with movement. Food rewards are a little more difficult to grab unseen. However, verbal praise and petting can be the start of the reward process as you proceed to retrieve the treat.

Be careful when you know the location of the source during practices, as handlers have been known to change their stride and slow down or stop as they approach the aid. Being aware of this tendency should help correct the behavior.

Finally, handlers have been observed countless times taking shortcuts to training aids when they know their location. Instead of conducting grid searches by covering the full perimeter of the area—including corners—they direct their K9's search patterns in ways that are often angled and spaced wider than if placement of the source was unknown. Setting up problems where training materials are concealed in corners or right on the perimeter—with the prevailing wind at times moving the odor out of the search area—may help handlers form the habit of consistent and thorough search patterns.

29

Training for Human Remains Detection

This chapter expands on specific training related to human remains detection.

Crime-Scene Preservation

When a live victim is injured, medical personnel are not concerned with what happens to the scene—their only thought is to treat the person and save a life. The location of a deceased victim is different.

Crime-scene preservation should be part of mandatory training and include much more than the basics: not touching anything, flagging the area, and leaving it. Some of the other important facets are discussed in this section. When a K9 finds a decomposing body, and the handler can see it, he or she should stop—the person is beyond medical help and proceeding right to the body will contaminate the location. In training the dog is always rewarded as close to the target odor as possible with a toy, treat, or praise. On actual searches, crime-scene preservation takes priority over how to reward. A good idea is to reward your K9 immediately with praise and then call him to your position and physically reward him. When finding scattered remains, you must balance crime scene preservation and practicality.

> *"Crime scenes are corrupted the moment someone 'invades' the space. This invasion can change blades of grass, brush and dirt, and scattered remains, evidence." – Vernon J. Geberth, in* Practical Homicide Investigation, Third Edition

Learn to be vigilant of anything unusual where you are walking or standing and flag anything suspicious or out of place. Fragile evidence can be destroyed while other evidence can be disturbed or blown away. If you find something delicate, direct law enforcement (LE) to it immediately. All points of entry and exit at the crime scene must be controlled and cordoned off. This is usually done by a LE officer, who also logs the names and times each person enters the crime scene. Since this record may subject people to being subpoenaed for court, it deters many who are just curious. Many LE agencies require anyone who enters the area to file a report.

Remember, crime scenes are three dimensional: up, down, sideways—floor, walls, ceiling. Each of those areas may contain evidence that must be preserved, so it is important you don't lean on, brush against, drop, or disturb anything in the vicinity of the find.

Chain of Custody

Legally, chain of custody is defined as "the movement and location of physical evidence from the time it is obtained until the time it is presented in court."[1] Chain of custody requires documentation of anyone who has come in contact with the evidence to safeguard against allegations of contaminating, planting, or tampering with evidence and to ensure the integrity of the item. Anything touched or moved by a handler or K9 must be reported to the lead investigator. Once an item has been altered or moved it is impossible to restore it to its original position or condition.

Emotions on Searches

Searching for homicide victims involves many dimensions and emotions. With a large percentage of speculative searches, frustration may creep in—more so for the investigators than for others involved in searches. Some handlers become annoyed at the "hurry up and wait" situation when they arrive at a scene. However, that wait period may be necessary for all information, documents (e.g., a search warrant), or equipment to arrive.

Emotional attachment or association is something that all handlers should be warned against. The victim may bring to mind someone that age in your own family. Scenes can be grisly, and searchers will not be immune to all they may experience. For one thing, the odor of human decay is unforgettable. The olfactory bulb, part of the brain's limbic system, is an area closely associated with memory and feelings, and is sometimes called the "emotional brain." Smells can bring on a flood of memories and powerful reactions that can affect your mood and work performance.

This does not mean that to be a handler you must harden your heart. Instead, you must learn coping strategies and responses, such as focusing on the positives—the value of finding the victim, knowing the job was completed successfully, and, while tragic, the family's torment of the unknown has ended. Still, you must be prepared for the times when focusing on the positive will not work so you can avoid an emotional collapse on the scene.

Viewing colored pictures or slides of bodies in all stages of decomposition and circumstances will give you an idea of what may be found on a search. Yet, this exercise might not prepare you for the reality of what you see and the overpowering, accompanying smells—smells that can be different from those of training materials. Requesting permission to watch an autopsy, visit a morgue, or, if possible, participate in a training session at one of the several, highly restricted "body farms" now in existence (similar to Dr. William Bass's original Anthropological Research Facility in Knoxville, Tennessee) will be advantageous. Training at a "body farm" is a privilege and should be done for the right reasons, with integrity and respect for the "residents." Photos should be taken only with permission.

Dogs Eating Remains

It is paramount that training includes a command for the dog to immediately drop what he has in his mouth. Handlers may claim their K9s do not eat remains, yet they train only with aids in protective containers. Unless they expose their dogs to unprotected remains during training in an assortment of exercises, they have no idea what their dogs will do on a real search. Consuming remains is a critical problem for the following reasons:

- The substance will be destroyed or obliterated—consider a blood droplet the K9 licks that may have belonged to the killer.
- Forcing a dog to vomit up the piece, by giving her peroxide, may not work and even if it does, there will still be damage to that portion of remains.
- The victim may have died from poisoning, an infectious disease, or a drug overdose, and if a dog ingests those chemicals, they could prove fatal a second time.

"Where Was It?"

Out of excitement, or for reasons unknown, a K9 that has never done so may pick up or move a piece of remains or evidence. Training the "Where was it?" command—after praise and reward for the find—is all important so your dog will take you to the original site and alert again. Regrettably, the object has been moved, but its initial place can be identified, and the object is not destroyed.

Search Strategy Training

Searching for HR is different in each circumstance. It is up to you to direct your K9 to all areas of the search location in such a way that he will be able to detect if the target odor is present. Some situations will require the K9 to work on lead, which is why occasionally training that way is necessary. If not accustomed to searching on lead, and only put on the leash for total control or obedience training, the dog's search tenacity may be suppressed when required to work on lead.

How the dog is worked depends on the object's size or odor concentration; the type of soil, if HR is thought buried; how that soil affects human remains; and the presumed depth—which can relate back to the type of soil and terrain. Even if you implement a sound search strategy, always remember that the terrain, obstacles, or wind and weather conditions may be such that your dog will not be able to locate the source unless other factors emerge or change. Following are search strategies for a few situations you might encounter at a scene: creek beds, buildings, and vehicles.

"Obstacles don't have to stop you. If you run into a wall, don't turn around and give up. Figure out how to climb it, go through it, or work around it." – Michael Jordan, in Dr. T. J. Allan, "How Michael Jordan's Mindset Made Him a Great Competitor"

STRATEGIES FOR SEARCHING CREEK BEDS

Strategies for searching creek beds differ depending on whether the bed has flooded or not. You need to consider how many times the creek has flooded since the victim went missing, to what height, and if any of the flooding was a flash flood. Flash-flood waters can travel 140 cubic feet (43 m^3) per second, which equals 1 mile (1.6 km) per hour! That force can carry a body far downstream. In addition, flash floods can wash remains up into brush on high banks and even into trees. If flood waters caused erosion, the remains might now be buried, so tight grid searches of highly suspect locations may be necessary.

STRATEGIES FOR SEARCHING BUILDINGS AND VEHICLES

Use set search patterns for buildings and vehicles, so no area is missed. A building search pattern may involve always beginning to search right to left after entering, and checking each room and objects in it thoroughly before moving on to another room. Another pattern might be having the K9 do a hasty search of all rooms in attempt to locate an area of interest, then begin with that room, before conducting a room-by-room detailed search.

When searching vehicles, always start your exterior search in the same place, and work in the same direction—clockwise or counterclockwise each time. Vehicle windows and doors should be closed if closing them does not disrupt the scene. Searches of vehicle interiors should be conducted by opening only the door on the downwind side of the car and employing one specific method to search the inside and trunk so no area is ever missed.

Vehicles have a lot of scent traps. To identify one vehicle among several, vehicles in scent lineups should be positioned so the dog can work crosswind to prevent the dog from detecting odor from a neighboring car.

Training in junkyards can be helpful, but neither you nor the employees will know for sure which vehicles already contain blood or decomposition odor from accidents. Therefore, a dog may alert on a vehicle because of contamination from its previous history and not just vehicles where you concealed training aids.

Search Strategies and the Ecosystem

Unlike changing your search strategy based on wind and terrain conditions, there may be other times when you need to alter your search strategy for a very short period. Some handlers have been so set in their mental search pattern that they call their dogs back when they deviate from that course of action. For example, a K9 can be scenting something behind an obstruction yards away but is recalled to finish the grid pattern. Or the dog that, while conducting horizontal grids on a hillside, suddenly rushes to the top of the slope, but is commanded to return to the handler. This exact situation has happened and, yes, the victim was found where the dog had been going (but much later). Think about this before you call your dog back from an area he wants to explore. Other instances in which you may need to alter your search pattern include the following:

BIOTURBATION

Bioturbation is the stirring, mixing, or channel-making in soil by living organisms, which allows scent to vent and escape. It is the scientific word to describe the activity of plants or insects that move compounded soil particles to levels higher than the location of a burial. Examples of bioturbation are anthills, animal burrows, earthworm activity, insect activity, and root expansion and contraction. In the context of HRD, do not ignore your dog if he becomes focused on a moving line of ants or even an ant hill. The ants may have a trail from their mound to a burial site yards away. Ants also prefer looser soil, so they have been known to build mounds over buried bodies. Let your dog investigate.

TRANSPIRATION

Transpiration is the process by which plants absorb and distribute water (including nutrients and minerals) through their root systems. Unneeded water is released into the air as vapor through pores in the plants' leaves. Transpiration rates vary greatly by temperature, soil type, precipitation, land slope, and other influences. Many handlers believe dogs sniff and use their second olfactory system—Jacobson's organ—to "taste" vegetation on or near buried bodies or where body parts have decomposed. Dogs have also been known to alert on the vegetation on burial sites rather than at the bare dirt covering the body. Remember that when humans smell something, they perceive one odor. When they smell a hamburger with condiments, they smell a hamburger. When the dog smells a hamburger with condiments, he smells each individual odor—the meat, bun, catsup, cheese, and all the elements in those ingredients. It is the same with flora. All plants have smell producing organs throughout, although flowers have certain compounds that tend to dominate. While a human smells one fragrance emitted by a plant, the dog analyzes each layer of the chemical compounds of the plant.

Some people argue that plants do not take up decomposition materials from the soil, disputing the belief that dogs detect the odor of decay through transpiration. However, the US Geological Survey (USGS) Water Science School article on capillary action states: "Plants and trees couldn't thrive without capillary action. Plants put down roots into the soil which are capable of carrying water from the soil up into the plant. Water, *which contains dissolved nutrients*, gets inside the roots and starts climbing up the plant tissue. As water molecule #1 starts climbing, it pulls along water molecule #2, which, of course, is dragging water molecule #3, and so on."[2]

Other factors appear to support the theory that K9s can sense decomposition via transpiration. After all, a human body is 55 to 60 percent water. Decomposition results in the liquefaction of soft tissue, thereby generating a liquid from a solid. Liquefied or other remains can be affected by ground water, the water found underground that can carry nutrients from a decomposing source to the roots of a plant.

Another factor to consider is a comparison between the most abundant elements in the human body—major elements: 65% oxygen, 18% carbon, 10% hydrogen, 3% nitrogen, 1.4% calcium,

Figure 29.1 K9s alerted on this cedar tree while it was standing, and again after it had been cut down and put in a different area among other like trees.

1% phosphorus, 0.50% magnesium, 0.34% potassium, 0.26% sulfur, 0.14% sodium, 0.14% chlorine, 0.004% iron, and 0.003% zinc; trace elements: arsenic, chromium, cobalt, copper, fluorine, iodine, manganese, nickel, selenium, silicon, and vanadium[3]—with the 12 essential nutrients plants must take up from the soil—nitrogen, phosphorus, potassium, calcium, magnesium, sulfur, iron, manganese, zinc, boron, copper, molybdenum, and chlorine (there is debate about the necessity of silicon, nickel, and cobalt).[4] Nine of those 12 vital nutrients are elements of the human body, so the decay process provides plants with a rich source of those mineral substances.

Figure 29.2 The dogs did not show interest in the other trees but again alerted on the same cedar tree as before. It was later learned that soil with human decomposition from a nearby clandestine grave—found and excavated three years earlier—had been dumped close to that tree. That information was not initially available.

It is not known exactly what chemical compounds an HRD dog identifies as the target odor, but it is fact that plants absorb nutrients, trace elements, toxins, and poisons from the soil if the molecules are not too large or fragile. It is also known that plants growing in areas of chemical spills will indeed transpire those chemicals through their leaves. Thus, it does not seem plausible to firmly say the chemicals that dogs identify as human remains are not absorbed by plants and detectable based on a K9's olfactory capabilities and odor threshold.

I have presented this information with precision here to indicate exactly what is being questioned in arguments disputing the dog's ability to detect HR via transpiration. When discussing this subject with research scientist and forensic anthropologist Dr. Arpad Vass, he agreed that further research on the chemical analysis of plants growing in soil saturated with human decomposition/burials and those that are not will provide more insight into the target odors of human decay.

SCENT MIGRATION

Scent can play strange tricks, and a dog can only tell his handler where the strongest scent is. According to Dr. Arpad Vass, "Odor from a decomposing body does not always migrate straight upward, particularly in the desert environment . . . . The hard, crusty layer below the surface tends to block odor rising from below, deflecting it laterally through the loose, fine gravel lens that exists a meter or so down."[5] No one really knows how far odor can traverse this way, but Vass believes it could travel as much as 33 feet (10 m) or more sideways before finding a way to the surface. Bodies wrapped or enclosed in some object can also force odors to filtrate laterally.

Hanging Victims

Hanging victims have been found in a variety of positions, from low, with their toes barely touching the ground to high, suspended at great heights. For realistic training, it is necessary to estimate the odor strength of the training materials versus the elevation they will be hung along with the time needed to produce a scent cone or scent pool. A full body, 15 feet (4.5 m) up in a tree, will not only create considerable odor but also decomposition fluids that might seep down to lower branches or the soil below. While training should be challenging, does affixing a weak source high up in a tree—with a short interval before the K9 team works the problem—meet an objective, or is it only a weak, elevated odor exercise? To simulate real situations, you need to study what occurs with tree drip lines (the outer circumference of a tree's branches) and scent voids or "dead spaces" (areas that lack scent although they are in close proximity to the target odor).

Recognizing Clandestine Gravesites

Bodies are not always buried in a long, narrow, "typical" type of grave. Neither is there always a depression indicating a burial site. Or, there could be two depressions—one from digging and a second depression within, caused when the decomposed chest cavity collapses. There can also be ground disturbance next to the grave where the soil had been placed during digging. One theory is that the size of the disrupted area next to a grave is an indicator of the depth of the hole. However, the size of that area may be due to the type of soil and number of people involved in the burial.

Further, the amount of vegetation alone is not a sign of a burial. Vegetation can be more or less abundant than in the surrounding area, or it can be absent. The colors of plant life also do not determine that there is a burial—it may be greener at a burial site, but that is not always the case. The vegetation can also be yellow or brown from too much nitrogen in the soil. Compact soil also reduces the ability of plants to utilize the nutrients, which affects their color and growth.

SOIL TYPES AND THEIR EFFECTS ON SCENT

Soil can affect the decomposition process, the availability of decomposition odor, or the ability to visually detect a burial site.

Sandy soil has large particles. It is dry and gritty to the touch. Because the particles have huge spaces between them, they cannot hold water. Fluids will leach out and create a larger area of soil affected by decomposition. Bodies will decompose faster or mummify.

Silty soil has much smaller particles than sandy soil and is smooth to the touch. When moistened, it is soapy slick. It retains water and can easily compact, so it is poorly aerated. Silty areas are usually close to creeks and at bottoms of hills because of the looser soil washing down. The more silt (or sand) in a soil, the less likely you are to see a grave depression.

Clay soil has the smallest particles and good water-storage qualities. It is sticky when wet but smooth when dry. The small particles tend to settle together, and little air passes through the spaces. Clay soil is cold, and it takes longer for the moisture within to warm up when the weather changes from cool to warm. It has shrink/swell potential, is very heavy, and especially during the summer months can turn hard and compact—it can seal over and prohibit air exchange, making it the most difficult soil through which a K9 can detect the odor of a body.

Loam soil consists of three textural components—sand, silt, and clay—that are normally present in equal parts and are mixed with organic matter, air, and water. Loam soil is the most frequently used in gardens due to its characteristics, which encourage plant growth. If there is more of one textural component, the soil will be further described, sandy loam, for example, means it contains more sand and may be less likely to compact. More clay would be clay loam, which might increase the characteristics of clay soil.

Caliché soil, also known as hardpan, is a layer of soil in which the soil particles have been naturally cemented together by lime (calcium carbonate, $CaCO_3$). It generally occurs on or near the surface but can be found in deeper subsoil deposits. Layers vary from a few inches to feet thick, and multiple layers can exist in a single location. An extremely old burial can exist under a few inches of caliché that has had time to form. That situation may cause the scent to migrate before it reaches the surface. Thus, the burial may be a distance from the dog's alert. Caliché is usually light colored, but its color can range from white to light pink to reddish-brown, depending on the impurities present in the soil.

Because of these influences and to get a better understanding of what you will be contending with in searching for buried remains, you may want to ask the investigators if they know or if possible check with the USDA Natural Resource Conservation Service, so they can provide you with soil survey information for areas you are searching.

GROUND WATER MOVEMENT AND ITS EFFECT ON SCENT

Ground water, the water beneath the land surface, is found in the pores between soil or rock particles and occurs almost everywhere. It

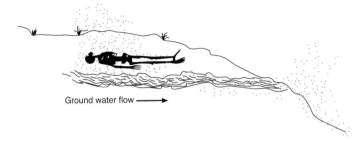

Figure 29.3 Because ground water flows, SAR/R dogs may detect primary and secondary scent cones and pools.

consists largely of surface water that has seeped down. Decomposition from a buried body also permeates the soil. If the two meet, the mixture can leach (drain) and cause the decomposition molecules to travel to areas distances away from the burial site where they can vent, causing your dog to alert at that point. In that occurrence, the terrain should be examined for even the slightest upward change in grade. If so, it is suggested to probe up the slope and have your dog sniff every probe hole to determine if there is more scent and the body at a higher elevation. If the area is flat, probing around the area of the alert may identify the grave farther away.

MULTIPLE SOURCES AND THEIR IMPORTANCE IN TRAINING

Detecting and alerting on multiple sources is a special skill that requires training, especially when it comes to a searching for disarticulated remains. This type of situation requires K9 teams to find more than one piece of remains without a lengthy reward interval before searching for more. It is not unusual for dogs that are trained to make only one find in exercises to shut down after that initial find, believing they are done. This is especially true with play-reward dogs that will be either so animated at the spot they can destroy or disturb the scene or dash away in anticipation of a thrown ball, neither of which is acceptable behavior at a scene. Variable rewarding in training is helpful, but not sufficient when dealing with the amount of remains that can be present.

Figure 29.4 In this case, officers spent two days searching for bones before a K9 was called in and found 27 additional pieces of bone and evidence nearly invisible to the human eye. The search area was about 5 acres—this image shows the widely scattered markers where evidence was found in about one of those acres.

In these situations, even if your K9 is a play-reward dog, you could both praise her and offer her a tiny food treat before telling her to continue searching. You can read more about this subject in the chapter on mass fatality training (Chapter 34).

Multiple-source training should vary with problems that have only one training aid to prevent your dog from always expecting there to be more than one source to find.

Disarticulated remains may or may not be spread out over a large area. However, knowledge of scavenger and predator habits, their ranges, and forensic taphonomy are indispensable to the handler in locating areas of scattered remains.

Documentation

Handlers should complete a training log for each training session. Although TEAMs may have different log formats, they must all contain pertinent information: the handler's and dog's names; the date and location of the training; the type of search (rural, hanging, building, fire scene, etc.); the type of soil and depth of training material if buried; the size of search area; the type of terrain; the wind direction and speed, and temperature when the search began; how long the training material had been in place; if the dog found the source; a description of the search; brief comments on how the dog worked. Brief, objective comments are best.

In addition, the handler should include information about the training problem; the instructor who set up the training problem should provide information about the type, age, and size of the training material; the training material's location; and the temperature and wind speed/direction at the time the problem was set up. The goal of the exercise should also be noted so the instructor can ascertain if that goal was met; and instructors may want to add their estimation of how the scent will travel, given those conditions. This will provide a picture to compare if there is a difference in how the dog worked to what was expected when the problem was created.

In live-victim searches, some logs include the instructor's comments and signature/signoff as well as the "victim's" description of the dog's reaction to him or her at the find. Did the dog immediately acknowledge the victim, or did it get sidetracked by something interesting in the area? Did the dog lick the "victim," bark, or act frightened because of his or her strange behavior (crying, screaming, etc.).

Setups for HRD Training Problems

Dragging a training aid from one point to another spot yards away will help you teach your dog to work to the highest concentration of odor and not alert on the first faint target odor he finds. Situations such as this happen when bones are scattered and residual scent is on the ground. In some situations, the odor in or on the ground is stronger than the skeletal remains; in this case, a dog may step over a bone and alert where the body or body part had decomposed. It is your responsibility to direct your K9 to search the area thoroughly. The following are a few suggestions for setting up HRD problems.

- Put the training aid in a location for several hours, then move it a couple of yards away.
- Dig dummy holes.
- Make negative piles of rocks, leaves, branches, or other matter.
- Conceal training materials in organic or inorganic rubbish piles.
- Put a clean bone in a mud puddle.
- Put only negative containers or only animal remains in the search area.
- Place blood on objects to simulate murder weapons—a thick piece of wood, a brick, baseball bat, knife, and so on. (Decomposition placed on a knife should be cleaned off the blade after use to prevent corrosion.)
- For temporary placement, use cricket cages, bird feeders, or similar objects to suspend or submerge training aids.

There are a multitude of locations HR aids can be placed, concealed, or suspended. Keep in mind that night searches are not generally conducted for suspected homicide cases, so night training is not a priority in searching for human remains.

Training in Addition to TEAM Sessions

Extra-TEAM training is often done with just two handlers. A fun and creative exercise to practice in this context follows.

1. Select three wooded or brush-filled areas approximately 200 yards away from each other and mark boundaries.
2. Each handler uses six human remains training aids of their choice.
3. Handler 1 goes to the locations and conceals whatever number of aids he or she wishes in each one and also

walks throughout each area to avoid a scent trail. Handler 2 then goes out and conceals her or his aids, not knowing Handler 1's arrangement and also walks around to contaminate each area. While each knows where and how many aids they placed in each location, they have no idea what the other has done. Handler 1 may conceal an aid at the base of a tree while unknowingly Handler 2 suspends one in the same tree. The object is to make sure each area is thoroughly searched and to trust the dogs.

4. After an agreed-upon period, each handler searches separately. The one not searching should wait at an established base location. After both have searched, they exchange information about how many aids each found in the different areas, if they missed any training aids, how their dogs searched, and if they trusted their dogs.

HRD Training Scenarios

HRD training scenarios involve the handler's knowledge and thought process, not only the dog detecting odor. These exercises should simulate as many realistic portrayals as possible. Following are some points to consider.

Training materials that represent the full spectrum of decomposition may not be available, but scent pictures will change regardless of the type of sources, which is why the environments in which the K9 team trains are equally as important as the materials. For example, swamps produce methane gas, but that methane is different from methane produced by human decay.

Make sure you add proofed-off items and distractions to the training area, which involves having a live person, at times, in the search area. While it is best to have a search location clear of LE and other searchers, that is not always possible; for instance, an investigator combing the property may get close to the K9's search section. Many investigators are not pleased if dogs are distracted by their personnel.

Finally, remember that the person placing the training aid *must* walk all around and crisscross his or her own tracks to contaminate

Figure 29.5 A tampon, covered with the strong odor of human decay or sprayed with diluted decomposition fluid, is secured to the tip of an arrow. It is then shot it into a field of high grass or brush.

the entire area with his or her scent. If not, the K9's ability to find the target odor is not proven—the dog may merely be following the scent of the person carrying and placing the training aid directly to the source.

SETUPS WITHOUT LIVE HUMAN SCENT

Suggestions on how to place training sources without any live-scent trail from the person setting up the problem are:

1. Toss, throw, or project a securely contained training aid via a ball launcher into an area.

2. Use a bow and arrow. The wind can make this problem very challenging. The K9 team must find and return with the arrow.

Anytime a source is launched by whatever means, the one doing so must attentively watch and diagram the landing area so the source will not be lost or overlooked when training aids are collected.

Reading the Dog: An Outside-the-Box Exercise

This unusual exercise can reveal your K9's slightest suggestion that something is different. The objective is to determine how well the handler can observe changes in the K9's behavior and body language.

1. Bizarre-smelling items, not overwhelming in odor, are randomly placed in a small, not previously used outdoor area. Examples of what has been used include legally acquired matter from a zoo or wildlife park: exotic animal feces, urine-soaked pads, hair and feathers, or anything else containing animal odor. Participants are not told what the materials are until all have finished the exercise. No human remains are in this section. However, a training aid is planted yards away, where its odor cannot contaminate the above-mentioned area.

2. Handlers work one at a time and are not permitted to observe other teams' work until they complete the exercise.

3. Handlers understand that the location does not contain human remains; however, handlers should still give their K9 the HR command and search the area thoroughly, as they normally would. If their dog alerts, handlers should correct the dog and continue searching.

4. Handlers are told that their job is to let the monitors know each time they see any physical change in their dogs—body language or behavior—by pointing to each place as it occurs, and verbally indicating "here" or "there." The dog should not be acknowledged, only told to "Get to work" if necessary, and he should continue to search until the handler feels the team has covered the area.

5. When the handlers say they are finished, they are told to expand their search toward the spot where the HR training material has been placed. This gives handlers the opportunity to once again observe their dogs' body language as they encounter human decay and the exercise will end on a positive note for the dog.

Two individuals monitor the proceedings using a check sheet for each handler. The sheet indicates the handler's and K9's names, the places and types of each exotic substance, and two columns under each substance—one to check if the handler noticed a change in the dog, and one for the monitors to note if they saw a change in the dog. The monitors also note what behavior change they saw. Not all K9s have a reaction to each exotic item, and not all handlers recognize differences in their dog's body language.

Handlers who have completed the exercise are allowed to observe. These handlers often notice gestures and behaviors as they watch the other dogs work, becoming more aware of the variety of changes a dog can display. A common observation is handlers that are so concerned with walking their grid pattern that they get in front of their K9s and miss a head turn or other nonverbal communication.

Visual Awareness of Remains in Different Stages of Decomposition

Having a basic awareness of what human remains, whether tissue or skeletal, might look like in different stages of decomposition is significant in HRD. Photos from books and websites can help you build your knowledge. In addition, attending a basic anthropology workshop or seminar can provide a brief, hands-on experience of the strange configurations of some skeletal body parts. However, seeing a bone or other remains in a clear photograph can be totally different from recognizing it when the body part is in vegetation or partially covered with dirt or debris.

Figure 29.6 This photo gives a closer look at mummified skin. The arrows point to two pieces—the rest is tree bark.

Bones can show marked and complex alterations and can deteriorate at different rates depending on the surrounding environment. The type of soil and circumstances they are exposed to can also change the coloration of bones, so they may not be readily identifiable. A handler should not make a definitive judgment about whether a found bone is human or animal, or what part of the body it may have come from. A week-long class in

Figures 29.7 One of these photos shows a patella (kneecap)—the other is a rock.

anthropology is not sufficient to learn the differences. Identifying what has been found should be determined by an anthropologist, who at times may take a manual into the field for reference. That said, basic visual awareness of remains in different stages of decay is important for handlers because many have corrected their dogs when they felt the dog was taking too long checking an object— because *they* thought it was a stone, wood, or other such matter. Always remember that remains can be contaminated by animal scent and other substances, and it is the dog that makes the determination, out of all the chemical compounds he senses, whether or not it is the target odor.

A Clue Mindset

Giving handlers a "clue mindset" means teaching them to recognize whatever is different or out of place, such as wood shavings, cigarette butts, a small area of gravel where no other gravel exists, a strange chunk of wood, a piece of fabric, a button, broken branches, a tire track, a footprint, a pile of dried human feces, and so on. All curious objects in the search area should be flagged. For example, the presence of human excrement, even if the dog doesn't alert on it, can be a clue. What is it doing in that area? DNA can be extracted from feces, so it can be a significant find. Some handlers allow their dogs to alert on human feces, while others proof their dogs off of it, feeling excrement contains only human scent—not the odor of human decay. However, remember that a dog trained to ignore feces is correct in alerting if she detects blood in the stool, so the handler should not automatically assume the dog is wrong if she alerts on human feces.

ILLUSTRATING A CLUE MINDSET IN A TRAINING SCENARIO

Consider this training scenario to highlight the clue mindset process: a mummified body is found in a clearing of low grass. Law enforcement wants the adjoining small, wooded area searched for any missing pieces of the victim.

The scenario was set up by placing three large, dry cow patties about 12 feet (3.7 m) apart along a path in those woods. Partially tucked under the third patty is a six-inch (15-cm) long piece of mummified human skin.

The K9 team started searching in the field at a pathway and continued into the group of trees. The dog came across the first cow patty, gave a brief sniff then left and continued searching. He did the same with the second cow patty. However, at the third one he stopped, sniffed much longer and had a change in body language. The handler was about to correct the dog and pull him off when he was stopped and questioned. "What did your dog do at the first cow patty?"

He answered, "Nothing."

"Did he do anything at the second patty?"

"No."

"Well then, what is so special about this one that his body language changed and he's checking it longer?"

That's a clue. The piece of mummified skin protruding from under the patty, and almost indistinct from the dry tree bark and other detritus, was then pointed out.

After being allowed to sniff a few more seconds, the dog alerted on the skin.

Without specific training to develop a clue mindset, a handler may not observe or understand the significance of his or her dog's changing body language. The end result may be the handler unwittingly pulling the dog off human decomposition.

When dogs exposed to a new source or stage of decomposition do not immediately alert, handlers may say that their dogs had "never smelled that before." Instructors may retort that "HR is HR," so it should not make a difference. That is true, but the scent picture and odor layers are different from what you have been using as training aids. Initially, the dog should be allowed more time to investigate the object. Remember the K9's olfactory process must take place for him to confirm the target odor, which signifies an alert. This may also explain why dogs are able to alert quickly on the same training materials used repeatedly. They are familiar with those specific scent layers.

Other Aspects of Training

TALKING TOO MUCH

Regardless of the search discipline, some handlers seem to feel they must constantly encourage their dogs with chatter: "Where is he?—Where is he?" "Find it—Find it!" and so on. Much of the time, the handlers speak without realizing they are. Handlers compelled to give commands repeatedly are often not doing so for their dogs' benefit but for their own assurance that their dogs are working. The chatter may be more disconcerting than motivating. Asking talkative handlers to wear a recording device— sensitive enough to pick up whispers too—during a training session and then playing it back may help them realize the extent of their chatter. Another way to illustrate how disruptive talking is, would be to select a paragraph—any paragraph—and ask talkative handlers to read it out loud. Just as they finish reading the first line, repeat the command, "Read this paragraph," and point to the beginning. As they start to read, again interrupt them and repeat, "Read this paragraph," pointing to it. Usually by the third time the command is issued, they get the idea of how they sound to their dogs.

MICROMANAGING AND SECOND GUESSING

Second guessing and micromanaging do not allow your dog to work on his own. The result of micromanaging is a K9 that looks to his handler each time before moving forward. If your dog is going in a direction *with purpose* (not if she is running off in "critter mode") and you want him to check something, let the dog check out whatever he is scenting first. By stopping and waiting, or taking a few steps in the direction your dog is going, you allow him to investigate. That area can be confirmed or rejected, or investigating it may result in loss of odor. If nothing is found, the spot should be marked, and the original search pattern continued. That area can be revisited, from a different direction, when searching the location is completed.

VIDEOTAPING

Filming training sessions is helpful for handlers to watch their dogs' different behaviors as well as their own movements as they search. Handlers who are against videotaping are concerned with legal issues and surmise footage could be used in court against the K9 team. The problem is not so much the video but the interpretation and conclusions of the person(s) viewing it. Thus, each TEAM has to decide if it wants to video training sessions and what to do with the video after viewing.

> *"Never trust the translation or interpretation of something without first trusting its interpreter." – Suzy Kassem*, Rise Up and Salute the Sun: The Writings of Suzy Kassem

NEGATIVE AREAS

Negative areas are an integral part of HRD training. Negative areas are as necessary as longer search problems. The K9 should not always find something or make a find in an accustomed period. If he is used to making a find at a certain time in training, he may false alert during a longer work period, or he could shut down after the usual duration of time has passed.

Negative searches must be conducted in true negative locations, not where previous training has been done. Some say you should be told the area is negative when you *first begin this training*, so you can comfortably focus on your dog's body language and actions. Another view is the handler should *never* be told, because if he or she knows the area is a negative before searching, the handler may unconsciously work the dog differently. Knowing an area is negative should be limited to the first few sessions of negative search training.

The object of these exercises is not to just complete a search but also to study the dog's behaviors while adhering to search strategies. You must search the area thoroughly with no shortcuts. At this stage of training, the instructor or flanker will be familiar with how the dog is handled when searching. Any differences should be pointed out to the handler immediately. This also helps the handlers realize how they may subconsciously alter their search of an area based on what they think or believe. This can happen when a team is called to search a speculative area that investigators say is "highly unlikely but has to be checked out." Handlers should train to search locations thoroughly every time and not base their strategy on conjecture.

After the introduction to negative searches, future periodic negative exercises would involve the handler thinking there is the probability of a find. Regular and successful completions of these scenarios will increase the handler's confidence in the dog's abilities.

TRAINING AID RESPONSIBILITY

Areas where training aids have been buried or spilled should be noted and cleaned up at the completion of each training day. It is not advisable to pour blood on the ground for a training problem, though this has been done. If so, that spot should be dug out to remove the fluid-soaked dirt, which can be reused as a training aid. Sites not cleared can contain HR odor, and in subsequent exercises in this area a K9's alert would be correct although the handler may believe it to be false.

Forgetting training materials at a location is shameful. To prevent this, an option is to put one person in charge of collecting all the materials, because if others are involved, miscommunication as to who picked up what easily happens. Some teams mark training aids with TEAM information for possible return if found. This system will, however, create two outcomes. First, the markings add to the scent picture, and second, the TEAM is identified as being careless or incompetent for leaving biohazardous materials behind. The best approach is simple: the person setting up the training problems should sign out each source with name, date, and time, note their exact location, and ensure they are all accounted for when leaving the area.

"It is not only for what we do that we are held responsible, but also for what we do not do." – Molière

Understanding What Happens to Victims of Fires

Depending on the length of time and fire temperature, the following can occur to victims of fire.

- Shrinkage. As muscle burns and chars, it physically moves joints, which retract along the bones of the arms and legs. Rapid dehydration from intense heat causes tendons and muscle fibers to shorten and produce what is called the "pugilistic posture." Bodies can appear much smaller than expected.

- Burning. The thickness of skin and tissue determines how a body burns. Less soft tissue protection on the forehead and hands cause them to burn faster than other portions of the body. However, this principle does not apply to homicide cases when an accelerant is poured on the victim.

- Detachment. Prolonged extensive exposure to fire can detach appendages from the torso—even the deeply embedded bones of the thigh and lower torso.

- Fragmented or "exploding" skulls. These were once believed to occur due to pressure buildup inside the cranial vault. Now, studies have determined that this happens because skulls have a thin layer of tissue that protects but is quickly burned away, revealing the bone. Once that covering has been breached, bone is exposed to thermal degradation. It soon becomes brittle and is broken easily by cold water hitting it or by falling debris.

- Changes in bones. Bones can twist and bend. Compact bones can split, and teeth, although durable, can crack. Facial bones rarely survive intact in a fire. When in contact with heat or fire for a relatively short period, bones become charred or blackened. Bone that is in contact with heat for long periods, or is repeatedly heated and cooled, attains the white appearance of calcined bone. Cremated bone fragments are a variety of colors—from brown to gray-blue, black, gray, gray-white, and chalk white. Other colors less frequently noted are green, yellow, pink, and red.

SEARCH STRATEGIES FOR FIRE VICTIMS

The strategy you use in this situation depends on the type of structure you are searching and the information you have received about the possible location of victims. However, victims' locations can change depending on their level of mobility. A perimeter search of a single-family home before entering is often a good start.

Before you begin, ask which side the fire had been attacked by firefighters or if it was extinguished from all sides. Pressure from fire hoses can blast pieces quite a distance from the structure, and those areas must be searched. It's important to search beyond the structure for other reasons too. For example, perhaps an injured victim escaped the fire but has collapsed in the surrounding area.

Explosions have a push-pull effect and blow remains away, and then negative pressure pulls them back. Scattered or fragmented body parts can thus be everywhere.

Following are key considerations when searching after a fire:

1. If the skull is missing it may be fragmented.

2. Small skeletal pieces of fingers, hands, and so on can break up and fall off below the body—they do not burn away but are camouflaged in the ash and debris around the victim. These remains are still present at the scene and can contribute valuable information.

3. Expect broken glass, nails, and tangled wires covering the ground.

4. For safety, watch for hot spots, unstable floors, overhead beams, and objects.

5. Fire suppression foam is sometimes composed of just liquid soap and water. Other types of foam may contain carcinogens. Ask what has been used and if any known hazardous chemicals are at the location.

Water Search

Water search is an HRD specialty. As with land HRD, many variables affect HR scent in water graves. Water HRD is not simply about putting your dog in a boat and going for a ride to see if he can detect odor. To conduct efficient and safe searches, you should know how to read and work your dog in the conditions of competing prevailing wind, top currents, and undercurrents to determine the location of HR and assist divers for recovery. You must also understand thermoclines, eddies, strainers, the possibility of feeder creeks, and other topics pertaining to this discipline to form the best search strategies. K9s need to learn that the target odor can come from beneath the water.

Some water searches are by the shoreline; others are conducted via whatever type of boat is available. Boats with bows that ride low

Figure 29.8 A four-month-old puppy detecting a bone in a puddle.

in the water are best because they permit a dog's nose to be closer to the water's surface. Dogs may, naturally or by training, perform a different type of alert than they do on land. Dogs have jumped into the water—some swimming in circles in the area of the body. However, entering the water can be dangerous, and if your dog is wearing a collar, she can get hung-up in strainers or on other objects.

Water HRD handlers have their own preferences regarding whether to work their dogs on or off lead, and whether or not the dog should wear a collar or a floatation device. Many handlers begin training by using divers—in which case rebreather diving equipment is used to prevent surface bubbles, or underwater communication is used to notify the divers to hold their breath as the K9 gets closer so they do not visually key in on the location. Other handlers use scent pumps or specially made scent machines.

A simple first step to show a dog that scent can be underwater is to place a bone in a deep puddle or bucket of water in the training area.

Figure 29.9 This photo shows Bear's exhalation as he retains odor in his olfactory path lines. The shaker contained teeth. (Courtesy Micky Blain)

Some studies state that once a body begins to sink, it goes directly to the bottom—others claim that bodies sink in incremental steps. Not all bodies will float. Bodies have positive, negative, and neutral buoyancy. If a body does not have enough gas buildup due to its condition when it was disposed of in the water, or low water temperature inhibits decomposition, it may not float or it may only rise to a certain level but not up to the surface. In addition, at a certain depth, external water pressure will counteract the decomposition gas.[6]

Because attributes of the underwater environment, along with temperatures and currents, interfere with and are influential in locating bodies, there have been varied reports regarding the duration of odor availability for K9 detection.

Humanmade lakes usually contain old structures, vehicles, and other items, so divers are subjected to more dangers than in

Figure 29.10 Lake and aquatic rakes, though expensive, are available for sale. Fishing nets and butterfly nets can also be helpful but have their own limitations, such as the strength of the net when trying to recovery something covered in silt or dirt or by collecting underwater life. This "cadaver rake," created over 20 years ago, has been used by many agencies. It is an extendible pool-cleaning pole with a piece of slightly curved metal and tenpenny nails attached.

natural lakes. Using unqualified dogs for water searches can put divers in perilous situations, cause them to make repeated dives in negative areas, and waste time and resources. In the last several years, departments have begun using sonar equipment to locate victims—some before deploying dogs, some after, and others use only sonar. Ponds and stock tank bottoms can present problems in searching for and recovering dismembered or skeletal remains. Searches may be limited to dogs only conducting searches from the banks or by swimming because the water may not be deep enough to safely use any type of watercraft. Although dogs may enter the water, take caution if you attempt to walk in and follow your K9. A deep silt bottom creates suction capable of pulling off boots or other footwear and can temporarily trap you. Draining a pond is not recommended, since surface algae will blanket the bottom of the pond. And finally, be aware that raised dirt/rock banks (berms) often contain snake dens!

30

Law Enforcement and SAR/R

"People's minds are changed through observation and not through argument." – Will Rogers

Law enforcement's major concerns often stem from trust. On occasion, one law enforcement (LE) agency may have trouble trusting another agency, so it should be understandable that they can be skeptical of civilian, volunteer SAR/R teams. That said, investigators who have worked with a good K9 team have said they would rather use a dog to assist them in searching than any other equipment.

Confidentiality is paramount when working with LE, and violating an agency's trust is a sure way of never being requested again by that agency. This is especially true in criminal investigations where a comment, even if seemingly harmless, may compromise an investigation.

Previous bad experiences with a SAR/R team are another factor. LE agencies share information. Some LE K9 handlers are against using civilian K9 TEAMs, opinions that can affect their agency's feelings too. Others may share favorable opinions about certain handlers or teams, which increases the likelihood of them being called to help.

There is a difference between law enforcement officers (LEOs) who put their lives on the line every day and see the worst in people, and a K9 handler who is not only a civilian but is *volunteering* his or her services free of charge. It is logical that LEOs might be doubtful about volunteers' motivation. At times, some LEOs use the word "civilian" in such a way that it sounds like a dirty word. LEOs who feel this way may be reacting, and holding fast, to their encounters with poorly trained K9 teams rather than acknowledging the excellence in others. Sometimes it is difficult to change a person's perspective, but it can be done. Civilian handlers must work hard to gain respect and trust—which are earned and may take time.

"Claiming that you are what you are not will obscure the strengths you do have while destroying your credibility." – Tom Hayes

Note that mentioning a friendship you have with an officer or investigator from one agency to a LEO from another may seem like a way to show knowledge or camaraderie in LE, but this action can result in an uncomfortable situation. If the two agencies or officers do not get along, whoever you are speaking to may reply with a caustic comment.

Call-Outs

Agency authority differs among cities, states, countries, and/or the location in which you are working. I will continue to use the terms "law enforcement (LE)," "agency," or "department" interchangeably in this chapter.

Rule Number One: Do Not Self-Deploy

There is a difference between a "self-deploy" and a "justifiable responder." A justifiable responder can be any person in the immediate vicinity of a tragic event who provides instant help or equipment to assist those in peril. A justifiable responder can also be an individual who travels to a disaster scene with personal watercraft or other vehicles needed to assist in the immediate rescue of victims. These responders are usually monitored, in some way, by LE or fire departments.

"Self-deploy," in this context, is a K9 team that shows up at scenes without being summoned. Handlers have reported strange dogs suddenly appearing in their search sectors with the accompanying people saying they are trained in search and rescue. These people believe they are assets, but their unauthorized presence reveals their lack of training, which can hurt the overall search effort.

Local, state, and federal agencies all have call-out procedures for different types of resources, some of which require certain accreditations. Even if your TEAM has built relationships with agencies, that does not mean you are automatically granted access to an incident. You still must receive a call-out. If you have not been called, it is acceptable to contact the agency to advise them of your TEAM's qualifications and availability and then wait for any directives. Whatever qualifications teams claim to have must be supported by documentation. As a wise person once said, "If you lie or exaggerate, everything you say afterwards loses credibility." As with every search, teams pay for all their costs incurred unless otherwise determined.

Do Not Criticize Other TEAMs in Front of LE

Any feelings of distrust harbored by LEOs are exacerbated when they hear one TEAM berating another TEAM that is providing assistance. This has occurred during call-outs when one TEAM learns a particular TEAM has also been called, or in some cases, TEAMs have refused to work together at a search scene. *A search is a cooperative effort and does not "belong" exclusively to one TEAM.* A TEAM's "turf" is not being invaded when another TEAM has also been called. Attitudes betraying contempt, resentment, or superiority expose poor character and are unprofessional at a search site. Those berating others may not know the relationship the agency has with the TEAM they are criticizing or why that TEAM was requested. Investigators are capable of seeing differences in the professionalism and quality among TEAMs.

Some say LE agencies should be advised diplomatically of their TEAM's concerns about a particular TEAM and then leave the scene. This can be unsound advice. After all, if the other TEAM is that bad or unreliable, the ones making accusations are forsaking all that SAR/R symbolizes by leaving. Rather than withdrawing from the search, it would be better to fulfill their agreement to respond and, at a later date, provide factual evidence of improprieties to LE investigators. The agency will then make its own determination for future call-outs.

"A sharp tongue can cut your own throat." – Unknown

Different Types of Call-outs

Not all call-outs require the full-scale response of a SAR/R incident commander along with a TEAM mobile command post. For searches in homicide cases, for example, only one or two K9 teams may be requested, with others on scene limited to LE.

TEAM Signage

The sensitivity of a mission may require TEAMs to remove all identifying signs from members' vehicles. This is a problem for those who have permanent identifiers rather than magnetic signs. Ask what the agency wants before arriving on scene. Uniforms are another issue. The team may be required to search in plain clothes to avoid unwanted attention.

Independent Outreach Search Centers

On occasion, one of the several Independent Outreach Search Centers formed to help find missing persons may be handling the call-outs. Some offer assistance only to the state in which they operate, but typically these centers respond nationwide, and a few become involved internationally. Independent centers should not be confused with any association officially designated as the state or emergency management SAR/R resource. Independent Outreach Search Centers can be very helpful in locating missing persons and witnesses, providing comfort to the family and, especially, keeping the missing person's name in the public eye. They can also be beneficial in supplying K9 teams; however, each organization operates according to its own bylaws, procedures, and standards. Their services and allocation practices may vary, as is the way they obtain, screen, and qualify volunteers.

TEAM Responsibility to LE

All SAR/R centers/organizations should focus on being dependable resources for LE and victims' families. They should not be working to garner personal media attention. Investigators have stated that there are a few centers guilty of giving false hope to families by making unrealistic claims and assurances when they know there are no new leads. One even had the audacity to tell the media it had new information and was going to search a location but the center refused share that new knowledge with LE.

In areas with relatively few volunteer SAR/R dogs, LE agencies may be so highly pressured by overwhelming attention about a case that they feel something is better than nothing, and they may welcome any resource, even if that team is not well-trained in the discipline required. K9 teams must be brutally honest with themselves when gauging their capabilities and limitations to LE. Turning down a mission is difficult. If a team has *not had any training in the conditions presented,* the handler must weigh the risks not only to the team but to law enforcement. Inherent dangers and uncertainties already exist on searches. Accepting a mission and placing your untrained team members or TEAM in perilous circumstances because you do not want to lose the call-out can be harmful to the team, the mission, and the agency's future use of SAR/R dogs. Referring another team that is qualified, even if it is from another state, shows professionalism and concern for the mission.

31

Search Briefings and Searches

Search briefings may give minimal or detailed information and are conducted so all responding individuals understand the nature of the mission.

Search Briefings

Prior to searching, law enforcement (LE) may provide a briefing to all TEAM members or discuss issues only with the TEAM's incident commander and staff, who in turn relay what they think is necessary to the K9 teams.

The information shared may depend upon the proven trustworthiness of the individual teams involved and the agency's confidence in them. Regardless of trust, some agencies give no information other than the area to search and the words, "See what the K9 does." This might be their strategy to determine the validity of previous information and prevent the possibility of the handler subconsciously giving the dog cues. One example of this kind of minimalist instruction from LE involved a handler asked to have a dog search the bed of a pickup truck. Although the bedliner had been thoroughly cleaned, the K9 alerted in one corner of the truck bed. The handler then learned that the alert corroborated information about where the victim had been killed. Bedliners are applied in different ways so they do not absolutely inhibit odor detection. Some bedliners are very porous due to their high elasticity and are both waterproof and breathable.

Complete information is not always available. Sometimes the information provided about the victim by family, friends, or informants is wrong or lacking. Families may be embarrassed about emotional issues of the missing; friends may be covering up for the person; and an incarcerated informant may just want a day out of jail, which can lead LE to a bogus search location. In addition, information about old cases presents major challenges since terrain features change and locating a site can be extremely difficult.

LE's restrictions on information are also a matter of "need to know" and "nice to know." This is not arrogance on their part— they are protecting the case. They may not know the backgrounds of all the responders and they all know stories of self-serving or irresponsible individuals who have gone off on their own to investigate, talked to the press, or sold their stories to tabloids.

"Just because you don't feel guilty doesn't mean what you are doing is okay." – NarcissistProblems.com

Landowner Consent to Search or Search Warrant

A search of private property may be limited to specific areas. Because of this, you should ask the following questions:

1. Does the designated search area include everything on the property, including out-buildings?

2. Can you enter the buildings, or only search their exteriors?

3. If told the search is of the "curtilage," it means the area around a home where the occupants spend most of their time living their day-to-day lives. The curtilage includes the front porch, driveway, front yard, side yards, backyard, swimming pool, and any other area close to the house.

4. However, the curtilage can also be determined by the means used by the occupants to guard their privacy: Did the occupants put up a fence, gate, or signs warning people to keep out of a specific area? Does the property have any cross-fencing? Can you cross those fences or enter fenced-off areas? When in doubt, ask if those areas are included in the owner's consent or in the search warrant.

Remember, the search could be for the victim of a violent crime and the landowner may not be welcoming. Remember, too, that with human scent detection, a K9's alert is only one indicator for reasonable suspicion of "wrongdoing." Other corroborating evidence must exist for LE to develop probable cause (PC).

Other relevant questions to ask, pertinent to the type and age of the case, are already outlined in other books, so below I only provide questions and suggestions related to safety. However, there will always be risks to the search team, regardless of the amount of information provided and gleaned.

Questions and Suggestions for Outdoor Searches

- What types of scavengers or predators are in the search areas?
- Are there open wells/shafts?
- Are there animal traps/snares?
- Watch for camouflaged or baited poison stakes for varmints.
- Be alert for loose dogs.
- Are there any known septic tanks or sinkholes?
- Keep your eyes open for booby traps or devices set by homeless individuals to protect their gear.
- Was the area previously a landfill?
- Does the area have a heavy snake infestation or rat populations?
- Have pesticides recently been applied?
- Be wary of chemical spills and creosote-soaked areas.

OUTDOOR METH LABS AND MARIJUANA FIELDS

Drug areas are highly protected and can hold a multitude of safety issues. Stay vigilant and increase situational awareness. Be aware of tripwires—some are attached to alarms while others are rigged to shotgun triggers. Also watch out for PVC pipe for irrigation in pot fields, empty plastic bottles (used to transport water), booby traps, fertilizer, chicken wire, coolers, and anything out of place or that does not look right. Do not disturb any object or place that seems suspicious, but notify LE immediately.

Recognizing Building and Structure Hazards

Watch for the following dangerous situations as you search:

- Contaminated needles.
- Broken florescent light bulbs.
- Elevator shafts. Partly open elevator doors in dim, vacant buildings can be difficult to see. An opening a foot wide might look like a doorway to the dog and is enough space for him to fit through and fall down the shaft. This has happened.
- Exposed electrical wires—they can be live.
- Glass and other sharp objects
- Objects you are tempted to move aside. Do not push or move anything out of the way—even a fire extinguisher can be a bomb. Use caution when investigating objects in wastebaskets.
- Laundry chutes.
- Missing stairs or landings.
- Possible narcotics/weapons/explosives.
- Structural failures.
- Toxic chemicals or vapors.
- Trap doors.

- Unsafe flooring.
- Caution should also be taken with dogs jumping over objects or barriers—indoors or outside—when you do not know what is on the other side. This can be deadly.

COMPACT FLUORESCENT LIGHTBULBS

Compact fluorescent lightbulbs are marketed as "safe," but that is only as long as the glass remains intact. If the bulbs are cracked, broken, or not disposed of properly, they pose a serious health hazard. The amount of mercury they contain—although miniscule—is extremely dangerous.[1]

When your dog is searching the exterior of structures and alerts on a spot by the foundation or side of the building, check for conduits, piping, electrical/phone boxes or other such objects that could be channeling the odor from inside the house. Tracing the connection to the interior location may help you discover the room or area where the odor originates. It may require a search warrant to search inside the building, so ask LE before you do anything.

Many TEAMs throughout the world begin each search with a simple prayer such as, "Dear God, we ask You to protect us and our K9 partners. Guide us and give us strength and courage to overcome challenges in all our efforts and help us on this mission. Amen."

Many LE officers use the word "hit" to describe a dog's interest or alert. If the word "hit" is used, it should be made clear what the handler means—did the dog identify the source of the odor or did he just show a great deal of curiosity in a location?

A field commander or incident commander (IC) will sometimes ask a team to try the impossible. When determining whether to accept or decline a difficult mission, you must take into account the type of area and the particulars of the search and compare it with your training and ability to work safely in such a context. If

you advise that the requested mission is beyond your level of training, you may still state you are "willing to try" because your trying
does not pose a big safety threat to you. The IC or lead investigator
must then consider your disclosure and make a decision by weigh-
ing the risks against the immediate needs of the search.

Considerations Regarding the Search

Since a great number of search personnel have not grown up on
a farm or ranch where these actions are second nature, they must
remember: *If a gate is opened it must be closed!* The same if it was
locked and then opened—it must be closed and relocked. Following are some other tips and important issues, though sometimes
overlooked.

ACTIVITIES IN THE AIR

Sometimes a helicopter or fixed-wing aircraft is used in conjunc-
tion with search parties on the ground. In those cases, the helicopters are searching—not hovering. Other times the activity in the
airspace is due to news helicopters that have not been restricted to
a certain altitude or distance from the search area. While the noise
can be a factor for search teams, the main problem is the "wash" of
airflow caused by the rotors as news helicopters hover to film the
activity below. This wash disrupts the scent at ground level where
K9s are working and hampers search efforts. Chief Pilot Bill Hogg
explains that helicopters associated with the search usually circle at
about 60 knots (about 70 miles [113 km] per hour) at between 200
and 500 feet (61 and 152 m) above ground and move in circles laterally in any direction needed—not hovering—so downwash does
not interfere with scent.[2]

DOG GPS TRACKING COLLARS

Dog GPS tracking collars are very useful. The downloaded data
shows the K9's travels and can confirm the search area has been
covered—from the perspective of the GPS, not the capabilities

of the dog's nose. With that in mind, relying on that information alone may not be accurate. If you are not close enough to direct your K9 relative to wind-direction changes, funneling due to terrain features or obstacles, human-remains or live-victim odor may be undetected because the scent was not accessible to the dog in the pattern he worked.

THE RELUCTANT MISSING PERSON

Searching for live victims includes searching for those who may not want to be found, sometimes for reasons no one would ever imagine. When a four-year-old boy went missing in a small, rural Texas town, sheriff's deputies and a group of townspeople, including the mayor, set off to search for him. They searched the extensive, harsh countryside surrounding his home for several hours—calling his name repeatedly. There were no sightings and no answers to their calls. As dusk began to settle in, their fear grew. Then the mayor caught sight of a dog's head sticking out of a large bush. A bush they had passed numerous times. When he approached the dog, the mayor could barely see a child's foot deep within the branches and again called the boy's name. This time the child replied and crawled out. When asked if he had heard them calling, the boy said, "Yes." When asked why he did not answer he said, "Because I was deer huntin' and my daddy told me when you're deer huntin' you have to be *real* quiet!" The child had only his imaginary gun and his dog, but in his mind, he was doing the right thing—"being *real* quiet."

FINDING THE SCENT TRAIL: NOT ONLY FROM THE POINT LAST SEEN

While always starting a trailing dog at the point last seen (PLS) may seem logical, circumstances at that location should be evaluated first. It is well-known that most times K9 teams are the last ones to be called for assistance after foot searches, and searches made using ATVs and horses, among other methods. At that point, even after just one day, the PLS and immediate area will be heavily contaminated by, at times, over 100 people. If the dog does not pick up a solid trail within 20 yards of the PLS, begin doing searches on all sides and at a distance from the PLS. This is similar to "drop trailing," in which the dog is taken to locations, paths, and crosspaths to see if it can detect the victim's scent. A search pattern of concentric circles from the PLS, expanding each circle by another 25 or so yards is another option. The distance between each circle will vary with the terrain and other conditions. The object is to minimize the time it takes to locate a direction of travel by reaching less-contaminated land to search for the matching scent and possibly find the victim faster.

FACTS AND THEORY

The job of a K9 SAR/R team is to search and report the results of their efforts, even if they do not match the information received or LE's beliefs about the case. It is the facts, not the theory that matters. Do not be concerned about whether your team's results exonerate or condemn someone.

> "It is a capital mistake to theorize before one has data. Insensibly one begins to twist facts to suit theories instead of theories to suit facts." – Arthur Conan Doyle, "A Scandal in Bohemia"

TOOLS NEEDED ON A SEARCH

Not every agency has CSI-type forensic units, equally trained personnel, or all the implements that may be needed on a search. It is prudent for teams to carry items such as tree and shrub pruners, loppers and hedge shears, saws, rakes, and pliers. HRD handlers should also carry entrenching tools, from mini-trowels to small shovels, as well as probes and soil core samplers. Probes help you check for differences in soil compaction, aerate soil to create an air exchange, break through vapor barriers, and delineate burial sites. Soil core samplers indicate if strata have been disturbed.

All tools should be clean from previous use. Consider affixing bright-colored flagging tape to the handles with your name written on each item. Remember, though, to only use tools with LE approval.

RECOVERY EFFORTS

Never risk a life to make a recovery! Recovery efforts should be conducted by professionals trained for that type of dangerous task.

TRAINING MATERIALS

Bringing training materials on a search to use to reinforce your dog during long or multi-day missions is a delicate issue. Due to prominent fraud cases (see page 176), bringing training materials to a search scene (which used to be a rather common practice) is now regarded with suspicion and controversy. If you bring something for a short, encouraging exercise or to determine if a tired K9 is still working, make sure you show it to LE upon arrival at the scene. The problem setup should be done outside all search areas and away from the media, whose members can misinterpret or exaggerate what you are doing.

RECOMMENDATIONS

It is best that your thoughts about a search area, before fielding your K9, is that "something is there, and we must find it." Viewing the location as though it is impossible for the victim to be there or other negative thoughts could cause a less-than-thorough search of the area. If you are asked how you want to conduct your search, you should be able to offer a tactical plan and make recommendations. But it is the agency's call as to what they do and in what order they want to do it.

BOUNDARIES

Searching farther than the assigned area without permission can create major problems for the case, as anything found outside the established boundaries may not be admissible in court. Ask before you go out of your assigned area.

AVOID CUING DURING CHECKS

If you are asked to have your dog check something, let the dog work into the object/area rather than taking him right to the spot and command him to "check." This method helps you avoid subconscious cuing or any accusation of cuing an alert.

SCATTERED REMAINS

Investigators have their own methodologies when dealing with scattered remains. It is wise for the handler to ask what procedure to employ. Ask if you should:

- continue searching after flagging the spot with *one* flag, even if it contains more than one object/bone close together;
- flag *each* bone or piece of evidence at the point of the alert and continue searching;
- place *one flag marked with the number of remains or objects you have observed* within inches of the K9's alert(s). (This method has been done to assist in confirming the number of pieces of skeletal remains/evidence that blend completely with groundcover or debris, and when windy conditions move leaves and obscure the sight of the objects. You may see five small bones at the point of the alert, but the individual collecting the items might see only four. Thus, if a flag is marked "5," a minimum of five things should be procured.); or
- stay at the spot until an investigator or member of the forensic unit arrives to make the collection.

BONE WITHOUT TISSUE

If clean bone (bone without any tissue) is yards away from where it decomposed, and wind conditions are not favorable, the dog's nose may have to be just a few inches away before he can detect it.

WHEN A BODY OR A BONE IS FOUND

If your dog finds a body missing skeletal components, or if you find just one bone or several of them clustered together, it is advisable to continue searching that immediate site in a tight methodical manner rather than continuing your original search pattern. There is a good probability there will be more bones or evidence in the vicinity. Even if the body was found and removed earlier, and a visual search and collection of items has been completed, start your search at that spot (where the body was found) and work outward. There are 206 bones in an adult human body, so there is a lot to miss if searching is done only visually. If a shredder has been used to chop up a body, look in trees and brush for pieces that were flung there.

THE WORK OF SCAVENGERS

Scavengers begin their activity on humans by chewing pieces of the limbs. Phalanges—the small bones of the fingers and toes—are usually missing, even in the case of a life-sized surgical manne-quin, stuffed with training materials, hidden in brush for a training exercise and left undisturbed for six weeks. When the K9 made the find, the fingers and toes had still been nibbled away and the glass eyes were missing, even though the "body" was not human. Only one of the training materials had been dislodged, so it appeared no large scavengers/predators had been in the area.

The mandible (lower jaw) is usually a distance from the skull because it detaches from the cranial vault during decomposition and is easily carried away. Also, upper and lower limbs can often be found a long way off from the main find and may have been buried by large scavengers.

Look for animal resting areas where critters take food to eat in safety or where they can watch the area around them. Bones or evidence may be in the soil or grass in such places. Rodents and varmints will also take pieces of remains into dens of sticks, into brush or holes. Despite the danger of the hole being occupied, it is important to have your dog check each possible hiding place, with-out sticking his head deeply into any openings. If you read your dog's body language as he nears the den, it may help determine the existence of HR and avoid danger if the burrow is occupied. If HR

Figure 31.1 This cultivator has been successful in retrieving bones and evidence from critter holes on numerous searches.

mannerisms are exhibited or the K9 alerts, you can stop your dog and use a five-prong telescopic cultivator to explore the den. This great tool helps you extract the contents of holes, but only use it if you have permission from LE. Remember to listen for sounds within the den before attempting any extraction.

Do not ignore animal scat. Consumed bone fragments or evidence may be contained within. Ribs are some of the easiest marrow-filled bones to consume.

When a "Find" is made, it is considered scene disruption if other TEAM members go to the location. Curiosity is no excuse.

CRIME SCENE LOCATIONS

There is not always just one crime scene. Additional crime scenes may include where the assault leading to the death took place—this can be yards away from the body or at a completely different location. Large animals might have dragged the body from its original dump site, and there may be physical or trace evidence of remains at the original spot where the body was buried or concealed. Handlers must remember that if they move around in the surroundings when a find is made, footprints, tire tracks, or drag marks could be destroyed. Always follow the instructions of the lead investigator.

SEARCHING UNDER CONCRETE

When searching for burials under concrete, there are less-invasive methods than the jack hammer. The first, and most used, method is to probe, at an angle, around the concrete base and allow the holes to vent for several minutes. Direct your dog to check each hole for the odor of decay. LE can also have someone drill vent

Figure 31.2 After cutting and removing a narrow strip, the backhoe can slide a large slab of concrete away from the area.

Figure 31.3 Compare dirt taken from different locations around the slab or base of a house.

holes in the concrete or cut a narrow strip out to slide away a piece of the slab. After holes are drilled or strips cut, be sure all concrete dust is blown away before setting your K9 to work to prevent him from inhaling fine particles.

THE K9'S BEHAVIOR IN PLACES OF VIOLENCE

Hesitant or fearful behaviors have been exhibited by K9s in places of violence. One handler commented that the K9 was very apprehensive approaching a search area that had signs of animal bones, strewn feathers, and wild boar diggings. Another handler had a similar experience of skittish behavior at a site of satanic worship. After a few minutes of acclimation to the areas, however, the K9s cautiously continued to search. No human remains were found in either case.

> *"The starting point of all achievement is desire. Keep this constantly in mind. Weak desire brings weak results, just as a small amount of fire makes a small amount of heat." – Napoleon Hill*

The Media

During a search, the media can be everywhere and anywhere. High-profile searches will bring reporters and photographers to search locations—staking out the scene in personal vehicles, lawn chairs, and media trucks with satellites lining the roads. Wanting to be the first to get the story, they can at times pop out of the bushes where least expected. Although kept at a distance from the search area, the media has a variety of tools at their disposal to gather information. Some media use high-powered zoom lenses that can capture images from hundreds of feet away, or even simple binoculars.

CAMERAS AND CONVERSATIONS

Because a camera is facing a particular area or subject does not mean those in the periphery of a wide-angle lens shot are not in the photo. Actions can cause embarrassment, as when a photographer focused on two rescue personnel in a rather remote area. Not until the photo appeared on the front page of the local newspaper was it noticed that another male searcher, a distance away, was obviously relieving himself. Handlers should also be mindful of how loud they speak and the topic of their conversations. Sophisticated listening devices can pick up and filter sounds—some from a surprisingly long distance.

TALKING TO REPORTERS

"The character of a man is known from his conversations." –
Unknown

Talking to reporters should be left to LE. Depending on the agency's policy, the point person could be the lead investigator, the LE public information officer (PIO), or the sheriff/chief—all of whom may respond, "No comment at this time." They have been trained how to respond to questions, and reporters are trained how to interview to get the details they want. The minute action stops on the search site, media scramble toward searchers—especially those with K9s. But some cunning reporters do not rush with the crowd, and instead meander off to a lone handler to get a different angle for the newscast. Avoiding the media can be difficult, and you should try not to be rude. Politely referring questions to the lead investigator or LEO in charge may work, but reporters can be persistent. If one handler is respectful and excuses herself, reporters will seek out others, possibly hoping to find someone looking for the notoriety of being on camera or seeing his or her name in print.

At times you may get trapped when questions start out benignly, "What is your dog's name?" "How long have you been a volunteer?" Then suddenly a reporter may ask about the search, taking you off guard. It is important to maintain control and stick to the original question. It does not matter if you do not give your name to a reporter. One handler answered, "I prefer not to say," to one question, which was followed by the question, "What is your dog's name?" The handler replied, "I don't mean to sound rude, but I prefer not to say—I believe the only name important here is that of the victim." Nevertheless, both the handler's and dog's names, along with telephoto-lens pictures of them working, appeared in the next day's newspaper. Another handler described a reporter taking a picture of their license plate and calling their home the next day. If reporters really want to know a handler's name, they will find it.

Every so often, LE may want a handler to speak with reporters; caution is necessary. Discussion of what occurred during the search efforts is off limits unless you are given explicit approval by the lead investigator, along with instructions related to content. Some TEAMs request that a representative from the LE agency be present during the interview to witness what was said and to correct any misunderstandings the media may have as reporters start to craft their stories. It is critical that you *offer no personal opinions or perspectives!* Some reporters twist words, sensationalize, or engage in creative editing to support their slant or specific point rather than relay what was actually said. "On the record" means the comments are attributed to a person by name. Even so, purported quotes have been altered or taken out of context to fit a purpose. "Off the record" is often a statement wielded by reporters, as in, "Off the record, what do you think?" This gray area does not mean the comments will not be used, but that they will not be ascribed to a certain person—instead, the comments will be preceded by "sources say." This can be disastrous to a case. It is best to think of yourself as being "on the record" whenever you speak to the media.

Taking all the credit when credit is not due has been done far too often by some handlers. A K9's alert on a flagged, small area identified through months or years of work by investigators should not translate to the headline: "K9 Team Finds Body" and aggrandize that dog and handler. The investigators on the scene know the truth and remember those self-serving remarks. There are times when that headline is correct, but when the investigators did all the work to get to that point, then the dog has *confirmed* their information or *assisted in the find.*

> *"Don't tell fish stories where the people know you; but particularly, don't tell them where they know the fish." – Mark Twain in* Mark Twain at Your Fingertips: A Book of Quotations

Debriefings

Team debriefings cover occurrences in search areas after a team returns from the field. Even a search that concludes with a find does not mean problems did not exist. Reviewing what went right and what went wrong are both necessary. Not addressing any problems is a failure to learn from them. There are usually three forms of debriefing—one done with the teams, incident command, and LE; another that LE conducts only with their personnel; and finally, the debriefing each TEAM has privately.

Search Reports

Handlers should provide a search report as soon as possible after each search day. Do not wait to submit an all-inclusive report at the conclusion of your involvement in ongoing searches. A small fact recalled after debriefing but included in a search report may be important to the agency. Search reports must contain only facts—no thoughts, beliefs, or feelings. Measurements of remains or evidence found should be left to the agency so there is no conflicting information. Documentation of items found should be described according to what they resemble. For example: a ring might be "gold colored" not "gold." If you or another handler was directed to do something, note the LEO's name and the instructions in the search report.

FACTS ABOUT DEATH AND DECAY
- Bodies may not swell very much when they are in hot and dry climates. The skin slippage may also be dry rather than wet and slippery.
- Degloving happens when the skin on the entire hand slips off. This is caused when liquid from cells gets between the layers of skin and loosens them. Fingerprints can still be obtained from the "glove."
- The first cells to die are in the brain. Each tissue and organ shuts down at its own pace.

- Body fluids can be released from a deceased victim at different times relative to the conditions surrounding the death and handling of the body after death. If, for example, great pressure is asserted on the abdomen, the bladder and bowels may release. In addition, skin will blister during the decay process, and fluids may seep from those blisters.
- Bodies can split and burst depending on the degree of gas built up and the tension/elasticity of the skin. Arms tend to split when extremely bloated.
- Teeth are the only portion of the human skeleton visible while a person is alive. Teeth may look different based on their country of origin, the person's cultural traits and dental aesthetics, not to mention oral health and diet.
- Residual scent can last for years in a building depending on the source of the odor, ambient conditions, and the type of material on which the source was originally placed.
- HIV can survive up to 15 days in a dead body.

Embalming

Embalming is done to restore a body to a "lifelike" appearance and temporarily preserve it for viewing at a memorial service. The effects of embalming do not last forever. The length of time a body is preserved depends on the culmination of embalming fluid distribution in the body and how well it was dispersed; type of embalming fluid used—before 1900, arsenic was used; type of casket and the kind of container/vault in which the casket has been placed. Dogs can still smell the dead tissue and body fluids of an embalmed body.

Lime and Decomposition

Some killers believe lime will accelerate the decomposition of soft tissue. However, although more studies are needed about how lime and soft tissue interact with other variables in the environment, observations by forensic investigators suggest that lime tends to slightly slow down decay of buried remains.

Snake Bites

You may not immediately be aware your K9 was bitten by a snake. The dog may not cry out but just jump back a little. If bitten on the face or neck, he may initially only shake his head. If the bite is on another part of his body, your dog may show lameness or a change in body carriage. Bites on the torso have a poorer prognosis than others.

It is critical that you to pay attention to your dog's body language and mannerisms.

First, K9s that range out of sight need careful observation when they return into the field of vision. Snake bites can happen any time one is encountered. Your dog does not have to have been nosing around rocks or dens; simply passing by an undetected snake could lead to a bite.

If your dog has been bitten, he will be highly sensitive and in extreme pain when you touch him near the location of the bite. If you find a bite, thoroughly examine your dog, since there may be more than one bite wound.

All handlers should have training in emergency responses to a suspected snake bite. Undertake this training from a veterinarian, and make sure it is applicable to all the types of snakes in the area in which you and your dog live and work. Depending on the snake, the fang marks can be large or small. There may even be only one fang puncture. Don't take chances; check your K9 thoroughly for other signs that may indicate snake bite.

Despite the dangers, it is suggested that handlers not carry antivenin kits for a couple of reasons. First, most antivenin products are for specific types of snakes and may not have any effect if the correct serum is not used. Second, they do not have a long shelf life and are so expensive that even many animal hospitals do not keep supplies on hand. At times, veterinarians do not use antivenin. This can be because the level of toxicity from the bite is not that high or because of other exigent factors. Instead the

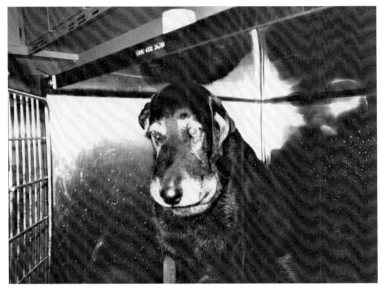

Figure 31.4 Swelling 15 minutes after Mercy arrived at the vet clinic, 30 minutes after two wet rattlesnake bites to the face. The swelling got worse. After ten days, areas across Mercy's nose and down her throat lost hair and had to be shaved and debrided of necrotic tissue. Deeper areas of necrosis were still highly visible. After two weeks, Mercy was completely back to normal and assisted in a homicide search. She showed no hesitation in searching among rocks, where she found critical remains identifying the victim. I, on the other hand, was very cautious and let her range only a few yards.

vet may administer IV fluids and other medications believed necessary.

Flies

Flies, as well as other insects, play an active part in the decomposition process. Fly species and their abundance differ from region to region, season to season, and habitat to habitat.

Usually a swarm of flies on searches draws your attention and signals possible decomposition. However, when you are searching for deceased hurricane victims, flies won't help you locate bodies because the forceful winds will have blown the flies away for a while.

Vultures

Circling vultures do not necessarily mean something below is dying or dead—the birds may just be enjoying a wind thermal or looking for something to eat. Also, numerous vultures in trees or on power lines can mean nothing more than they have just found a roosting place they like. But, when they circle and then dive toward the earth, carrion is present. Vultures have reduced corpses to skeletal remains in less than 24 hours.

Bears

I add this information here because of the common instruction to "play dead" when encountering a bear. Brown bear attacks differ from those of black bears, and the way to ward off the two types is *not* the same according to the National Parks Service. Searchers should know the species of bears in the areas in which they live and are searching, as well as how to tell the differences between species. This is also of importance for teams that search nationwide. Different species require different responses. What to do about wildlife safety encounters should be learned through research from experts in that field and not from hearsay.

Part V

Disasters and Disaster Teams

32

Major Disasters and Mass Fatalities

"If we treat a dead body as if it were no more than an inanimate thing, we dehumanize not just the person who died, but ourselves and our fellow human beings too." – Silas Boadu, "Let's Treat the Dead with Dignity"

There is a difference between mass fatality and mass casualty incidents. An incident is referred to as a mass casualty when the number of people injured far exceed the number of emergency responders, which can make all the difference in terms of how many victims survive and how many do not. A mass fatality incident, however, can involve as few as five lives lost if the situation overwhelms local resources and their capabilities—including the number of bodies the medical examiner's office can handle and process.

After each major disaster, SAR/R online discussion groups light up with comments about self-deployment, untrained teams being deployed while qualified teams are not called to assist, disorganization at incident command for not having complete control or knowing qualifications of teams in the field, and FEMA (Federal Emergency Management Agency) canine teams in the United States.

The number of agencies involved in any disaster depends on the type of disaster, its scope, and whether it has been declared a "national disaster" requiring federal assistance. County or state agencies do not automatically relinquish all authority to FEMA task forces and may sanction their own resources. Thus, in widespread disasters, local emergency operations centers (EOCs) or incident command posts (ICPs) might be established in each individual jurisdiction. Those additional ICPs are not always formed by FEMA or whatever agency is managing the entire search operation. There have been times they were established by the local sheriff/chief in that area, as happened with Hurricane Katrina. While additional posts may be needed, adding them can lead to duplicated efforts and conflicted guidance and activities.

Where and how additional K9 teams are acquired has been a predicament. The overwhelming need for help can supersede verifying qualifications of those offering assistance, resulting in bogus and shoddily trained K9 teams being granted permission to deploy, based only on verbal assurances of expertise. The responsibility in this situation lies with the integrity of each team. However, the aftermath of a disaster is no time to try to educate an agency on K9 teams. Neither is it a time for partly trained teams to expect IC to figure out where to send them based on their capabilities. "Wanting to help" is usually the reason for being part of the effort, but offering a K9 service you are not fully trained for can be dangerous for all involved. For the most part, self-deploying and unqualified K9 teams appear without communication apparatus, equipment, or the ability to be self-sustaining, which can cause chaos and major logistical problems, and burdening the system.

Media reports of a major disaster trigger vigilance among K9 teams. This is a difficult period of anticipation and desire for teams trained for those conditions. They are eager to respond but must wait to see if they are called. It is a time of growing anxiety, but their professionalism and training restrain them from self-deploying, even as their desire to help increases. Some teams might demonstrate their feelings with a level of anger, unfavorably judging the teams deployed. However, any team that self-deploys makes its lack of training evident.

> *"Expectation feeds frustration. It is an unhealthy attachment to*
> *people, things, and outcomes we wish we could control, but don't." –*
> Dr. Steve Maraboli, via Facebook

FEMA USAR Canine Teams

FEMA Urban Search and Rescue (US&R, commonly known as USAR) Task Forces are occasionally predeployed to a staging area pending a potential disaster such as a hurricane gaining strength in the Gulf of Mexico. But they are not allowed to enter the area until given the order by FEMA.

The subject of FEMA canine teams being used instead of qualified local teams has made for a hotbed of viewpoints among SAR/R K9 handlers. The animosity felt by state and local TEAMs stems from their frustration at being excluded as soon as FEMA is called. Their negative feelings have not developed because of rumors, but because of first-hand comments—including those by FEMA canine search specialists, after-action reports, and media statements. While not seeking the limelight, qualified local handlers can feel disheartened when their hard work and contributions are ignored or rejected in favor of FEMA dog teams. According to the 2006 general audit of the US&R system, "FEMA never intended to have an in-house rescue capability of its own and recognized that the best sources for urban search and rescue knowledge and skills resided at the State and local levels. Therefore, the National US&R Response System was established as a federal–state–local partnership, based on Memoranda of Agreement and Individual Cooperative Agreements between FEMA and the Sponsoring Organizations for the task forces."[1] Even though state and local teams have been recognized as "best resources," highly trained and experienced teams not part of FEMA task forces, but granted permission by state legal entities, have been turned away, prohibited from searching and even evicted from sites. This has caused resentful feelings toward FEMA.

A unified command in incidents involving multiple jurisdictions or organizations ensures effective coordination, planning, and interactions. When unified, the different organizations can make joint decisions and speak as one voice. Each responder reports to a single supervisor within that responder's area of expertise. State and local emergency-management agencies (EMA) develop response rosters of SAR/R teams. EMAs in states with K9 SAR/R standards require certain qualifications to be met before a team is added to their roster. EMAs in other states list any teams that submit their information. Some of these EMAs include a disclaimer that the individuals or organizations, private or public, have not been confirmed by any agency or person.

If verification of K9 SAR/R teams for capabilities and credibility was done before they were rostered, agencies could have confidence in their abilities, leading to increased efficiency in searching. Although this may not eliminate who has the highest authority for approval of deployment, it would ensure a level of competence and might alleviate a few challenges. Umbrella organizations can be more difficult to verify. Made up of K9 teams from various organizations, umbrellas must rely on what a handler claims unless they conduct their own evaluations before accepting membership and then periodically test the resources they represent.

A common question is "Why are FEMA K9 teams deployed to search for human remains in disasters when their mission is 'live-victims only'?"

Some have responded, "Because of the media reaction if they did not assist when requested."

To which others retort, "So what? If not trained for a specific discipline, the teams should not deploy."

Many knowledgeable SAR/R personnel believe the directives from FEMA headquarters to deploy task-force K9 teams beyond their scope of expertise are more to present a positive veneer for political perception than to support the mission in question. A FEMA photographer is always on scene to capture photos of task-force K9 teams—not others—which propagates the impression that only those dogs are capable. It is true that FEMA K9 teams train hard and have extensive live-victim and rubble search training. However, FEMA team qualifications do not mean there are not state or local K9 teams with exceptional skills and teams more qualified to search for deceased victims. Another possible reason why on-site officials may not allow help from local teams is because of communication challenges after a disaster. Those challenges can range from no cell phone reception to poor or broken up transmissions, which can slow or prevent permission to field local teams.

The other frequent question is "Why are non-certified or unqualified FEMA K9 teams allowed to deploy?" The answer: because a FEMA member in charge of deployment says so. Many non-FEMA handlers say this behavior degrades SAR/R, and that the standards that apply to them should be the same, or even more stringent, for FEMA K9 teams. However, FEMA USAR K9 teams respond because it is their obligation to follow orders as members of the USAR Task Force. The April 2002 issue of FEMA's *Dog Talk* newsletter gave a "heads up" to task-force handlers, saying, "It is not official yet, but there is a big push for a Task Force requirement of CERTIFIED TEAMS ONLY going out the door on deployments."[2] Two years later, it was stated in another issue that "7-1-04 was the projected date requiring canine teams to be certified in order to be deployed."[3] It has not been ascertained if FEMA is upholding that principle. Searching for live victims in disasters has always been FEMA USAR canine teams' one and only official mission. Searching for the deceased in disasters is a different discipline. As discussed in the next section, deployments of FEMA and other search teams in mass fatality incidents (MFIs) have caused problems.

The Disaster Mortuary Operational Response Team and Search Dogs

The federal Disaster Mortuary Operational Response Team (DMORT), experts whose mission is the identification, processing, preparation, and disposition of victims to their loved ones, voice many concerns about working with SAR dogs following a disaster. Their grievances through the years include the following:

- the time wasted because of the number of objects dogs alerted on, which required someone going into the field to collect them, taking them to the medical examiner's office where they had to be logged in as received along with their descriptions and the locations where found, then taken to the correct forensic experts only to determine they were not of human origin;

- the duration other personnel had to stop working when searching for bodies so live-victim and cross-trained K9 teams would not alert on them;

- down time for "depressed dogs," who needed to be emotionally boosted by having someone hide for them to make a live find;

- dogs observed "snacking" on food items in the rubble and, worse yet, handlers reporting a "find" but when personnel arrived to make the recovery they learned the dog had eaten the object; and

- wasted time dismantling piles of debris because of K9 alerts and finding dead animals or rotting food instead of human remains.

DMORT, initially a part of the United States Department of Public Health Service (USPHS), Office of Emergency

Preparedness (OEP), and National Disaster Medical Systems (NDMS), is divided into the same 10 regions as FEMA. DMORT is composed of forensic anthropologists, pathologists, forensic odonatologists, fingerprint experts, medical examiners, coroners, X-ray technicians, investigative personnel, embalmers, funeral directors, medical records technicians and transcribers, computer professionals, security, and administrative support staff. DMORT members leave their normal jobs and become federal employees when deployed to a MFI. For a long time, most of these hundreds of specialists believed dogs could not help find deceased victims in MFI situations.

A HISTORY OF THE DMORT MASS FATALITY K9 PROGRAM

In 1997 DMORT members' perception of SAR/R dogs began to change. At that time, I was a DMORT member and an HRD K9 handler who had trained a dog specifically for MFIs. DMORT's national commander, Tom Shepardson—the "father of DMORT"[4]—a couple of regional commanders, a forensic expert, and I believed in and diligently promoted the use of dogs to expedite DMORT's mission. We began to collaborate on the development of a mass fatality K9 program to support DMORT's mission criteria. Each concern of the forensic experts had to be addressed and countered. Some needed proof of the value of K9s. Many still did not believe that specially trained dogs could find deceased victims in MFIs without slowing down the mission or alerting on anything other than human remains.

In 1998 four more K9 handlers (with stellar reputations), were contacted for their input about the program. As standards and requirements were being written, the advantages of DMORT K9s were being recognized by other commanders and in the upper echelons in Washington. The four K9 handlers who had been contacted were later approved as DMORT members in other positions for which they were qualified, as were four additional veteran handlers, due to impressive recommendations. Subsequently, Washington placed a "freeze" on adding any more handlers to DMORT until the program was complete.

Toward the end of 1998, a national non-government organization (NGO) contacted the United States Public Health Service (USPHS), offering to write the DMORT standards and requirements in the official USPHS "Management Directive" format. This proposition, reluctantly received by DMORT commanders and other DMORT experts, was nevertheless okayed by USPHS management. All the standards, procedures, and requirements written thus far by the DMORT K9 group, along with DMORT's criteria and fundamental information, were transferred to the NGO.

By 1999, I had been unofficially deployed, with my dog, to two MFIs. Both deployments were beneficial to DMORT's mission. However, setbacks occurred because of problems with a few of the other teams involved in searching for deceased victims after the Oklahoma City / Moore tornadoes. Those problems were the same ones DMORT had issues with previously—dogs slowing down the mission, snacking on food from freezers and other places rather than searching, and alerting on animal remains. One local team contacted the medical examiners (ME) office to report that his dog found human remains, but when the ME's investigator got to the scene, the handler confessed his dog had just eaten the material. It was never determined what that dog consumed.

Unfortunately, these problems reinforced the doubt of the forensic experts not yet convinced dogs would be beneficial to DMORT. Some emphatically voiced their concerns. Even so, and while waiting for the draft of written standards and requirements to be submitted by the NGO, the DMORT K9 group continued to work on and resolve additional program issues. In 2000, the long-awaited standards and requirements draft proposal was submitted to the 10 DMORT commanders and a few non-DMORT handlers.

However, the template the NGO used for the DMORT program was the one for FEMA USAR canine teams. The mention of dogs having to find human remains was added toward the end of the documents—rather than being the *first* requirement. This draft was rejected by all the DMORT commanders, as was the second draft in January 2001, which was basically the same. Neither draft included any of the standards and requirements that had been created by DMORT and passed along to the NGO. After the second draft failed, USPHS put the DMORT Mass Fatality K9 Program on hold. However, this did not stop the DMORT K9 group (whose years of work on the program were unpaid and done on the own time) from pursuing its goal.

In January 2002, at a meeting at USPHS headquarters, Dr. Robert Knouss, director of USPHS/OEP/NDMS, directed me to form a committee to develop DMORT's Mass Fatality K9 Standards and Requirements and appointed me the national chairperson. The committee was made up of nine DMORT members / HRD K9 handlers who had the combined K9 SAR/R experience of over 200 years. The committee, along with Tom Shepardson, consulted with dozens of subject-matter experts and federal departments to follow and meet government regulations, protocols, and specific wording, while still conforming to DMORT's needs and requirements.

Late that year Dr. Knouss, who had become a staunch supporter of DMORT's K9 program, was diagnosed with cancer and stepped down from his position. There were also several changes in personnel at USPHS/OEP headquarters that required the program, written thus far, to be reviewed again, this time by the new individuals involved. The Office of General Council (OGC) also had to examine the program, as did the Office of Human Resources (OHR). A few issues had to be addressed to be in legal compliance. After several months, the DMORT Mass Fatality K9 Program was agreed upon by the K9 committee and Tom Shepardson.

The program then moved further up the chain of command for additional review.

In 2003, as the Shuttle Columbia tragedy recovery efforts came to conclusion, Tom Shepardson, stationed at headquarters in Washington, DC, for this mission, stated that when he returned home to New York, the last steps of the DMORT Mass Fatality K9 Program would be taken, finalized, and submitted to the assistant secretary of the United States Department of Health and Human Services for signature. Two days later, Tom died of a heart attack.

Through 2003 and 2004, there was more government reorganization, and DMORT was moved from under USPHS/OEP/NDMS to the Federal Emergency Management Agency / Department of Homeland Security / Office of Emergency Response / National Disaster Medical Systems (FEMA/DHS/OER/NDMS). In July 2004, final revisions to the program were made to comply with additional federal regulations, and those revisions were signed off on by each member of DMORT's Mass Fatality K9 Committee.

Following that achievement, I was notified that a subcommittee had to be formed to work with the Operations Working Group (OWG) to discuss portions and details of the program. The OWG represented all areas of the country and consisted of individuals from DMORT, FEMA, WMD (Weapons of Mass Destruction), VMAT (Veterinary Medical Assistance Team), DMAT (Disaster Medical Assistance Team), and NDMS (National Disaster Medical Systems). The K9 subcommittee included five members: a regional commander, a veterinarian/VMAT member, me, and two other K9 committee handlers. After months of conference calls and a few more revisions, the OWG signed off on the program and passed it to the Management Working Group (MWG).

Chairs from 11 federal departmental groups made up the MWG. After weeks of consultations, the MWG approved the

DMORT Mass Fatality K9 Program and sent it to Washington. The proposal was finally approved in May 2005 under FEMA/ DHS/OER/NDMS, and DMORT K9 "Units" (the term decided upon rather than the word "teams," which was opposed by Washington) were rostered as a NDMS resource. No handlers/teams, other than the eight K9 committee members, me, and our K9s were ever affiliated with the program or a DMORT Mass Fatality K9 Unit, contrary to a few claims.

AN OVERVIEW OF DMORT'S MASS FATALITY K9 PROGRAM

Since finding remains is the first step in managing the dead, the foundation for DMORT's program focused on experienced handlers with at least five years' involvement working a dog in K9 SAR/R. Those handlers had to have proven HRD K9s that were competent in locating remains in all situations and stages of decomposition, and proofed off other biological substances. The training methods did not matter as long as they were not abusive. Any type of alert—although some were thought better suited for disaster—was acceptable if it did not destroy the source. There was no need to change things that had been successful. Naturally, there was more to the process. Additional elements and skills would be evaluated and verified through teams' training records, information, accomplishments, and written recommendations (vouching for the team's skills, character and abilities)—from a few agencies they assisted, and an unedited test video of specific content demonstrating proficiency. Regional commanders would also interview the handlers before submitting them for government background investigations and approval. As a member, a K9 unit would be required to complete additional training and periodic assessments. Because of DMORT's worldwide reputation for expertise in MFIs, a comprehensive education in its principles and system would also be mandatory. This K9 program was developed to be efficient, logical, rational, and fair.

FIRST DEPLOYMENT

In September 2005, DMORT Mass Fatality K9 Units were deployed by the DMORT Commander of Region IV and FEMA/NDMS to the catastrophic wreckage of Hurricane Katrina. It was their first official mission, although not all the elements of the Mass Fatality K9 Program were implemented and not all outlying areas and satellite command posts were aware of the availabiity of the K9 units. But the magnitude of this disaster created the need for qualified K9 teams in the mass fatality detection discipline. The DMORT K9 units were initially assigned to work with FEMA task force members who would assign the units to areas they felt needed to be searched again. The K9 units and task force members worked very well together. However, there was a problem with DMORT K9 units having to wait each day for FEMA to conduct morning briefings with the task forces. It was not necessary for K9 units to take additional time to travel to the FEMA base command (logistically established in a different location than DMORT's command and morgue unit) to listen to the FEMA debriefings—all they needed to know was what area to search that day. In addition, search areas were dangerous, as were road conditions, and DMORT K9 units were allowed to travel only with a police escort. These delays meant searching didn't begin until later in the morning when temperatures had risen. Some afternoons, the temperatures rose to 105°F, which meant the dogs' temperatures had to be checked about every ten minutes so they would not succumb to heat exhaustion or heat stroke. Veterinarians (VMAT) on site provided any necessary treatments, and the dogs were frequently placed in an air-conditioned vehicle until their temperature returned to the normal range. There were other challenges, as well, such as a shortage of handheld radios, which made communication difficult. After FEMA task forces were deactivated, DMORT members in the field were challenged with identifying areas to search; without specific information, they could only speculate by what they observed.

Figure 32.1. Sleeping quarters for five of the DMORT K9 units deployed was a "reefer" (semi-trailer), the type of refrigerated trailers used by DMORT to hold and transport bodies of the deceased. If the trailer had been needed for more victims, the K9 units would have had to move elsewhere. Cardboard was placed on the floor to help the dogs walk on the corrugated aluminum floor.

Despite the challenges, the K9 units worked well and successfully accomplished their mission in the areas they searched.

GOVERNMENT REORGANIZATION

In January 2007, DMORT was transferred back under United States Department of Health and Human Services (previously USPHS, but now called HHS, which included the Department of Health and Human Services / Office of the Assistant Secretary for Preparedness and Response / Office of Preparedness and Emergency Operations / National Disaster Medical System / Disaster Mortuary Operational Response Teams. Or, for abbreviation purposes: HHS/OASPR/OPEO/NDMS/DMORT).

The K9 program approved by FEMA/NDMS now had to be approved by the assistant secretary of HHS, but in the meantime,

DMORT Mass Fatality K9 units remained rostered as an NDMS resource. Late in 2007, discussions of DMORT's function in search and recovery began at HHS headquarters. One question was whether DMORT's role should be restricted to the jobs of identification and preparation of the deceased (removing search and recovery from its mandate). Talks at HHS extended through 2008.

In 2009, despite the overwhelming support and documentation for DMORT to continue with search and recovery—roles they had fulfilled, with exceptional skill, ever since the teams' inception in the early 1980s, and the need for DMORT to use specially trained dogs to expedite its mission was proven—HHS headquarters decided DMORT would no longer be involved in search and recovery operations.

FEMA STEPS IN TO FILL THE NEED

DMORT cannot perform its duties of identifying and processing victims if the victims have not yet been found. This means families of the missing must wait longer to hear news of their loved ones. Although experienced DMORT members and Mass Fatality K9 units would expedite the mission's capabilities, HHS did not change its decision, even after a few years of appeals by DMORT experts. Consequently, FEMA'S USAR canine teams changed their mission to include HRD and created their own standards and requirements. But, because FEMA canine teams report to FEMA/USAR, not HHS/DMORT, it will be necessary for both agencies to cooperatively manage searches to avoid problems. Hopefully, politics will not play a part and the mission will be the only focus—with the USAR canine teams able to achieve complete and expedient results that will benefit the duties of DMORT and the return of victims to their families.

33

Searching in Mass Fatality Incidents

Building Markings Systems

Two marking systems are extensively used—FEMA's in the United States and the International Search and Rescue Advisory Group's (INSARG's) in other countries. These markings are vital in search and rescue operations.

Searching for deceased victims is the last step before disaster sites are cleared. By this time reconnaissance/rescue personnel from either state or federal task forces have most likely searched for live victims and marked all structures in the affected fields. Standardized USAR markings on building exteriors are used to ensure uniformity and clarity. Handlers must understand all the marks for safety reasons. They provide information not only on structural conditions, any hazards found within or near the building, and other critical data, but also when, and by whom, a building has been searched for the living. Even so, each mass fatality incident (MFI) K9 team must be aware of the possibility of, and look for, other hazards and problems that may be inside or around the structures. Unmarked buildings have probably not been searched.

Fragmented Remains

The world, as most knew it, has changed since September 11, 2001. Bodies in some prior disasters were fragmented, but suicide bombings and the increase of explosives being detonated in heavily populated areas result in more situations in which bodies are shattered. MFI search requires the expertise of K9s to find human remains that may be severed into small pieces in an atmosphere pervaded by the odor of decay or exposed to the degradation of fire. Portions of bodies can be in areas saturated with blood, body fluids, and raw sewage, and even be inside crumpled sheets of metal or airplane pieces, as they were at the Pentagon in the aftermath of 9–11. One tooth or fingertip found can be crucial, as it may be all that is left to help identify a victim. Since body parts can be unrecognizable, the K9 must be trained to pinpoint each piece of remains and continue to work after each find.

MFI Search Strategy Particulars

Search strategies for the dead in a disaster setting differ, to a degree, from those employed in other instances and from live-victim searches. MFI dogs still climb rubble piles, walk planks, enter collapsed structures and the ruins of burned buildings; they still search through culverts, thick brush, and obstacles, and they still search in waters. But MFI K9 teams do not risk life to make a recovery. Climbing ladders and traversing precarious areas are not crucial in searching for the dead. If necessary, huge rubble piles can be dismantled in stages for the MFI K9 team to search each segment in a safer environment. Descending deep into pits or tunnels would not be suitable for a K9 to precisely locate a body part. A passive alert in such a location would be unseen and require a refind full of risks. In addition, entering the pit to retrieve the remains would be hazardous. Zone alerts or "zone barking" (in which a dog alerts on the target odor in a specific, small area or "zone" of a rubble pile) can work for live victims searches, whose bodies will be seen as the debris is removed. But considering how small—and possibly unrecognizable—a body part may be in an MFI search, zone alerts are usually not adequate. The K9 needs to pinpoint the exact location of a find.

Cameras developed to be worn by dogs have their own disadvantages. For example, many handlers do not want their dogs to wear anything while searching to prevent them from becoming hung up on protruding rebar and similar obstacles. As well, dogs can knock off or disrupt a camera as they often rub against debris. Collapsed structures can also interfere with signal strength as well as light levels, and visual interference caused by the dog moving through rubble formations means the video stream can be obscured or distorted.

Not all areas require the MFI handler be a distance away from the dog. Many times, the K9 must work close, or on lead to avoid dangers. MFI K9 teams must be accustomed to searching in the presence of loud noise, heavy equipment, and people working in the area, possibly near the dogs as the recovery process progresses. Whether the dog is on or off lead, situational awareness is vital for the handler. Airline and other transportation crashes add to the demands of MFI searches. Every major disaster of this type should be treated as a potential crime scene. Clue awareness is important. If anything is moved, it must be documented. The position a body is lying in and any items on or near the victim are critical for accident reconstruction to determine the cause of the disaster and increase safety factors.

Depending on the size of the remains and the strength of other odors in the search area, a solid alert may be difficult for the K9 to perform. It is up to the handler to read the dog's body language and properly proceed in the search of that location to find the source. It's worth noting that a search area may include more bodies than were victims of the disaster, especially after floods. Sometimes DMORT has had to find and identify remains of individuals who had been dead and buried for years, but whose caskets collapsed and expelled their bones and body parts into the surroundings.[1]

Many times, requesting agencies will require non-disclosure agreements that will prohibit handlers from discussing details of the mission. Another subject that must be addressed, whether included in an agreement or not, is the taking of photos. No TEAM member should ever, for any reason, take photographs of deceased victims or body parts. This reportedly took place after 9–11 at the World Trade Center by a non-federal K9 TEAM that said the photos were "for training purposes." It astonished and incensed forensic personnel at the New York City Medical Examiner's Office to think any search team could believe that was acceptable.

K9 teams responding to MFIs in other countries must realize that there are a considerable number of regulations to which you must adhere and may include quarantine of your dog for a specific time.

Regardless of a K9's proficiency during training sessions and on searches in their locale, they may need several minutes to acclimate in a disaster setting. Some handlers say that if the dog is properly trained, he should be ready to work immediately. But the dog just traveled, possibly a long distance, perhaps to a different time zone or climate. The accompanying unique smells and situation can have an effect for a brief period. However, in most cases, by the time the team is processed, badged, and has received its assignment, the dog is ready to work.

34

Mass Fatality K9 Team Training

Because mass fatality incident (MFI) training is beyond standard training practices, it is advisable to begin with only fully trained dogs committed to the odor of all stages of human decomposition. Teaching agility, obedience, and directional signals are necessary, and the team must be trained in and comfortable searching all types of environments and conditions. MFI K9 teams are usually not deployed until the searches for live victims have concluded. This could be hours, days, or weeks after a disaster. Thus, K9s should be proficient in finding remains with a short postmortem interval as well as those in advanced stages of decomposition. The handler must remember that decay begins when life ceases, and human remains that are hours old still emit some degree of decomposition odor. These are but a few of the differences between searching for cadavers in an MFI environment and searching for cadavers in less calamitous circumstances.

Types of Scenarios

Training must include as wide a range of potential scenarios as possible in order to prepare teams to work in real disasters. Earthquakes produce different scenarios than flash floods, for example,

so it is necessary to visualize a specific type of disaster when setting up training problems so you can be as realistic as possible. As
well, a single disaster can create a variety of destruction settings,
from rubble or pancaked piles to bodies in swamps. Settings can
include buildings, fields, and woods. Bodies could be under rubble,
in vehicles, on the surface, inside objects, or in swimming pools
covered with so much sediment and debris that the surface looks
stable but the dog will sink in a mire of unknown substances. A
scene after a hurricane or airline crash might include victims or
body parts in trees, brush, or elevated in strange places. The MFI
K9 team must be able to reliably search all of it, so training set ups
require detailed visualization of what situations the aftermath of
various disasters might include.

Training sessions must be conducted in different geographic
environments: residential, rural, urban, wilderness, and water—
such as creeks, lakes, or ponds—and a mixture of two or three of
those areas. Objects or obstacles are not only blocks of concrete or
empty collapsed buildings, but also piles of wood, downed trees,
drywall, furniture, household items, and the like. Take caution
when training with piles of debris that have been undisturbed for
a length of time. They may provide spaces for "victims" to hide and
be long-lasting places to use, but they can become overgrown with
vegetation that are home to wildlife. Piles of debris may also have
industrial waste in or on them.

Humanmade Disaster Piles, Tunnels, and HRD

Nature-made rubble piles can have debris crisscrossing numerous
tiny areas where airflow/odor can channel from the victim's location to the surface and escape as if through a straw. This is not
necessarily true with humanmade disaster sites that have tunnels,
voids for safety, and specific vented locations to provide air for the
people pretending to be "victims." Tunnel configurations can produce a set pattern of airflow/odor at certain times and temperatures.

Some structures and rubble piles have been designed so portions can be rebuilt or adjusted to produce different physical features.

Disaster sites are built predominantly for live-victim search and rescue efforts. Dogs may encounter difficulties in pinpointing the exact location of HR training aids in such tunnels for a couple of reasons.

First, air does not automatically move, and movement is needed to carry scent. While the live "victims" produce some air current by breathing or changing their body positions, HR training materials, although strong, can be in places with very little or no air activity. A column of cold air will not rise and vent at higher levels of debris—it takes the path of least resistance. If not rising, air may be stagnant or move horizontally through wider paths in the tunnels.

Second, hot air rises and cool air falls. Temperature inside the tunnel versus the outside temperature and wind velocity should be taken into account when you see your K9 having a problem with committing to one specific spot.

Training Setup Suggestion

Following is one suggestion for training your dog to work an MFI search area:

At the beginning of MFI training, a delineated area, *not a rubble pile*, should be scattered with uncontaminated HR materials. Strong-smelling training aids need to be placed in very close proximity to weak ones. A long delay between the setup and the search time helps the section to be filled with the smell of decay. Because human remains in MFI areas are highly contaminated, *as the team progresses*, you need to introduce training aids that have been tainted with animal and other odors. Later, dead animals (including fish), rotting food, and other odiferous substances must be added to the search area. Again, delay times before working the dogs should be extended for the various odors to intermingle.

When your dog consistently finds all the human remains in these settings, the complexities of finding the odor in rubble piles and disaster sites should be added. Again, the exercise should begin with you using only uncontaminated training materials and advance to contaminated ones and other objects.

CONSIDERATIONS FOR MFI TRAINING

Training for MFIs in the real world must, along with human remains, include several people walking around the area. This gets dogs used to numerous personnel in the vicinity while they search. Periodically position a live person inside the rubble/tunnels so you can observe your dog's reaction. You may encounter a live victim buried in the debris of a real search area.

Similarly, it is crucial in live-victim training to have very strong-smelling human decomposition close or next to live subjects. This authentic combination is the only way to accurately judge the competency of the team in finding a live victim amid the putrid odors of human decay.

Because it is possible an MFI K9 may pass over a faint-smelling body part and alert on one with a more powerful odor, you must make sure the area around those remains are thoroughly searched to find everything at that location.

Finally, rewarding with a toy can be troublesome in MFI search areas. The dog's anticipation of the toy may excite him on the rubble, causing it to precariously shift; the toy may be dropped in unknown substances; or the dog will leave the debris after each find and wait for his toy. In addition, decontamination of both dog and handler may be mandatory each time the team leaves the "hot area." In these situations, decontamination of the toy would also be necessary. Rewarding with a tidbit of a treat using a variable reward method is helpful, even if the dog's regular reward is a toy. Morsels of food reward in this type of search have not caused any problems—they provide a bridge to the big play reward when the K9 team leaves the search area.

K9 Well-being in MFIs

Searching for deceased victims in an MFI is intense nose work for K9s. You must determine how long your dog should work based on the temperature and difficulty of the areas. It may not be exceptionally hot out, but a dog's temperature can increase suddenly, so it is important to know your K9's baseline temperature. Ask your veterinarian to show you what signs to look for in your dog to check for overheating. The indications are different for different dogs—you may need to look at your dog's gums, inner eyelids, breathing, and changes in behavior. This is another reason being able to read your dog's body language is critical. It is wise to do these types of evaluations in training sessions so you will become accustomed to recognizing your dog's behavior before it becomes deadly.

A break may be needed after only 10 or 15 minutes of searching. If the dog is overheated, wait until your dog's temperature is back within normal range (between 100 and 102.5°F [37.8–39.2°C]) before fielding him again. However, remember your dog's temperature may vary according to his age, breed, and level of activity. Regardless of the ambient temperature, you must closely watch your dog for hydration issues and prevent him from drinking standing water that may be contaminated with infectious diseases or toxic chemicals. Even though your dog has been given water, he may also need fluids administered intravenously (IV). You should also carefully monitor your dog for any signs of distress or injury both while searching and each time he returns from the field. Furthermore, it is advisable to have your dog's blood chemistry and liver function baselines checked before and after deployment to determine if health problems exist because of the search efforts.

35

Emotions, Stress, and Post-Traumatic Stress

All types of searches can create emotional disturbances for the handler, but disasters tend to trigger more. Constant contact with the dead or severely injured, death or serious injury of a fellow searcher, children's toys strewn about, and family photographs now in ruin, are all part of the circumstances. Then there are the bodies of pets still chained in yards and dead farm animals that did not have a chance—all tears at the heart.

Professional-level emotional distance is necessary. Identifying with the victims or their families can make you a victim too. Difficult as it is to disassociate yourself from the sights and smells of the search area, focusing on the job at hand and viewing each victim found as a contribution to the mission is a way to help curb your grief about what has happened. Regardless, extended deployments can take their toll.

Understand your normal stress reactions. Take inventory of your feelings during a mission and note if there are any significant changes in how you perceive your work. Anger, hostility, and irritability are common signs of stress. Remember, emotions travel down the leash to the dog. If your dog is not working properly, you need to not only check your dog for physical problems but also look to yourself and your frame of mind.

Stress Debriefing

Critical Incident Stress Debriefing (CISD) is performed in accordance with a fixed, structured method for first responders, fire fighters, and police, and has been extended to other disaster-response personnel. Its purpose is to review stressful experiences in a disaster and should be conducted only by experienced, well-trained practitioners. Disaster survivors and their relatives take part in a different type of debriefing.

CISD was never intended as a substitute for therapy but is meant to be performed in a group format that is combined with the multicomponent, crisis-intervention system called Critical Incident Stress Management (CISM). Stress can come from the work the responder is doing as well as from additional factors (e.g., tensions with someone in a supervisory position or other searchers, family or job concerns). Mental associations with the tragedy may appear weeks or months later and are mentally and physically harmful. Objects, sounds, or smells you would not think important—like the sight of a teddy bear—may rekindle the emotions you had when you saw one next to a child's body. Nightmares, anxiety, insomnia, lack of concentration, emotional numbing, and other problems may be related to post-traumatic stress disorder. Handlers should rate themselves monthly after a deployment. Followup referrals may be necessary.

Some stress-reducing techniques include:

- talking with someone who understands the experience you've had;
- slowing down—being nice to yourself;
- lowering your shoulders and taking deep breaths; and
- thinking positive thoughts. A person can only have one thought at a time—a positive thought replaces a negative one.

Remember that stress reduction takes time, so manage your workloads.

Part VI

Additional Issues

36

K9 Teams and Court

Anyone can be called to court as a witness. A person's involvement in a case may be as simple as knowing a person or having been at a location.

Legal precedents and trends change; therefore, it is important to keep abreast of those pertaining to your K9's search discipline in your jurisdiction. The most well-regarded information on this subject for handlers has been Terry Fleck's *Canine Legal Update and Opinions* website. Remember: a ruling made in one state does not mean it will apply in others. Because of the complexity of legal issues and different courts' interpretations of evidence and findings, this chapter offers only some points for you to keep in mind.

Seminars

Seminars that include district-attorney or prosecuting-attorney instructors who teach handlers about courtroom procedures provide a wealth of information. Classes conducted by a K9 handler can offer insight about being on the witness stand, testimony, and the proceedings, but regardless of how often that handler has appeared in court, he or she is still a layperson in the judicial arena. The handler's explanations about testimony and findings from non-related case transcripts may be correct or just his or her interpretation.

Alerts, Probable Cause, and Accepted Methods

Human scent is not a contraband substance. Unlike narcotics-detection K9s, whose alert is considered probable cause (PC) and reasonable suspicion of wrongdoing, an alert performed by a live-victim or HRD dog does not constitute PC and needs corroborating evidence.

Many handlers ask how to explain what an HRD K9 is trained to find. Although K9s are trained to find and alert on the *odor* of HR—not on human remains themselves—that odor must come from a source of human decay, be it a body or residual scent. Thus, the dog does alert on something with physical properties, even if microscopic.

If you deviate from accepted methods (industry standards) in K9 training, you may have to articulate, in court, your reason for doing so and be able to show that your methods meet or exceed industry standards.

Terminology

To avoid confusion, know your terminology. Because SAR/R terminology differs across the United States, you should be able to define not only the terms that are recognized in the region in which you live, but also those where you have searched, if terms and their definitions are not the same.

Images

The defense may ask you if you took any photos of the search scene, who authorized them to be taken, and what you did with the photographs. If such photos were not provided to the investigators, they will not be a part of the prosecution's files but can be requested by the defense in an attempt to discredit other information. Extra problems may arise if images were posted on social media.

Certifications, Logs, and Notes

Courts have used terms such as "bona fide organization" and "formal certification" as legal language. A bona fide organization can be a non-profit or for-profit training institution that meets industry standard guidelines. Not all certifying groups' testing standards and protocols meet industry standards. This can be problematic. You should know if your certifications are "bona fide" or just pieces of paper that equate to participation in an exercise.

Because certifications do not demonstrate reliability or consistency, it is crucial to keep good documentation of all training and search work as a way to offer proof of your skills and experience. Handlers often train by themselves, but training logs should not be just from your perspective. You may know the most about your dog, but your opinion may be biased. Periodic validations by an experienced SAR/R handler or evaluator should be included in your training logs.

Logs should not be embellished. They should truly represent the work of the dog and the dog and handler as a team. The K9 may do well, for example, but the handler does not and lacks knowledge in essential components. Logs must include failures and weaknesses and plans to correct them. Defense attorneys will most certainly call "wonder dogs" to task.

If notes from the search are kept in your "case file," you should make sure they do not contradict what was written in your search report. Retained notes are considered part of the record, and all documents must be given to the investigators if the case is going to trial. All documents are in turn provided to the prosecution, which must then give all case-related information to the defense attorney in the discovery phase of a trial. Anything not given to the investigators, but in possession of the handler, may be regarded as withheld information.

The Handler as Prosecution Witness

"I am for truth, no matter who tells it. I am for justice no matter who it's for or against." – Malcolm X, Malcolm X

The following is an example of the process after a handler is called as a witness for the prosecution. Guidance in answering questions are only suggestions. The prosecutor will give specific instructions.

The District Attorney's (DA) office normally contacts the handler to gather information and discuss questions the handler will be asked if summoned as a witness. Not all those notified to appear will be called to take the witness stand, and not all K9-involved cases require the handler to testify. Honesty and openness about abilities and qualifications are imperative. Prosecuting attorneys must know your answers to potential questions so they are not blindsided in court.

Should you be called as a witness, remember that your dress for a court appearance should be neat and business appropriate. In some instances, you may be told to wear your uniform.

While on the witness stand and in court, regardless of snide remarks and seemingly foolish questions the defense attorney may ask, you must be respectful and composed when replying. The defense will sometimes attempt to confuse witnesses, suppress evidence, and discredit anyone involved in the investigation.

When answering questions, even those posed by the prosecution, replies should be brief—"Yes" or "No" if possible. If the prosecution wants further explanation, their attorney will ask you to elaborate. Defense inquiries can be tricky on purpose. Do not rush to answer, and first give careful thought to what was asked. Again, responses should be short and to the point. This can be difficult, since not everything is black and white. Those gray areas are fraught with opinions. If the prosecutor thinks the answer given to the defense was not sufficient, confusing, or sounded contradictory, he or she will question or ask for clarification of your response during the redirect examination. Long replies give defense attorneys more information to scrutinize, and they will key in on every word. Even if you believe an answer is detrimental to the prosecution, however, you must reply honestly.

Whether you are called to be a witness for the prosecution or the defense, the truth is still the truth. When you are knowledgeable, able to justify your actions, and are confident in your training and documentation, it does not make any difference which side calls you to testify. Some handlers think that testifying for the prosecution is being on the "right side" and testifying for the defense is being on the "dark side." This is not the case. Remember that "colleague loyalty," "professional courtesy," or SAR/R TEAM–accepted preference has no place in a courtroom—but integrity does. Integrity separates good from bad.

However, a few handlers are known to be frequent defense expert witnesses. Other handlers have questioned their intentions because their "expert witness" testimony has been routinely slanted in favor of the defense. But remember, what those handlers say is only their opinion or interpretation of events and can be countered by the prosecution.

"Facts are stubborn things; and whatever may be our wishes, our inclinations, or the dictates of our passions, they cannot alter the state of facts and evidence." – John Quincy Adams

37

Websites and Social Media

Websites

"I'd rather be able to face myself in the bathroom mirror than be rich and famous." – Ani DiFranco

Although the most common way law enforcement (LE) locates resources is through other agency's referrals, websites can help to promote a TEAM and gain the attention of agencies. When agencies do review a TEAM's website, they want easy navigation and clear information about the organization, the people in it, and its capabilities. Several sites I reviewed gave no indication of how long a TEAM had been in existence, who the members are, or even the name of a contact person—just a phone number. Websites like this may offer impressive words but are devoid of substance.

Investigators do not like to waste time. They do not want to contact phantom handlers who may be people they have had problems with in the past. A couple of handlers explained they did not want their names publicized because of their involvement in working homicide cases. This appears to be undue worry, as numerous LE agencies list their divisions and investigators by name and include contact information on their websites.

Listing the names of agencies a TEAM has assisted but not the individual contacts at these agencies is ambiguous. Was the agency the one that requested your TEAM or was it just present at the scene? There is a big difference. If you are concerned about listing names of specific law enforcement officers, possibly adding a statement that "names and contact information will be provided upon request" would be more forthcoming.

Outlandish claims, though unfortunately believed by some people, are often exposed and the organization or handler discredited. Other times it is only the SAR/R community that recognizes the deception and, without much recourse, dishonest ways continue. It could be that those handlers or TEAMs convince themselves no one will be any the wiser, or maybe they do not care.

Remember that posting photos of search scenes on websites and social media should be done only with permission from the agency in charge of the case. Confrontational statements, or statements badmouthing other TEAMs or LE are also inadvisable.

Social Media

Some handlers make glowing, but untruthful comments about themselves or members of their TEAM on the Internet. Experienced SAR/R personnel usually recognize fabrications. You or your team can lose your reputation or credibility if you fail to realize that those in SAR/R are not the only ones reading your posts. LE and attorneys also explore all forms of social media—not only websites—for various reasons, including for use in court cases. They are aware that people can portray themselves in misleading ways on social media; however, your comments often yield much about your character, attitude, and truthfulness or that of your TEAM—as do posts on Facebook and the Internet group discussion lists discussed next.

Cyberspace Forums and Groups

Prior to Facebook being a major source of social media, there were numerous SAR/R email discussion groups that included members from around the world. Some groups were for specific disciplines and others were for K9 SAR in general. Cyberspace forums and groups are wonderful for problem solving and the exchange of ideas and information. Although information has been electronically available for years, our exposure to it has increased dramatically, and what used to be collections of statements or comments made on monitored discussion lists are now accessible to the world. Some groups are public and others are private, but restricting posts to "friends only" is not a safeguard that they will not be disclosed to "friends of friends," to another group—and beyond. The majority of those in SAR/R are passionate about their work and share information and insights. However, some handlers who possess a great deal of knowledge admit they do not make comments in cyberspace forums and instead "lurk" or reply privately. They do not want, nor do they have time for, snarky backlash—as opposed to constructive feedback—and hidden agendas that turn into off-topic arguments.

> *"There are two ways to be fooled. One is to believe what isn't true; the other is to refuse to believe what is true."* – Soren Kierkegaard, Works of Love

Basic Internet etiquette should govern all online interactions. There is a difference between having a strong opinion and being judgmental. Share your ideas without insulting or condemning those with other opinions. Acting impulsively with a quick reply or email containing hurtful words or an attack is a big mistake. Pausing and thinking first can help you compose a reply that is framed in a more purposeful and professional way.

SHUTTLE COLUMBIA SOCIAL MEDIA FUROR

Social media and discussion groups can be a great source of valuable information after a major disaster, but they can also provide a forum for false claims, exaggerations, and accusations. The aftermath of the Shuttle Columbia explosion is a case in point.

In 2003 the Shuttle Columbia, carrying seven astronauts, exploded upon re-entering the earth's atmosphere. The National Aeronautics and Space Administration (NASA) and the FBI were in charge of the search and recovery mission and established an Incident Command Post. However, the size of the area involved with debris precipitated response from multiple local jurisdictions in the immediate aftermath of the tragedy and later during the mission. The resources requested through Incident Command were known because of their federal or state agency association or through recommendations by trusted individuals. Even so, that does not mean all those teams, agency affiliated or otherwise, were qualified for this type of search. Thousands of other people volunteered, including unknown SAR/R teams.

In the aftermath of the search efforts, a high-level agency representative, who served in an oversight capacity at the NASA/FBI command post, asked me to post an email to message boards for the SAR/R community. The posting pointed out serious issues that occurred during the searches, such as dogs indicating on non-human remains and, when the errors were discovered, their handlers continuing to work the dogs instead of attempting to correct the problem before returning to the field. Also, handlers were seen working their dogs past the point of fatigue, raising doubt about whether things were missed. In general, the email wanted to provide frank feedback on the search efforts while thanking the teams for their response. In addition, the message addressed false claims posted by many handlers, on various discussion lists, that stated their dog found remains of the astronauts.

That email was intended to prompt honest self-evaluation for the entire SAR/R community and to inform handlers that agencies do read postings on the Internet. Instead, it was met with anger, defensiveness, and accusations—online—while the majority of those with positive comments (agreeing with the content and thanking the writer for the honest feedback) were sent to me privately. The number of responses received—approving replies and all the harsh comments, demands, and attacks—compelled me to write and post a followup message. Both messages are reproduced below in their entirety and are done so to provide a service to all teams. I want to note clearly that the first email is not about *all* those who volunteered to help with their SAR dogs—it is about problems with *some* K9 teams.

> Just received the following message. Cross-posting of this message is granted.
>
> To: Vi Hummel Carr
> K-9 Specialty Detection
> Date: Wed, 26 Feb 2003 05:10:16 EST
> Vi, please post this to your SAR lists.
>
> For those dog teams that responded to the shuttle accident in Texas, I want to sincerely thank you for your response. It does a heart good to know so many wanted to help. Now comes the difficult part: I served in an oversight capacity in the shuttle disaster and I wanted to provide feedback to those teams that were there in addition to setting the record straight to those who were not.
>
> The majority of the human remains (99%) were found by ground pounders. The reason for this is two-fold, how the teams were deployed and the areas searched, and unfortunately the quality of the dogs and handlers fielded. One should be cautious in believing all the claims being made about dog teams finding HR. I received the information regarding dogs' alerts, and with few exceptions, the vast majority of them were on pig, deer and other animal remains. This is a fact not conjecture.
>
> Some dog teams were imminently qualified and others were not. I have heard feedback that some teams were thrown together and sent with no verification of their qualifications. Besides the fact that it undermines the credibility of the organization asked to obtain dog teams for the operation, I think we can all agree that this is disturbing based on the mission we needed to accomplish.
>
> Additionally, handlers must be careful about the fatigue factors with their dogs. Handlers were working their dogs without significant breaks or reinforcement problems. As a result, dogs shut down and handlers continued to work them which benefited no one and did not accomplish the mission at hand. What needs to be asked is how much was left behind because of this.
>
> There were at least two handlers whose dogs did not alert on verified HR and continued to work the dogs. The excuses presented for their mistakes were appalling and disconcerting and they will not be called again if I can help it. This is where credibility and integrity, and the consequences

of the lack thereof, comes into play. It would have been completely appropriate for the handler to remove the dog from searching for a day or two and then redeploy. Unfortunately, due to their inaction, that decision was made for them. These issues were viewed by law enforcement agencies who talk to each other and NASA, and relayed the stories to me. I was able to confirm the veracity of their accounts.

As a result of what I saw and what was reported to me, I am compiling a report and deployments by my agency will be handled differently. If you are offended by the presentation of these facts, I am sorry. I am sorry because rarely is there any frankness in feedback received or accepted and maybe that is what dog handlers want. However, for those who want the truth, these facts were presented for you to utilize for the betterment of your team and to caution handlers about playing the "claim game" [falsely saying they have found remains] when it comes to claiming finds. Besides it being perceived as disrespectful in this case it may very well be erroneous.

Again, credibility and integrity are at stake. The more educated law enforcement becomes about canine teams, the less they will be fooled by handlers with inadequately trained dogs who continue to make excuses for unaddressed training issues. Thank you for your time and your service.

(Name withheld due to agency restrictions)

Following was my only reply after reading 81 posts and private messages.

The message sure has generated some interesting posts, both positive and negative. I believe that was the goal of the writer, besides wanting to provide feedback, and being able to sleep at night again. (That is the level of concern they are dealing with.)

For those of you who have posted negative feedback, I encourage you to open your mind and read the message again. In addition to comments on the list, I received private emails. It was interesting that some saw it as an affirmation of how they conduct themselves and others saw it as an attack. Whether you accept what was written or not, for whatever reason, the writer stands by it.

The message sent is nothing new. It brings up issues that have been discussed time and again on this list. Has everyone forgotten all the critical comments posted about dog teams surrounding 9-11? No names identified the offensive individuals—only generalities—as did this message. The only difference is this message came from someone outside the list, someone in a high capacity of those agencies we serve. The person who requested I post the message is one of exemplary honesty, integrity, character, and SAR dog knowledge. In addition, the author of the message is in a top-echelon position of Incident Command on the shuttle recovery mission. All information they have is documented. Those who know me know, or should know, that if I had even the slightest doubt [about the writer's credibility] I would not have posted the message.

The message was not backstabbing (as is often done by dog teams behind closed doors and in whispers). The message was open and forthright, a service to credible dog teams and a wake-up call to those playing the "claim game." I was advised that by the number of HR "finds" claimed by some teams there would have had to be 87 people on board the shuttle rather than seven.

The list moderators say we shouldn't "flame" anyone on this list, yet here are messages asking for exact names of the teams that committed the offenses. In addition, they are asking for credit for the good teams. Each team that was deployed knows where it stands in this message. Has everyone forgotten the words "I sincerely want to thank you" and "imminently qualified dog teams" that were a part of the message?

For those of you who asked what the specific problems were—they were addressed in the message.

For those of you who suggest the writer make suggestions to correct the problems—the problems were stated—the policies are out there and are a part of every credible team—and you know the answers.

For those of you who are demanding to see the documentation or verification of the facts by comments such as: "...Provide me that information and we will have something to discuss..." or "...but much of the information appeared to be withheld," etc., I am not privy to that and do not hold myself in such high regard that I think I am entitled to be provided with that information. If you had the qualifications and security clearances needed to be a part of that government "inner-circle," you would already know what facts the documentation contained. The message stated the problems that occurred for your benefit and to learn from.

In the aftermath of 9-11, a common quote on the list was "Good intentions do not make a search team." If your dog is not trained for the mission (as Rick and others in the past have mentioned), don't field your dog. Help in another capacity. The designation "cadaver dog" has become a very loose term. And yes, there is a difference between a "cadaver dog" and a cadaver dog / mass fatality dog that is capable and consistent in the quality of their work in mass fatality situations. Both Rick and Bruce made excellent points.

To those of you, both on and off the list, who want me to forward your messages and expect replies from the author—please read again "Name withheld due to agency restrictions."

Confidentially is a major part of SAR work and the government, and I am bound by that. Your messages/comments will be passed on but that is all I can do. No individual on this mission was flamed (other than the author and myself—by some of you). The author of the message is dismayed by those of you who only want kudos and not constructive feedback which stated the problems. But on some level, that was to be expected.

Knowing the author's identity will not change what was written or the facts, which were witnessed and verified. It only allows those who want to, to "throw rocks," and again that was also to be expected.

If you have responded to searches before and done so in a professional manner with properly trained dogs, the agencies will know the quality of your team and call you again.

I was advised that the author will pursue what they feel is the proper path which will hopefully ensure the mistakes of the past are not repeated— that has always been the goal. This is the last I'll say on this issue.

Sincere regards,

Vi Hummel Carr

38

Politics, Egos, Glory Seekers, Frauds, and Misunderstandings

They are out there in every walk of life, regardless of how noble the profession. This chapter serves a cautionary purpose for both those who are guilty and for those who are quick at finger pointing and labeling others. Teams that adulterate SAR/R are few in comparison to the thousands of honorable handlers devoted to the SAR/R mission and undergo so much to become handlers and maintain the level of skill required to be a quality operational resource. But even a few deceptive handlers are of great concern to the K9 SAR/R community. Many handlers and organizations believe legitimate SAR/R personnel should "police themselves" to abolish dishonest teams. Methods offered for "policing" have been: legislation, a national anti-fraud protocol, the creation of a database listing the names those individuals, and specific tests conducted by state or national organizations. The next questions are usually "Who will critique the evaluators to ensure they are not part of the problem?" followed by "Who will pay for these programs?" The task of preventing and exposing fraud is a dilemma for all K9 SAR/R professionals.

"One of the greatest delusions of the world is the hope that the evils of this world are to be cured by legislation." – Thomas B. Reed, in George W. Stimpson's A Book About American Politics

Assessing Others

Handlers are accustomed to assessing things—a search scene, a dog's performance, and so on—so it is only natural for them to pay attention to and assess other handlers and TEAMS. However, their assessment may be swayed by what others have told them about, for example, a handler who is a glory seeker or fraud, or who has an over-sized ego, or a TEAM member who initiates destructive politics. Or maybe they heard that an entire TEAM might be guilty of misconduct. Rather than agreeing with the brand others have placed on someone, each person ought to reach his or her own conclusions, based on facts. That is the only way to be fair and not later regret your attitude or actions. Do not make observations when you are angry, as anger tends to seek out only that which confirms it. Being able to look at things from other viewpoints could show fraud, belittlement due to a personal vendetta, or something as simple as a misunderstanding.

Politics

> *"Most people can bear adversity; but if you wish to know what a man really is give him power. This is the supreme test." – Robert J. Ingersoll on Abraham Lincoln, in* Unity, *April 1883*

In SAR/R, the word "politics" carries negative connotations, meaning problems with members or organizations: crafty tactics or unprincipled methods, ploys to undermine other TEAMs, scheming for power and status, and dishonest practices. Dishonest practices include appointing friends or family members to positions they are not qualified for, patronage / double standards, and paid-to-play politics in which TEAM officers, members, and K9s with bad ethics and poor capabilities are condoned because the TEAM does not want to lose the "toys" or types of benefits that member provides.

Potential, new, and old members alike have been shunned, criticized, and demeaned by false, even malicious, rumors spread about them by others in their organizations or by members of another TEAM. When members direct a venomous attitude toward a handler in their own organization, it could be because of jealousy or insecurity. That handler may be working and studying harder than the others on the TEAM and receiving quality training elsewhere. Arrogant members may want a person to do well but not better than them, and they worry that somehow their positions on the TEAM will be diminished by others' success. Or, those in power fear another handler will learn they are not all they profess to be and worry their control is threatened. All these scenarios poison an organization. The mindless conformity of members going along with the inequity may not be illegal, but it is immoral and cruel, contagious conduct. What is allowed is encouraged, and trust deteriorates.

> *"False words are not only evil in themselves, but they infect the soul with evil." – Plato*, Phaedo

Sadly, there are groups of good handlers who are more of a clique than a TEAM. While both TEAMs and cliques are focused on a goal, the goals are different. The clique has an inward focus, such as elitism, and the TEAM has an outward focus, such as wanting to serve their communities. Cliques can grow in the shadows of an organization and promote an "us versus them" attitude, or even lack of impartiality when it comes to testing and certifying other teams. Unwritten rules tend to flourish in cliques, as members work to secretly gain a desired end, usually to become a monopoly—or the most prominent—in their area. Before any problem can be corrected, it must be recognized by the organization in which it occurs.

Ego

> *"Talent is God-given; be humble. Fame is man-given; be thankful. Conceit is self-given; be careful." – John Wooden*, They Call Me Coach

Everyone has an ego—ego is the awareness of one's own identity, one's own self-image. A positive sense of self-esteem gives a person confidence. However, there is a difference between confidence and conceit. If ego is not well-managed, it becomes inflated and arrogant, and that arrogance encourages a person to adopt prejudicial views and believe other people are not as good or as smart. Egotists find it hard to admit they are wrong; they tend to crave power and like to control things; they feel that anything bad they might do is justified; and they are unreceptive to change unless they are the ones with the idea to change.

A K9 team that has a find very early in its SAR/R career—at times, as some have said, a find that is more like a "tripping over the victim"—is not necessarily a legend in the making. Exaggerating capabilities thereafter disproportionately bolsters the handler's ego. Several good and extremely confident handlers have made statements about their dogs' ability to *always* find, and alert, on live victims first, regardless of whether there are several deceased victims on top of them. This is said mostly by those with dogs cross-trained to find both live and dead victims in disaster situations. Others have wondered if that is ego, bravado, bias, or fact, and if those handlers feel the value of their confidence is worth risking human life.

> "Be wise instead of overconfident. One leads to unexpected failure, the other to unexpected success." – Jerry Corstens, from his website TheGoldenMirror

When you are involved in SAR/R, you are faced with a litany of questions, but one of the most frequent ones is "How many people/victims have you found?" Creating an answer that broadens that discussion to generalities can provide information without sounding evasive, falsely humble, or boastful. Perhaps say something like, "A few" or "Several" (if finds have been made), then add, "but a lot of people are involved in a search, and we're all working toward a common goal." It becomes a little more delicate if you are called a "hero." A good reply I've heard is "Well, thank you. But I've never considered myself a hero. I am just doing what I love to do."

> *"It is better to deserve honors and not have them than to have them and not deserve them." – Mark Twain*, Mark Twain's Notebook, 1902–1903

Glory Seekers

> *"Don't confuse visibility with credibility." – Harvey Mackay,* The ABCs of Networking

Glory seekers tend to be different from publicity hounds. The *Urban Dictionary* defines a "publicity hound" as someone who "seeks attention from the media by participating in stunts that generate [negative] attention." Some glory seekers do nothing but show up on search scenes with their dogs and sign-embellished vehicles and congregate close to the media. Other such teams may search for a short time and then parade in front of the cameras. It can be difficult to avoid the media, but when a handler is always doing things to draw their attention, he or she will soon be called a glory seeker.

Glory seeking behavior also includes other distasteful acts. Some handlers have notified their local media before departing on a high-profile search or a disaster—many times self-deploying. This displays a lack of training and professionalism. Some have gone so far as to make assurances that they "will find the victim!"

Another action that can be seen as glory-seeking is when TEAM members wear their TEAM uniforms to a victim's funeral. Some believe this is a "kind and supportive action," while others think it is a display for publicity. Attendance at the behest of the family is one thing, but going to a funeral to make a show is inappropriate.

If the TEAM is truly there to support the family and friends of the victim, members should appear in civilian clothes.

Mistakes, Misrepresentations, and Frauds

There are mistakes, foolish mistakes, honest mistakes, misrepresentations, and then there is fraud. A mistake is usually accidental—it is a choice made that turns out to be wrong. An honest mistake is something done wrong because the person did not know any better. Admitting a mistake and accepting accountability is honest and an important part of professionalism.

> *"When a man who is honestly mistaken hears the truth, he will either quit being mistaken, or cease to be honest." – Unknown*

Misrepresentation is a misstatement innocently made. People who misrepresent may be repeating what someone else taught them was true. This can happen with handlers who receive inadequate or misguided training. Fraud is willful misrepresentation—deceptive acts done intentionally to cheat. Fraudulent people know they are lying and have specific motivations for their actions, but all lack ethics and are single-mindedly out for themselves.

The fraud resides with the handler(s) or TEAM(s)—the K9s can be very well-trained but the intentions of the human components are repugnant. Many veteran handlers recommend that background checks and screening of handlers' characters and motives should be done before investing time in training, including all members, even TEAM officers. In one case, two TEAM officers were wanted in four states for theft! Also, being a TEAM founder does mean you are above reproach. Although outright frauds represent only a very small minority, they can degrade the entire SAR/R community in the eyes of law enforcement and the public. The disgusted feelings handlers have about frauds are not just about the credibility of legitimate teams being unfairly maligned. The bigger issue is the indifference frauds display regarding victims and their families, and the suffering they cause, which can include innocent people convicted of crimes.

Independent Handlers

"It's better to walk alone than with a crowd going in the wrong direction." – Diane Grant

I discuss working as an independent handler in this chapter because allegations are sometimes made that independent handlers are glory seekers who like being "one-person shows." To tar all independent handlers with such unsavory labels is unjust and defamatory. Some independent handlers may just live in a rural area where attempts to form a quality TEAM have been unsuccessful. Becoming an independent handler does not mean they are trying to circumvent the requirements and standards of a quality TEAM.

Some might want to be independent because of the particular TEAM(s) in their area: their politics, unethical behavior, or poor training. Political abuse by TEAMmates may influence a handler who is dedicated to training and the mission (not dealing with personal agendas, egos, and hypocritical behavior) to become an independent team. While wanting to be a member of a TEAM, this person's trust factor—necessary in SAR/R work—has been destroyed by other members.

However, before deciding to become an independent handler, careful thought and self-examination are necessary. Working independently is difficult. Following your passion—what you believe is your calling—does not mean it will be easy. There will always be hard work, obstacles, and adversity, even as an independent team. In addition, your reputation is strictly based on you and your K9(s). There are no collective capabilities of other members to strengthen your team's stature.

"There is an immense difference between training to do something and trying to do something." – John Ortberg, The Life You've Always Wanted: Spiritual Disciplines for Ordinary People

TO BE INDEPENDENT

Training to be a quality, credible, independent resource means:

- a high degree of self-discipline and ethics. No one is there to confirm your dedication to the mission or your frequency of training and practice;
- increased study in all areas and SAR/R-related positions of the chosen discipline. Every part of the search effort may be up to you;
- communing with quality instructors and handlers and attending seminars and workshops for advancement and guidance on problems encountered. Undertaking the position of independent handler/team does not mean you are self-taught;
- being organized;
- developing and maintaining high written standards and protocols. Standards are what make one accountable. Without them, a lone handler can lose focus and slip into inferior behaviors and attitudes;
- structured training—there are no shortcuts. Training problems must progress in terms of difficulty and length;
- receiving evaluations and earning certifications from reputable organizations;
- paying for everything associated with the training and work, as there is no TEAM equipment, no TEAM website, and no TEAM funds to offset expenses for searches or to attend seminars as a representative. While some TEAMs do not offer such assistance, a great many do;
- not being satisfied with mediocrity;
- not being blind to your dog's flaws;
- keeping accurate and truthful training logs;
- generating awareness as a resource, which is more demanding for one person than TEAM members working in concert; and
- though you are wary, knowing the necessity of being cooperative when working with and referring other SAR/R teams when needed—and hoping they will afford the same considerations and place the victim first before their number of call-outs.

"If you want to be successful, you must respect one rule: never lie to yourself." – Paulo Coelho, personal papers

Red Flags

"Frauds and falsehoods only dread examination. Truth invites it." – Thomas Cooper, Lectures on the Elements of Political Economy

Red flags may be seen by handlers and K9 instructors, but they are seldom recognized by law enforcement. Even though LE passes along names of K9 resources to other agencies, they do not always share or compare details that may generate a true picture of the team recommended—a picture that might conclude with questions about honesty. Because of the lack of this information exchange, frauds and highly questionable teams continue to mislead authorities. It can be years before such handlers or TEAMs are exposed for what they are. By that time, the damage to the victims, their families, LE, and guiltless people can be momentous—and their behavior casts an ugly shadow over all of SAR/R. Past cases have shown that handlers can maintain excellent reputations—albeit built on lies and deceit—for years, and it can be hard to convince others of their atrocities. Officers have been chastised for even suggesting that offenses have occurred.

Red flags do not inevitably mean "fraud," but they are warning signs worthy of inquiry. Following are red flags handlers have mentioned—some are blatant lies while others are suspicious. Negatively labeling a handler in any fashion—even in your own mind—requires solid facts and verification of accusations. Mischaracterization is a serious matter. Reputation outlasts the person. Examples of red flags include:

- The K9 *always* finds something.
- The team self-deploys.
- The handler "guarantees" the team will find the person.
- The handler seems reluctant to call the dog's alert and mainly uses the indeterminate word "interest" when describing the dog's behavior. To constantly be non-

committal about the dog's alert or seem to not have the ability to work the dog to either confirm or reject an area is considered questionable behavior. Always using the word "interest" appears to be a ploy to make sure the team always ends up in a positive position. If subsequently nothing is found, the handler may say, "Oh, my dog *only* had an interest there." If the victim or something is found the emphasis changes to, "Oh, *my dog* had interest there!"

- The handler makes unrealistic claims. Even though dogs constantly astound people with their capabilities, some claims deserve scrutiny.
- The handler boasts a 99 or 100 percent "find" rate or claims an exorbitant number of "finds."
- The ratio of a team's number of searches/finds does not make sense related to the amount of time the handler and dog have been in SAR/R . . . or the days in one year.
- The number of disciplines the dog is trained or "certified" in does not correlate when you consider the age of the dog and amount of time involved between training and certifications.
- The handler fields an untrained dog.
- The handler will not produce documentation of qualifications.
- The handler's exploits and experience are too good to be true.
- The handler proclaims he or she has a "wonder dog" or the only dog in the world that can do something.
- The handler acts like "God" at seminars—placing him or herself on a figurative pedestal.
- The handler will not submit to independent testing and will not demonstrate the dog's abilities unless he or she sets up the problem, or has many excuses about why the dog did not work well if the exercise is set up by someone else.
- The handler argues with the requesting agency and then publicly criticizes it, other searchers, and investigators

about the way a search was conducted, even contacting newspapers with accusations of negligence or absurdities committed by LE and other teams.

- The handler pressures families to permit him or her to search, saying LE does not really care about the family member.

- The handler claims to represent the family of the victim on a search scene.

- The handler shows up at search scenes but spends more time in his or her vehicle, fiddling with gear and parading up and down instead of actually searching.

- The handler brags about being on searches he or she was not part of—especially disasters that can be hard to verify, and in reality, does not prove qualifications. Going on a search does not mean the team is qualified—a team could have self-deployed without others teams knowing.

- The handler boasts about finds never made.

- The handler is vulgar or sloppy in attire, has a non-professional demeanor, or his or her dog shows neglect.

- The handler is opportunistic and looks to profit financially or publicly, or to establish credibility from involvement—despite self-deployment—in a disaster or high-profile search.

- The handler fabricates the number or types of certifications he or she has.

- The handler proclaims affiliation with many LE or national agencies. There seems to be a misunderstanding with the word "affiliated" as it applies to LE and other agencies in a legal sense. If one trains with an agency, are friends with someone in an agency, have lectured/taught at an agency, or been deployed by an agency, one is still not "affiliated" with that agency. Unless a person is a bona fide member and has been issued a formal ID stating their position with the agency or department, he or she should not claim affiliation.

- The handler includes agencies' or investigators' names on a resume or website but in false context, believing no one will contact them to confirm.

- The handler has been ejected from searches because of behavior, or has actually been banned from search scenes.
- The handler has falsified SAR/R history, qualifications, and other information on websites and social media.
- The handler becomes very upset, evasive, or confrontational when asked to prove validity of claims.

Anyone displaying the above behaviors cannot go back and start over, but they can begin right now to make positive changes. SAR/R will never be completely rid of loathsome conduct—it occurs in all walks of life. But the conduct of some should not devalue the legions of outstanding K9 handlers throughout the world who are dedicated to serving others. They know they leave imprints on the lives of all those they touch and that the choices they make in SAR/R can cause pain and emotional scars to families. They also know their actions can be remembered as honorable, and that gives them the peace and satisfaction of knowing they have made a difference and have fulfilled the mission of SAR/R in their training and attitude—because they put the victim first.

A Final Note

These are just a few words of encouragement for all those who have a passion for SAR/R but are struggling and feeling rejected because of politics, egos, or betrayal by those you have trusted—there are things that happen in our lives and we don't know why. Often, we limit our thinking and our dreams. We set our minds in one direction—what we want to accomplish, where we want to go, and how we want to get there. When that does not work out, we mourn the loss. But those experiences are what define character and gauge true dedication. They can send us on a slightly different path if we open our hearts and minds—and if we embark on this new path for the right reasons, we may find more fulfillment than we could ever have imagined.

Here, you lead—my way isn't working.

Acknowledgments

The first individuals I must thank are the many handlers and instructors from around the world who through the years have both asked and answered questions, and dedicated themselves to SAR/R. *You* are the heart of this book. Next, my deepest gratitude goes to notable author Susan Bulanda for her confidence in me, her counsel, and her criticism, which helped me improve my writing skills, and to my publisher, Brush Education, and Tom Lore, Lauri Seidlitz, my wonderful editor Meaghan Craven, and all those whose efforts and expertise transformed my pages of words into this book.

I am also thankful to Sally Santeford, Sue Ellen Hillard, Billy Smith Sr., and Harold "Ben" Bennett for their insight and encouragement as I pursued this endeavor, and to John and Debra Hnath for the outstanding photo of Chase holding his leash. I will be forever grateful to forensics experts Dr. Bill Bass—a mentor, a friend, and the writer of the prelude to Section IV—and Dr. H. Gill-King for his advocacy and sharing from the very beginning.

My sincere appreciation to M. Alan Nash, district attorney and former defense attorney, who took time from his busy schedule to read the manuscript for legal aspects, and to Dr. Arpad Vass, Dr. David C. Dorman, Dr. Dennis J. Blodgett, Brent A. Craven, Dr. Joni McClain, and Jamie Hawthorne for their graciousness in thoroughly answering my questions. A special thanks to Todd Ellis, my past DMORT regional commander for his review of the major disasters and mass fatalities content.

Since the eight members of the DMORT Mass Fatality K9 Standards and Requirements Committee were only identified as a group, as committee chairperson I believe it is necessary to recognize each of those exceptional handlers who so enriched my life and the world of SAR/R: Terry Crooks, Charm Gentry, Lisa Higgins, Debra Hnath, John Hnath, Marcia Koenig, Andy Rebmann, and Dee Wild.

It is also with gratitude that I acknowledge all those in SAR/R, law enforcement, fire departments, and my fellow DMORT members for the invaluable lessons they taught me. And thank you to Jeff Burns who first introduced me to SAR/R, and I also cannot forget to thank my current partner True, who seemed to know when it was time for me to take a break and move away from the computer and would not leave me alone until I did so—and my precious previous partners: Mercy, Grace, Spirit and Omega—you are forever in my heart.

Notes

K9 Search Disciplines: An Overview

1   N. Lorenzo, T. L. Wan, R. J. Harper, Y. L. Hsu, M. Chow, S. Rose, and K. G. Furton, "Laboratory and Field Experiments Used to Identify *Canis lupus* var. *familiaris* Active Odor Signature Chemicals from Drugs, Explosives, and Humans," *Journal of Analytical and Bioanalytical Chemistry*, 376 (2004): 1212–1224.

TEAM Standards, Procedures, and Bylaws

1   FEMA, 508–8, "Typed Resource Definitions: Search and Rescue Resources," May 2005, https://www.fema.gov/media-library/assets /documents/25923.

2   See https://swgdog.fiu.edu/approved-guidelines/.

Evaluating Puppies and K9 Selection

1   Dan Estep and Susanne Hetts, "Are Dogs Ruled by Their Drives and Instincts?" *Temperament or Personality* (2013), http:// animalbehaviorassociates.com/blog/dogs-ruled-drives-instincts/.

2   Daniel Estep and Suzanne Hetts, "The Trouble with Drives," http://www .animalbehaviorassociates.com/pdf/RMN_drive_troubles.pdf.

3   The renowned K9 trainer, Kevin George, was the founding member of the Search and Rescue Dog Association of Alberta, Canada, and the owner of Sentry Patrol Dog Service. Michelle Limoges, "Unfolding Our 25-Year History," http://hp177.hostpapa.com/~sarda983/pdf /SARDAAHistoryJan26_14.pdf.

4   Ivona Svobodová, Pavel Vápenik, Ludvík Pinc, and Luděk Bartoš, "Testing German Shepherd Puppies to Assess Their Chances of Certification," *Applied Animal Behavior Science*, 113, no. 1–3 (September 2008): 139–149.

5   For information about development, see Steven R. Lindsay, *The Handbook of Applied Dog Behavior and Training* (Ames: Iowa State

University, 2000). See Ellen Dodge, "The Urban Puppy Toolkit"; Clarice
Rutherford and David H. Neil, "How to Raise a Puppy You Can Live
With"; Clarence Pfaffenberger, "The New Knowledge of Dog Behavior";
and Dr. Ian Dunbar, "Instructor Training Course"—all at https://
weimaranerclubofamerica.org/. See also "Developmental Stages," *Diamonds
in the Ruff*, http://www.diamondsintheruff.com/developmental-stages.

The Dog's Nose

1   Brent A. Craven, Thomas Neuberger, Eric G. Paterson, Andrew G.
    Webb, Eleanor M. Josephson, Edward E. Morrison, and Gary S. Settles,
    "Reconstruction and Morphometric Analysis of the Nasal Airway of the
    Dog (*Canis familiaris*) and Implications Regarding Olfactory Airflow," *The
    Anatomical Record*, 290 (2007): 1325–1340. DOI: 10.1002/ar.20592.

2   Randy Kidd, "The Canine Sense of Smell: Sniffing Out the Source of
    Our Dogs' Remarkable Ability to Smell," *Whole Dog Journal* (November
    2004, updated February 24, 2016), https://www.whole-dog-journal.com
    /issues/7_11/features/Canine-Sense-of-Smell_15668-1.html.

3   Joseph Stromberg, "New Study Shows That Dogs Use Color Vision After
    All," *Smithsonian Magazine*, July 17, 2013, http://www.smithsonianmag
    .com/science-nature/new-study-shows-that-dogs-use-color-vision-after
    -all-13168563/.

4   Bill Tolhurst, "Carbon Monoxide Study," *Scent Study in Home of the Big T,
    Scent Research* (2002), http://www.angelfire.com/ny4/bigT/.

5   William G. Syrotuck, "Theory of Scent," in *Scent and the Scenting Dog*,
    Eden Consulting Group, Police Dog Home Page, https://www.policek9
    .com/html/theory.html.

Developments in Understanding Scent

1   Rex A. Stockham, Dennis L. Slavin, and William Kift, "Specialized Use of
    Human Scent in Criminal Investigations," *Forensic Science Communication,
    Research and Technology*, 6, no. 3 (July 2004), https://archives.fbi.gov
    /archives/about-us/lab/forensic-science-communications/fsc/july2004
    /research/2004_03_research03.htm.

2   Sichu Li, "Overview of Odor Detection Instrumentation and Potential for
    Human Odor Detection in Air Matrices," Human Odor Emission MITRE
    Nanosystems Group, M53 P0900, March 2009, https://www.mitre.org
    /sites/default/files/pdf/09_4536.pdf.

3   Monell Chemical Senses Center, "Odorprints Like Fingerprints?
    Personal Odors Remain Distinguishable Regardless of Diet,"
    Science Daily, November 3, 2008, https://www.sciencedaily.com
    /releases/2008/10/081030203247.htm.

4   Rex A. Stockham, Dennis L. Slavin, and William Kift, "Survivability of
    Human Scent," *Forensic Science Communication, Research and Technology*, 6,
    no. 4 (October 2004), https://archives.fbi.gov/archives/about-us/lab
    /forensic-science-communications/fsc/oct2004/research/2004_10
    _research03.htm; see also https://archives.fbi.gov/archives/about-us

/lab/forensic-science-communications/fsc/july2004/research/2004_03
_research03.htm.

5 Ibid.

K9 Trainers

1 Peter F. Cook, Ashley Prichard, Mark Spivak, and Gregory S. Berns,
"Awake Canine fMRI Predicts Dogs' Preference for Praise vs. Food," *Social
Cognitive and Affective Neuroscience*, 11, no. 12 (December 1, 2016):
1853–1862, https://doi.org/10.1093/scan/nsw102.

Basics in K9 SAR/R Training

1 U.S. Department of Justice, Civil Rights Division, Disability Rights
Section, "Service Animals" (2010), https://www.ada.gov/service
_animals_2010.pdf.

2 See "SARDA Registration" in *Scout Search and Rescue*, November 7, 2016,
https://scoutsardog.wordpress.com/2016/11/07/sarda-registration/.

3 Major Janice Baker, "Ear Protection of Dogs in Helicopters," USAR Group
Veterinary Document, http://usarveterinarygroup.org/usarvet/wp-content
/uploads/2016/08/Ear-Protection-in-Helicopters.pdf.

4 "Crates" (2015), http://www.centerforpetsafety.org/test-results/crates/.

5 H. D. Denham, J. W. Bradshaw, and N. J. Rooney, "Repetitive Behaviour
in Kenneled Domestic Dog: Stereotypical or Not?" *Psychology and Behavior*
128 (April 10, 2014): 288–294. DOI: 10.1016/j.physbeh.2014.01.007. See
also Anne J. Pullen, Ralph Merill, and John W. S. Bradshaw, "The Effect of
Familiarity on Behavior of Kennel Housed Dogs During Interactions with
Humans," *Applied Animal Behavior Science*, 137, no. 1–2 (February 2012):
66–73, DOI:10.1016/japplanim.2011.12.009.

Understanding Training Methods

1 J. Topál, R. W. Byrne, Á. Miklóski, et al. "Reproducing Human Actions and
Action Sequences: 'Do as I Do.'" *Animal Cognition*, 9 (2006): 355, DOI:
10.1007/s10071-006-0051-6.

2 Claudia Fugazza and Ádám Miklósi. "Deferred Imitation and Declarative
Memory in Domestic Dogs," *Animal Cognition* 17, no. 2 (March 2014):
237–247, DOI: 10.1007/s10071-013-0656-5.

3 Jamie Robinson, *Snake Avoidance Without Shock*, self-published, see http://
snakeavoidancewithoutshock.com/new-page.html.

Field Training

1 Lt. Weldon Wood, "Scent, that Magical, Elusive, Intangible Thing that
Eludes Our Every Effort to Trap, Contain or Identify It and Perplexes Us
at Every Turn. What Is It? Where Does It Come From? How Do Our
Dogs Utilize It?" National Police Bloodhound Association, www.vk9sar.org
/Scent_NPBA.doc.

2   Find the Beaufort Wind Scale at http://www.spc.noaa.gov/faq/tornado /beaufort.html.

The Scent Article

1   FBI, "Specialized Used of Human Scent in Criminal Investigations," *Forensic Communication/Research and Technology*, 6, no. 3 (July 2004). This article provides information on California vs. Flores, 2000; California vs. Willis, 2002; and California vs. Willis, 2004.
2   Ibid., California vs. Flores, 2000.
3   Ibid.
4   Ibid., California vs. Willis, 2004.

The Controversy over Cross-Training

1   Internationale Reddingshonden Groep, The Netherlands, "Scent Discrimination Tests in the Training of Search Dogs," http://www .reddingshonden.net/en-us/membersarea/research.aspx.
2   Lisa Lit and Cynthia Crawford, "Effects of Training Paradigms on Search Dog Performance," *Applied Animal Behaviour Science*, 98, no. 3–4 (July 2006): 277–292. 10.1016/j.applanim.soor.08.022.
3   See Lisa Lit, J. B. Schweitzer, and A. M. Oberbauer's "Handler Beliefs Affect Scent Detection Dog Outcomes," *Animal Cognition* 14, no. 387 (2011). SWGDOG's response can be found at https://swgdog.fiu.edu /news/2012/swgdog-response-to-lit-k9-study/swgdog_response_to_lit _study.pdf.

Prelude to Human Remains Detection

1   William M. Bass, DABFA, is Professor Emeritus and diplomate, American Board of Forensic Anthropology. He is the founder and former director of the Forensic Anthropological Center (FAC), University of Tennessee, Knoxville, also known as "The Body Farm."

Cadaver / Human Remains Detection

1   See http://www.corpus-delicti.com/forensic_fraud.html or https://www .justice.gov/archive/opa/pr/2004/September/04_crt_652.htm for more information.

Odor of Death

1   A. Wisman and I. Shrira, "The Smell of Death: Evidence that Putrescine Elicits Threat Management Mechanisms," *Frontiers in Psychology*, 6 (August 28, 2015): 1274, DOI:10.3389/fpsyg.2015.01274.
2   Arpad A. Vass, Rob R. Smith, Cyril V. Thompson, Michael N. Burnett, Dennis A. Wolf, Jennifer A. Synstelien, Nishan Dulgerian, and Brian A. Eckenrode, "Decompositional Odor Analysis Database," *Journal of Forensic*

Sciences, 49, no. 4 (2004): 760–769. See also Arpad A. Vass, Rob R. Smith, Cyril V. Thompson, Michael N. Burnett, Nishan Dulgerian, and Brian A. Eckenrode, "Odor Analysis of Decomposing Buried Remains," *Journal of Forensic Science,* 53, no. 2 (2008): 384–391.

3   TEDx, "CommonScents": Dr. Arpad Vass at TEDxYYC," filmed July 5, 2012, YouTube video, 15:31, posted July 5, 2012, https://www.youtube.com /watch?v=l0Qd2nxMC2Y.

4   Walker, D. B., J. C. Walker, P. J. Cavnar, et al. "Naturalistic Quantification of Canine Olfactory Sensitivity." Applied Animal Behaviour Science 97, no. 2-4 (2006): 241–54. https://doi.org/10.1016/j.applanim.2005.07.009.

5   From email correspondence with the author, May 31, 2016. Brent A. Craven is a research scientist in the Division of Applied Mechanics, U.S. Food and Drug Administration Computational Fluid Dynamics, Medical Devices, Biofluid Dynamics and Transport Phenomena. See D. B. Walker, J. C. Walker, P. J. Cavnar, J. L. Taylor, D. H. Pickel, S. B. Hall, and J. C. Suarez, "Naturalistic Quantification of Canine Olfactory Sensitivity," *Applied Animal Behaviour Science,* 97 (2006): 241–254, DOI: 10.1016/j. applanim.2005.07.009). See also B. L. Craven, E. G. Paterson, and G. S. Settles, "The Fluid Dynamics of Canine Olfaction: Unique Nasal Airflow Patterns as an Explanation of Macrosmia," *Journal of the Royal Society Interface* 7, no. 47 (April 26, 2010): 933–943, DOI:10.1098/rsif.2009.0490.

Training Materials or Scent Sources

1   Lindsey Bever (*Washington Post*), "Michigan Couple Allegedly Rented Out Diseased Body Parts from Cadavers," *The Star,* March 26, 2016, https:// www.thestar.com/news/world/2016/03/26/michigan-couple-allegedly -rented-out-diseased-body-parts-from-cadavers.html.

2   Jim Watson, master trainer, North American Police Work Dog Association (NAPWDA) contacted one of the popular sellers of bones and questioned them regarding the health and safety of their products. Posted on an email discussion list.

3   Centers for Disease Control and Prevention, "Extracted Teeth," especially "How should extracted teeth in the dental office be disposed of?" and "Can I give patients their teeth after they have been extracted?" https://www.cdc .gov/oralhealth/infectioncontrol/questions/extracted-teeth.html.

Training Materials Myths and Misconceptions

1   Seth Augenstein, "Decomposition Rates Between Humans, Pigs May Vary Wildly," *Forensic Magazine,* May 3, 2016, https://www.forensicmag.com /article/2016/05/decomposition-rates-between-humans-pigs-may-vary -wildly.

2   In conversation with the author.

3   Centers for Disease Control and Prevention, "Mold," https://www.cdc.gov /mold/faqs.htm.

4   Carey W. Pettus, sheriff at Young County Sheriff's Office, Graham, Texas, 1997.

5   David C. Dorman, DVM, PhD, DABVT, ATS, is a professor of Toxicology, North Carolina State University, College of Veterinary Medicine Department of Molecular Biomedical Sciences. Dorman also works with scent detection K9s used by the United States Marine Corps. Dennis J. Blodgett, DVM, PhD, diplomate, ABVT, is an associate professor emeritus in the Toxicology Department of Biomedical Sciences and Pathobiology, and a diplomate, American Board of Veterinary Toxicology, Virginia–Maryland Regional College of Veterinary Medicine. My conversation is quoted from private correspondence.

Introducing Odor, Imprinting, and Search Commands

1   Bill Tolhurst, *The Police Textbook for Dog Handlers* (Sanborn, NY: Bill Tolhurst, 1991), 11.

The Alert

1   U.S. Fish & Wildlife Service, *Migratory Bird Treaty Act*, list of migratory bird species protected by the MBIA as of December 2, 2013, in *The Greenwolf*, "U.S. State Laws," http://www.thegreenwolf.com/u-s -state-laws.

2   University of Veterinary Medicine, Vienna, "What Are You Looking At? Dogs Are Able to Follow Human Gaze," *Science Daily*, June 12, 2015, htttps://www.sciencedaily.com/releases/2015/06/150612091146.htm. See also, Teresa Schmidjell, Friederike Range, Ludwig Huber, and Zsófia Virányi, "Do Owners Have a Clever Hans Effect on Dogs? Results of a Pointing Study," *Frontiers in Psychology*, 3, no. 558 (December 26, 2012), DOI: 10.3389/fpsyg.2012.00558. See also, Lisa J. Wallis, Friederike Range, Corsin A. Müller, Samuel Serisier, Ludwig Huber, and Zsófia Virányi, "Training for Eye Contact Modulates Gaze Following in Dogs," *Journal of Animal Behavior*, 106 (August 2015): 27–35.

Training for Human Remains Detection

1   Definition retrieved from https://legal-dictionary.thefreedictionary.com/ chain+of+custody

2   Emphasis by the author. U.S. Geological Survey (USGS) Water Science School, "Capillary Action," https://water.usgs.gov/edu/capillaryaction.html.

3   Pennsylvania State University, Eberly College of Science, "Elements in the Human Body," in *CHEM 101: Introductory Chemistry*, https://online .science.psu.edu/chem101_activewd/node/3333Q2.

4   Agro Services International, Inc., "What Nutrients Do Plants Need?" http://www.agroservicesinternational.com/Education/Fert1.html.

5   Dr. Arpad Vass in Douglas Page, "Is Forensic Science Going to the Dogs?" *Forensic Magazine*, October 1, 2008.

6   William D. Haglund and Marcella H. Sorg, "Human Remains in Water Environments," in *Advances in Forensic Taphonomy: Method, Theory, and Archaeological Perspectives* (Boca Raton: CRC Press, 2002), 202, 204, 205.

Search Briefings and Searches

1 Consult the Environmental Protection Agency for more information about CFLs. See https://www.epa.gov/cfl/cleaning-broken-cfl#di and also the article "Understanding the Dangers of Compact Fluorescent Light Bulbs" from https://wakeup-world.com/2012/05/06/understanding-the-dangers -of-compact-fluorescent-light-bulbs/.

2 Chief Pilot Bill Hogg from Fort Worth, Texas Police Department, retired from Texas Department of Public Safety after 27 years as officer/pilot. He was commissioned as a special ranger. His comments here come from a private conversation with the author.

Major Disasters and Mass Fatalities

1 Office of the Inspector General, Department of Homeland Security, "Audit of the National Urban Search and Rescue Response System, OIG-06-54," December 22, 2011, https://archive.org/details/241301-audit-of-the -national-urban-search-and-rescue.

2 FEMA, *Dog Talk*, 5, no. 2 (April 2002): 31, www.disasterdog.org

3 FEMA, *Dog Talk*, 6, no. 2 (March 2003): 8, www.disasterdog.org.

4 Leah Nathans Spiro. "Dentists Pitch In When Disaster Strikes," *New York Times*, April 27, 2003, https://www.nytimes.com/2003/04/27/nyregion /dentists-pitch-in-when-disaster-strikes.html.

Searching in Mass Fatality Incidents

1 Isabel Wilkerson, "Cruel Flood: It Tore at Graves, and at Hearts," *New York Times*, August 26, 1993, http://www.nytimes.com/1993/08/26/us /cruel-flood-it-tore-at-graves-and-at-hearts. See also Mike Lear, "Officials Recall Hardin Cemetery Washout 20 Years Ago," http://www.missourinet .com/2013/10/15/officials-recall-hardin-cemetery-washout-20-years-ago/. And Lily Koppel, "Coffins and Buried Remains Set Adrift by Hurricanes Create a Grisly Puzzle," *New York Times*, October 25, 2005, http://www .nytimes.com/2005/10/25/us/nationalspecial/coffins-and-buried-remains -set-adrift-by-hurricanes.html.

Bibliography

Agro Services International, Inc. "What Nutrients Do Plants Need?" http://www.agroservicesinternational.com/Education/Fert1.html.

Augenstein, Seth. "Decomposition Rates Between Humans, Pigs May Vary Wildly." *Forensic Magazine.* May 3, 2016. https://www.forensicmag.com/article/2016/05/decomposition-rates-between-humans-pigs-may-vary-wildly.

Baker, Major Janice. "Ear Protection of Dogs in Helicopters." USAR Group Veterinary Document. http://usarveterinarygroup.org/usarvet/wp-content/uploads/2016/08/Ear-Protection-in-Helicopters.pdf.

Bever, Lindsey. (*Washington Post*). "Michigan Couple Allegedly Rented Out Diseased Body Parts from Cadavers." *The Star.* March 26, 2016. https://www.thestar.com/news/world/2016/03/26/michigan-couple-allegedly-rented-out-diseased-body-parts-from-cadavers.html.

Center for Pet Safety. "Crates." 2015. http://www.centerforpetsafety.org/test-results/crates/.

Centers for Disease Control and Prevention. "Extracted Teeth." https://www.cdc.gov/oralhealth/infectioncontrol/questions/extracted-teeth.html.

———. "Mold." https://www.cdc.gov/mold/faqs.htm.

Cook, Peter F., Ashley Prichard, Mark Spivak, et al. "Awake Canine fMRI Predicts Dogs' Preference for Praise vs. Food." *Social Cognitive and Affective Neuroscience* 11, no. 12 (December 1, 2016): 1853–62. https://doi.org/10.1093/scan/nsw102.

Craven, Brent A., Eric G. Paterson, and Gary S. Settles. "The Fluid Dynamics of Canine Olfaction: Unique Nasal Airflow Patterns as an Explanation of Macrosmia." *Journal of the Royal Society, Interface* 7, no. 47 (April 26, 2010): 933–43. https://doi.org/10.1098/rsif.2009.0490.

Craven, Brent A., Thomas Neuberger, Eric G. Paterson, et al. "Reconstruction and Morphometric Analysis of the Nasal Airway of the Dog (*Canis familiaris*) and Implications Regarding Olfactory Airflow." *Anatomical Record* 290, no. 11 (2007): 1325–40. https://doi.org/10.1002/ar.20592.

Denham, H. D., J. W. Bradshaw, and N. J. Rooney. "Repetitive Behaviour in Kenneled Domestic Dog: Stereotypical or Not?" *Psychology and Behavior* 128 (April 10, 2014): 288–94. https://doi.org/10.1016/j.physbeh.2014.01.007.

Diamonds in the Ruff. "Developmental Stages." http://www.diamondsintheruff .com/developmental-stages.

Dodge, Ellen. "The Urban Puppy Toolkit." https://weimaranerclubofamerica .org/.

Dunbar, Ian. "Instructor Training Course." https://weimaranerclubofamerica .org/.

Estep, Dan, and Susanne Hetts. "Are Dogs Ruled by Their Drives and Instincts?" *Temperament or Personality* (2013). http://animalbehaviorassociates.com/blog /dogs-ruled-drives-instincts/.

———. "The Trouble with Drives." http://www.animalbehaviorassociates.com /pdf/RMN_drive_troubles.pdf.

FBI. "Specialized Use of Human Scent in Criminal Investigations." *Forensic Communication/Research and Technology*, 6, no. 3 (July 2004). https://archives .fbi.gov/archives/about-us/lab/forensic-science-communications/fsc/july2004 /research/2004_03_research03.htm.

FEMA. "Typed Resource Definitions: Search and Rescue Resources." May 2005. https://www.fema.gov/media-library/assets/documents/25923.

———. *Dog Talk*, 5, no. 2 (April 2002): 31. www.disasterdog.org.

———. *Dog Talk*, 6, no. 2 (March 2003): 8. www.disasterdog.org.

Fugazza, Claudia, and Ádám Miklósi. "Deferred Imitation and Declarative Memory in Domestic Dogs." *Animal Cognition* 17, no. 2 (March 2014): 237–47. https://doi.org/10.1007/s10071-013-0656-5.

Haglund, William D., and Marcella H. Sorg. "Human Remains in Water Environments." In *Advances in Forensic Taphonomy: Method, Theory, and Archaeological Perspectives*. Boca Raton: CRC Press, 2002.

Internationale Reddingshonden Groep. The Netherlands. "Scent Discrimination Tests in the Training of Search Dogs." http://www .reddingshonden.net/en-us/membersarea/research.aspx.

Kidd, Randy. "The Canine Sense of Smell: Sniffing Out the Source of Our Dogs' Remarkable Ability to Smell." *Whole Dog Journal* (November 2004, updated February 24, 2016). https://www.whole-dog-journal.com /issues/7_11/features/Canine-Sense-of-Smell_15668-1.html.

Koppel, Lily. "Coffins and Buried Remains Set Adrift by Hurricanes Create a Grisly Puzzle," *New York Times*. October 25, 2005. http://www.nytimes .com/2005/10/25/us/nationalspecial/coffins-and-buried-remains-set-adrift -by-hurricanes.html.

Lear, Mike. "Officials Recall Hardin Cemetery Washout 20 Years Ago." http:// www.missourinet.com/2013/10/15/officials-recall-hardin-cemetery-washout -20-years-ago/.

Li, Sichu. "Overview of Odor Detection Instrumentation and Potential for Human Odor Detection in Air Matrices." Human Odor Emission MITRE

Nanosystems Group. M53 P0900. March 2009. https://www.mitre.org/sites/default/files/pdf/09_4536.pdf.

Limoges, Michelle. "Unfolding Our 25-Year History." http://hp177.hostpapa.com/~sarda983/pdf/SARDAAHistoryJan26_14.pdf.

Lindsay, Steven R. *The Handbook of Applied Dog Behavior and Training.* Ames: Iowa State University, 2000. https://doi.org/10.1002/9780470376874.

Lit, Lisa, and Cynthia Crawford. "Effects of Training Paradigms on Search Dog Performance." *Applied Animal Behaviour Science* 98, no. 3–4 (July 2006): 277–92. https://doi.org/10.1016/j.applanim.2005.08.022.

Lit, Lisa, J. B. Schweitzer, and A. M. Oberbauer. "Handler Beliefs Affect Scent Detection Dog Outcomes." *Animal Cognition* 14, no. 387 (2011): 387–94. https://www.ncbi.nlm.nih.gov/pubmed/21225441.

Lorenzo, N., T.L. Wan, R.J. Harper, et al. "Laboratory and Field Experiments Used to Identify *Canis lupus* var. *familiaris* Active Odor Signature Chemicals from Drugs, Explosives, and Humans." *Journal of Analytical and Bioanalytical Chemistry* 376, no. 8 (2003): 1212–24. https://doi.org/10.1007/s00216-003-2018-7.

Monell Chemical Senses Center. "Odorprints Like Fingerprints? Personal Odors Remain Distinguishable Regardless of Diet." *Science Daily.* November 3, 2008. https://www.sciencedaily.com/releases/2008/10/081030203247.htm.

Office of the Inspector General, Department of Homeland Security. "Audit of the National Urban Search and Rescue Response System, OIG-06-54." December 22, 2011. https://archive.org/details/241301-audit-of-the-national-urban-search-and-rescue.

Page, Douglas. "Is Forensic Science Going to the Dogs?" *Forensic Magazine.* October 1, 2008.

Pennsylvania State University, Eberly College of Science. "Elements in the Human Body." In *CHEM 101: Introductory Chemistry.* https://online.science.psu.edu/chem101_activewd/node/3333Q4.

Pfaffenberger, Clarence. "The New Knowledge of Dog Behavior." https://weimaranerclubofamerica.org/.

Pullen, Anne J., Ralph Merrill, and John W. S. Bradshaw. "The Effect of Familiarity on Behavior of Kennel Housed Dogs During Interactions with Humans." *Applied Animal Behaviour Science* 137, no. 1–2 (February 2012): 66–73. https://doi.org/10.1016/j.applanim.2011.12.009.

Robinson, Jamie. *Snake Avoidance Without Shock.* Self-published. http://snakeavoidancewithoutshock.com/new-page.html.

Rutherford, Clarice, and David H. Neil. "How to Raise a Puppy You Can Live With." https://weimaranerclubofamerica.org/.

"SARDA Registration" in *Scout Search and Rescue Dog.* November 7, 2016. https://scoutsardog.wordpress.com/2016/11/07/sarda-registration/.

Schmidjell, Teresa, Friederike Range, Ludwig Huber, et al. "Do Owners Have a Clever Hans Effect on Dogs? Results of A Pointing Study." *Frontiers in Psychology* 3, no. 558 (December 26, 2012). https://doi.org/10.3389/fpsyg.2012.00558.

Spiro, Leah Nathans. "Dentists Pitch in When Disaster Strikes." *New York Times*, April 27, 2003, https://www.nytimes.com/2003/04/27/nyregion /dentists-pitch-in-when-disaster-strikes.html.

Stockham, Rex A., Dennis L. Slavin, and William Kift. "Specialized Use of Human Scent in Criminal Investigations." *Forensic Science Communications, Research and Technology*, 6, no. 3 (July 2004): https://archives.fbi.gov /archives/about-us/lab/forensic-science-communications/fsc/july2004 /research/2004_03_research03.htm.

———. "Survivability of Human Scent." *Forensic Science Communications, Research and Technology*, 6, no. 4 (October 2004): https://archives.fbi.gov /archives/about-us/lab/forensic-science-communications/fsc/oct2004/ research/2004_10_research03.htm.

Stromberg, Joseph. "New Study Shows That Dogs Use Color Vision After All." *Smithsonian Magazine*. July 17, 2013. http://www.smithsonianmag.com /science-nature/new-study-shows-that-dogs-use-color-vision-after-all -13168563/.

Svobodová, Ivona, Pavel Vápenik, Ludvík Pinc, et al. "Testing German Shepherd Puppies to Assess Their Chances of Certification." *Applied Animal Behaviour Science* 113, no. 1–3 (September 2008): 139–49. https://doi .org/10.1016/j.applanim.2007.09.010.

SWGDOG. "Approved Guidelines." https://swgdog.fiu.edu/approved-guidelines/.

Syrotuck, William G. "Theory of Scent." In *Scent and the Scenting Dog*. Eden Consulting Group, Police Dog Home Page. https://www.policek9.com/html /theory.html.

TEDx. "CommonScents: Dr. Arpad Vass at TEDxYYC." Filmed July 5, 2012. YouTube video. 15:31. Posted July 5, 2012. https://www.youtube.com /watch?v=l0Qd2nxMC2Y.

The Greenwolf. "U.S. State Laws." December 2, 2013. http://www.thegreenwolf .com/u-s-state-laws.

Tolhurst, Bill. "Carbon Monoxide Study." *Scent Study in Home of the Big T, Scent Research*. 2002. http://www.angelfire.com/ny4/bigT/.

———. *The Police Textbook for Dog Handlers*. Sanborn, NY: Bill Tolhurst, 1991.

Topál, J., R.W. Byrne, Á. Miklósi, et al. "Reproducing Human Actions and Action Sequences: 'Do as I Do.'." *Animal Cognition* 9, no. 4 (2006): 355–67. https://doi.org/10.1007/s10071-006-0051-6.

U.S. Department of Justice, Civil Rights Division, Disability Rights Section. "Service Animals." 2010. https://www.ada.gov/service_animals_2010.pdf.

U.S. Geological Survey (USGS) Water Science School. "Capillary Action." https://water.usgs.gov/edu/capillaryaction.html.

University of Veterinary Medicine, Vienna. "What Are You Looking At? Dogs Are Able to Follow Human Gaze." Science Daily. June 12, 2015. https:// www.sciencedaily.com/releases/2015/06/150612091146.htm.

Vass, Arpad A., Rob R. Smith, Cyril V. Thompson, et al. "Decompositional Odor Analysis Database." *Journal of Forensic Sciences* 49, no. 4 (2004): 1–10. https://doi.org/10.1520/JFS2003434.

Vass, Arpad A., Rob R. Smith, Cyril V. Thompson, et al. "Odor Analysis of Decomposing Buried Human Remains." *Journal of Forensic Sciences* 53, no. 2 (2008): 384–91. https://doi.org/10.1111/j.1556-4029.2008.00680.x.

Walker, D. B., J. C. Walker, P. J. Cavnar, et al. "Naturalistic Quantification of Canine Olfactory Sensitivity." *Applied Animal Behaviour Science* 97, no. 2-4 (2006): 241–54. https://doi.org/10.1016/j.applanim.2005.07.009.

Wallis, Lisa J., Friederike Range, Corsin A. Müller, et al. "Training for Eye Contact Modulates Gaze Following in Dogs." *Journal of Animal Behavior* 106 (August 2015): 27–35. https://doi.org/10.1016/j.anbehav.2015.04.020.

Wilkerson, Isabel. "Cruel Flood: It Tore at Graves, and at Hearts." *New York Times*. August 26, 1993. https://www.nytimes.com/1993/08/26/us/cruel-flood-it-tore-at-graves-and-at-hearts.html.

Wisman, A., and I. Shrira. "The Smell of Death: Evidence that Putrescine Elicits Threat Management Mechanisms." *Frontiers in Psychology* 6 (August 28, 2015): 1274. https://doi.org/10.3389/fpsyg.2015.01274.

Wood, Lt. Weldon. "Scent, that Magical, Elusive, Intangible Thing that Eludes Our Every Effort to Trap, Contain or Identify It and Perplexes Us at Every Turn. What Is It? Where Does It Come From? How Do Our Dogs Utilize It?" National Police Bloodhound Association. www.vk9sar.org/Scent_NPBA.doc.

Additional Sources Consulted

Alley, William M., Thomas E. Reilly, and O. Lehn Franke. "General Facts and Concepts about Ground Water." In *Sustainability of Ground-Water Resources, Circular 1186*. https://pubs.usgs.gov/circ/circ1186/pdf/circ1186.pdf.

American Psychology Association. "Recovering Emotionally from a Disaster." August 2003. http://www.apa.org/helpcenter/recovering-disasters.aspx.

Ancic, Mario. "Drive and Instinct: Harness the Benefits for Training Your Dog and You!" http://www.training-your-dog-and-you.com/drive.html.

Auf der Heide, Erik. *Disaster Response: Principles of Preparation and Coordination*. St. Louis: The C.V. Mosby Company, 1989.

Australian Museum. "Decomposition: Corpse Fauna." https://australianmuseum.net.au/decomposition-corpse-fauna

Baxter, Kyle. *Extrinsic Factors that Affect the Preservation of Bone*. Lincoln: University of Nebraska, Nebraska Anthropology Department, 2004., http://digitalcommons.unl.edu/nebanthro/62/.

Berryman, Robert, and the University of Mississippi Department of Psychology. "Sensory Capacity of the Military Working Dog." Air Force Office of Scientific Research (AFSC) Contract F44620–69-C-0050. http://www.dtic.mil/dtic/tr/fulltext/u2/739989.pdf.

Claridge, Jack. "Understanding Trace Evidence." *Explore Forensics*. http://www.exploreforensics.co.uk/understanding-trace-evidence.html.

Concha, Astrid, Daniel S. Mills, Alexandre Feugier, et al. "Using Sniffing Behavior to Differentiate True Negative from False Negative Responses in Trained Scent-Detection Dogs." *Chemical Senses* 39, no. 9 (November 2014): 749–54. https://doi.org/10.1093/chemse/bju045.

Cornwell, Langley. "How Dogs Interpret Human Body Language." *Canidae*. https://www.canidae.com/blog/2015/05/how-dogs-interpret-human-body-language/.

Correa, Julio E. *The Dog's Sense of Smell*. Huntsville, Auburn: Alabama A&M and Auburn Universities, Alabama Cooperative Extension System, 2011.

Costandi, Moheb. "Life After Death: The Science of Human Decomposition." *The Guardian.* May 5, 2015. https://www.theguardian.com/science /neurophilosophy/2015/may/05/life-after-death.

———. "The Smell of Death." *Daily Mail.* May 6, 2015. http://www.dailymail .co.uk/sciencetech/article-3071037/The-smell-death-Scientist-reveals -bacteria-creates-heady-mixture-scents-rips-apart-rotting.

Curran, Allison M., Scott I. Rabin, and Kenneth G. Furton. "Analysis of the Uniqueness and Persistence of Human Scent." *Forensic Science Communications*, 7, no. 2 (April 2005).

Dautartas, Angela Madeleine. *The Effect of Various Coverings on the Rate of Human Decomposition.* Master's Thesis. University of Tennessee. 2009. http:// trace.tennessee.edu/utk_gradthes/69.

Department of Homeland Security Federal Emergency Management Agency. *FEMA Canine Search Team Certification Evaluation Handbook: Human Remains Detection – Passive Alert.* August 2015. http://disasterdog.org/pdf/ policies/Handbooks/CSTCEHandbook_HRD_PassiveAlert_Aug2015.pdf.

Desborough, J. P. "The Stress Response to Trauma and Surgery." *British Journal of Anaesthesia* 85, no. 1 (2000): 109–17. https://doi.org/10.1093/bja/85.1.109.

Disaster Mortuary Operational Response Team (DMORT). *Field Operations Guide.* August 2000. United States Department of Health and Human Services, Office of Emergency Preparedness, National Disaster Medical Systems.

Donahue, Amy, and Robert Tuohy. "Lessons We Don't Learn: A Study of the Lessons of Disasters, Why We Repeat Them, and How We Can Learn Them." *Homeland Security Affairs: The Journal for Homeland Security Defense and Security*, 13 (2006–2017).

Farricelli, Adrienne Janet. "Dog Training: Recognizing Different Drives." *PetHelpful.* https://pethelpful.com/dogs/Dog-Training-Recognizing -Different-Drives.

Federal Emergency Management Agency (FEMA). *Training Program Administration Manual National Urban Search and Rescue (US&R) Response System.* February 2013. https://www.fema.gov/media-library-data/ 1393958418794-405f9ed0b305ca8ee660cbe164f35321/508_Urban_Search _Rescue_Training_Program_Admin_Manual_Feb2013.pdf.

———. *National Urban Search and Rescue US&R Response Team Field Operations Guide.* September 2003.

Ferworn, Alex, Devin Ostrum, Alireza Sadeghian, et al. "Rubble Search with Canine Augmentation Technology." May 2007. https://doi.org/10.1109/ SYSOSE.2007.4304328.

Freedman, Rachel, and Ron Fleming. "Water Quality Impacts of Burying Livestock Mortalities (includes Environmental Impacts of Human Burial)." Paper presented to the Livestock Mortality Recycling Project Steering Committee. Ridgetown College, University of Guelph. August 2003.

Fugazza, Claudia. *Do as I Do: Using Social Learning to Train Dogs.* Wenatchee, WA: Dogwise Publishing, 2014.

Fugazza, Claudia, and Ádám Miklósi. "Deferred Imitation and Declarative Memory in Domestic Dogs." *Animal Cognition* 17, no. 2 (2014): 237–47. https://doi.org/10.1007/s10071-013-0656-5.

Fugazza, Claudia, and Ádám Miklósi. "Social Learning in Dog Training: The Effectiveness of the Do as I Do Method Compared to Shaping/Clicker Training." *Applied Animal Behaviour Science* 171 (2015): 146–51. https://www.appliedanimalbehaviour.com/article/S0168-1591(15)00236-1/fulltext.

Furton, Kenneth G., Norma Iris Caraballo, Michelle M. Cerreta, et al. "Advances in the Use of Odour as Forensic Evidence Through Optimizing and Standardizing Instruments and Canines." *Philosophical Transactions of the Royal Society of London. Series B, Biological Sciences* 370, no. 1674 (August 5, 2015): 20140262. https://doi.org/10.1098/rstb.2014.0262.

Gearin, Conor. "Hundreds of Mystery Human Skulls Sold on Ebay for up to $5500." *The New Scientist Daily News.* https://www.newscientist.com/article/2097171-hundreds-of-mystery-human-skulls-sold-on-ebay-for-up-to-5500/.

Graham, Hatch. "Probability of Detection for Search Dogs or How Long is Your Shadow?" Self-published handout. 1994.

Greene, Claudia L. "Human Remains and Psychological Impact on Police Officers: Excerpts from Psychiatric Observations." *Australasian Journal of Disaster and Trauma Studies* 5, no. 2 (2001).

Grow, Brian, and John Shiffman. "Special Report: In the Market for Human Bodies, Almost Anyone Can Sell the Dead." Reuters. October 24, 2017. https://www.reuters.com/article/us-usa-bodies-brokers-specialreport/special-report-in-the-market-for-human-bodies-almost-anyone-can-sell-the-dead-idUSKBN1CT1F5.

Hardy, Marian. "How to Develop and Train a Water Search Dog Team." Mid-Atlantic D.O.G.S. 1992. https://sites.google.com/site/midatlanticdogsinc/Home/Articles/How%20to%20Develop%20and%20Train%20a%20Water%20Search%20Dog%20Team.

———. "Water Search with Dogs." Mid-Atlantic D.O.G.S. 1995. http://www.pawsoflife.org/Library/Trailing%20Water/Water%20Search%20with%20Dogs%20-%20Marion%20Hardy.pdf.

Haugen, Krista. "Resilience Starts with You." Survivors Network: Air Medical Community. https://www.survivorsnetwork-airmedical.org/resources.

Haupt, Gary. "Drowning Investigation." FBI Law Enforcement Training Bulletin. https://leb.fbi.gov/file-repository/archives/feb06leb.pdf/view.

Hecht, Julie. "Dog of the Dead: The Science of Canine Cadaver Detection." *Scientific American* 9, no. March (2015): https://blogs.scientificamerican.com/dog-spies/dog-of-the-dead-the-science-of-canine-cadaver-detection/.

Horowitz, Alexandra, ed. *Domestic Dog Cognition and Behavior: The Scientific Study of Canis familiaris.* Berlin, Heidelberg: Springer-Verlag, 2014. https://doi.org/10.1007/978-3-642-53994-7.

Hrala, Josh. "Human 'Body Farm' Reveals We Need to Stop Using Pigs to Establish Time of Death." *Science Alert.* June 17, 2016. https://www

.sciencealert.com/pigs-may-not-be-the-most-amazing-forensic-tool-after
-all-finds-body-farm-researchers.

Hudson, David T., Allison Curran, and Kenneth Furton. "The Stability of
Collected Human Scent Under Various Environmental Conditions." *Journal
of Forensic Sciences* 54, no. 6 (November 2009): 1270–7. https://doi
.org/10.1111/j.1556-4029.2009.01153.x.

Hugo, Kristin. "After Amputation, You May Be Able to Take Your Body Part
Home." PBS News Hour. January 5, 2017. https://www.pbs.org/newshour
/science/took-amputated-leg-home-can.

———. "Human Skulls Are Being Sold Online, But Is It Legal?" *National
Geographic* 23, no. August (2016): https://news.nationalgeographic
.com/2016/08/human-skulls-sale-legal-ebay-forensics-science/.

Jia, Hao, Oleg M. Pustovyy, Paul Waggoner, et al. "Functional MRI of the
Olfactory System in Conscious Dogs." *PLoS One* 9, no. 1 (2014): e86362.
https://doi.org/10.1371/journal.pone.0086362.

Johnston, J. M. "Canine Detection Capabilities: Operational Implications
of Recent R&D Findings." Institute for Biological Detection Systems,
Auburn University. June 1999. http://barksar.org/K-9_Detection
_Capabilities.pdf.

Jones, Phillip. "Scents and Sense-Ability." *Forensic Magazine*. April 1, 2006.
https://www.forensicmag.com/article/2006/04/scents-and-sense-ability.

Kaldenbach, Jan. *K9 Scent Detection: My Favorite Judge Lives in a Kennel.*
Calgary: Dog Training Press, 1998.

Keller, Paul. *Searching for and Recovering the Space Shuttle* Columbia:
*Documenting the USDA Forest Service Role in this Unprecedented 'All-Risk'
Incident, February 1 through May 10, 2003.* https://www.fireleadership
.gov/toolbox/lead_in_cinema_library/downloads/challenges/Searching
_Recovering_Shuttle_Columbia_2003_Paul%20Keller.pdf.

Kesling, Joyce. "The Canine Senses." Responsible Dog Training and Behavior
Solutions, Bradenton, Florida. https://responsibledog.net/2011/03/21
/the-canine-senses/.

Koenig, Marcia. *Handler Strategies for Water Search Scenes.* Handout, 1990.

Leintz, Rachel. "Forensic Evidence: Types, Definition & Cases." Chapter 11.
Lesson 39. https://study.com/academy/lesson/forensic-evidence-types
-definition-cases.html#transcriptHeader.

Lothridge, Kevin, David Sylvester, and Alistair Ross. *A Simplified Guide to Trace
Evidence.* Largo, FL: National Forensics Science Technology Center, 2012.,
http://www.forensicsciencesimplified.org/trace/TraceEvidence.pdf.

Marsh, Tanya D., and Daniel J. D. Gibson. "Summary of State Laws Regarding
the Authority to Dispose of Human Remains." https://www.forgottenashes
.com/state-laws.

Meyer, Iben, and Jan Ladewig. "The Relationship Between Number of Training
Sessions per Week and Learning in Dogs." *Applied Animal Behaviour Science*
111, no. 3-4 (June 2008): 311–20. https://doi.org/10.1016/j.applanim
.2007.06.016.

Milner, Lt. Col. Robert. "Training Disaster Search Dogs." In *Disaster Search Dog Training Manual*. September 23, 2003. http://www.duckhillkennels.com /libraries/PDFs/TrainingDisasterSearchDogs.pdf.

Moulton, D. G. "Enhancement of Olfactory Discrimination." Defense Technical Information Center. March 1979. http://www.dtic.mil/docs /citations/ADA068752. https://doi.org/10.21236/ADA068752.

Oesterhelweg, L., S. Kröber, K. Rottmann, et al. "Cadaver Dogs: A Study on Detection of Contaminated Carpet Squares." *Forensic Science International* 174, no. 1 (January 15, 2008): 35–9. https://doi.org/10.1016 /j.forsciint.2007.02.031.

Page, Douglas. "Life in a Disaster Morgue." *Forensic Science Magazine*. December 1, 2005. https://www.forensicmag.com/article/2005/12 /life-disaster-morgue.

Pang, Benison, Karen K. Yee, Fritz W. Lischka, et al. "The Influence of Nasal Airflow on Respiratory and Olfactory Epithelial Distribution in Felids." *Journal of Experimental Biology* 219, no. 12 (2016): 1866–74. https://doi .org/10.1242/jeb.131482.

Pappas, Stephanie. "Human Body Language Can Mislead Dogs." *Live Science*. April 25, 2012. https://www.livescience.com/19906-human-body-language -mislead-dogs.html.

Physics Forums. "How Fast Does a Human Sink in H_2O?" https://www .physicsforums.com/threads/how-fast-does-a-human-sink-in-h20.168768.

Plonsky, Dr. M. "K9 Perception." www4.uwsp.edu/psych/mp/c/p275.htm.

Pope, Elayne J., O. C. Smith, and Timothy G. Huff. "Exploding Skulls and Other Myths about How the Human Body Burns." *Fire & Arson Investigator*, 54, no. 4 (April 2004).

Prada, Paola A., Allison M. Curran, and Kenneth G. Furton. "Persistence and Stability of Human Scent." In *Human Scent Evidence*. 69–73. Boca Raton: CRC Press, 2014.

Quinn, Woodrow L., Jr., and Nicholas Montanare. "Body Recovery Dog." In *Technical Report No. IWL-03B73*. Aberdeen Proving Ground, MD: National Technical Information Service, U.S. Department of Commerce, 1973.

Schotsmans, Eline M. J., John Denton, Jessica Dekeirsschieter, et al. "Effects of Hydrated Lime and Quicklime on the Decay of Buried Human Remains Using Pig Cadavers as Human Body Analogues." Originally published in *Forensic Science International*. 2011. http://citeseerx.ist.psu.edu/viewdoc/down load?doi=10.1.1.910.9097&rep=rep1&type=pdf.

Shirley, Natalie R., Rebecca J. Wilson, and Lee Meadows Jantz. "Cadaver Use at the University of Tennessee's Anthropological Research Facility." Knoxville: Department of Anthropology, University of Tennessee. http:// www.academia.edu/565984/Cadaver_Use_at_the_University_of_Tennessees _Anthropological_Research_Facility. https://doi.org/10.1002/ca.21154.

Simon Fraser University Museum of Archaeology and Ethnology. "Forensic Botany or the Uses of Plants in Criminal Investigations." *Investigating Forensics*. http://www.sfu.museum/forensics/eng/pg_media-media_pg /botanique-botany/.

Stefanuto, Pierre-Hugues, and Jean-Francois Focant. "The Case of the Decaying Cadaver." *Analytical Scientist* 51 (April 2017): 22–32.

Stepaniak, Philip C., Helen W. Lane, and Jeffrey R. Davis. *Loss of Signal: Aeromedical Lessons Learned from the STS-107 Columbia Shuttle Mishap.* National Aeronautics and Space Administration. https://ntrs.nasa.gov /archive/nasa/casi.ntrs.nasa.gov/20140008287.pdf.

Tebrich, Spencer. "Human Scent and Its Detection." Central Intelligence Agency Historical Review Program. September 22, 1993.

Thompson, Kalee. "Preparing for Disaster at First Responders Boot Camp." *Popular Mechanics.* June 4, 2012. http://www.popularmechanics.com /adventure/outdoors/a7535/preparing-for-disaster-at-first-responders -boot-camp-7588642/.

Titus, Roger. *Training Trails.* Sussex, NJ: National Police Bloodhound Association, 1983.

Vass, A. A., W. M. Bass, J. D. Wolt, et al. "Time Since Death Determinations of Human Cadavers Using Soil Solution." *Journal of Forensic Sciences* 37, no. 5 (September 1992): 1236–53. https://doi.org/10.1520/JFS13311J.

Vass, Arpad A., Rob R. Smith, Cyril V. Thompson, et al. "Odor Analysis of Decomposing Buried Human Remains." *Journal of Forensic Sciences* 53, no. 2 (March 2008). https://doi.org/10.1111/j.1556-4029.2008.00680.x.

Volhard, Wendy. "Dog Personality Profile: Discovering Your Dog's Personality." http://www.volhard.com/uploads/drives-2010.pdf.

Wade, Nicholas. "Sit. Stay. Parse. Good Girl!" *New York Times.* January 17, 2011. http://www.nytimes.com/2011/01/18/science/18dog.html.

Waggoner, L. Paul, Meredith Jones, Marc Williams, et al. "Effects of Extraneous Odors on Canine Detection." *Proceedings of the SPIE,* 3575 (1998).

Williams, Marc, and James M. Johnston. "Training and Maintaining the Performance of Dogs (*Canis familiaris*) on an Increasing Number of Odor Discriminations in a Controlled Setting." *Applied Animal Behaviour Science* 78, no. 1 (2002): 55–65. https://doi.org/10.1016/S0168-1591(02)00081-3.

Zubedat, Salman, Shlomit Aga-Mizrachi, Adi Cymerblit-Sabba, et al. "Human–Animal Interface: The Effects of Handler's Stress on the Performance of Canines in an Explosive Detection Task." *Applied Animal Behaviour Science* 158 (September 2014): 69–75. https://doi.org/10.1016 /j.applanim.2014.05.004.

Suggested Reading

American Rescue Dog Association. *Search and Rescue Dogs: Training Methods.* New York: Howell Book House, 1991.

Bryson, Susan. *Search Dog Training.* New York: The Boxwood Press, 1991.

Bulanda, Susan. *Ready to Serve...Ready to Save: Strategies of Real-Life Search and Rescue Missions.* Phoenix: Doral Publishing, 1999.

Bulanda, Susan, with Larry Bulanda. *Ready! Training the Search and Rescue Dog.* Allenhurst, NJ: Kennel Club Books, 2010.

Burnett, Patti. *Avalanche!* Phoenix: Doral Publishing, 2003.

Button, Lue. *Practical Scent Dog Training.* Crawford, CO: Alpine Publications, 1990.

Cooper, Donald C., Patrick Lavalla, and Robert C. Stoffel. *Search and Rescue Fundamentals: Basic Skills and Knowledge to Perform Wilderness, Inland, Search and Rescue.* Cuyahoga Falls, OH: National Rescue Consultants, 1996.

Foster, Steven, and Roger Caras. *Venomous Animals & Poisonous Plants.* New York: Peterson Field Guides, Houghton Mifflin Company, 1994.

Haglund, William D., and Marcella H. Sorg, eds. *Advances in Forensic Taphonomy.* Boca Raton: CRC Press, 2002.

———. *Forensic Taphonomy: The Postmortem Fate of Human Remains.* Boca Raton: CRC Press, 1997.

Jensen, Robert A. *Mass Fatality and Casualty Incidents: A Field Guide.* Boca Raton: CRC Press, 1999. https://doi.org/10.1201/9781420048797.

Johnson, Glen R. *Tracking Dog Theory & Methods.* Mechanicsburg, PA: Barkleigh Productions, 2012.

Neudeck-Dicken, Marilyn. *Cumulative Stress Management for Search and Rescue: A Workbook for All Emergency Personnel.* Palmer Lake, CO: Filter Press, 1997.

Prada, Paola A., Allison M. Curran, and Kenneth G. Furton. *Human Scent Evidence.* Boca Raton: CRC Press, 2014.

Pryor, Karen. *Don't Shoot the Dog.* New York: Bantam, 1985.

————. *On Behavior Essays & Research*. Thomastown, Australia: Sunshine Books, 1995.

Rebmann, Andrew, Edward David, and Marcella H. Sorg. *Cadaver Dog Handbook*. Boca Raton: CRC Press, 2000.

Schettler, Jeff. *K-9 Trailing: The Straightest Path*. Crawford, CO: Alpine Publications, 2012.

Smith, Cheryl S. *The Rosetta Bone: The Key to Communication Between Humans and Canines*. New York: Howell Book House, 2004.

Syrotuck, W. G. *Scent and the Scenting Dog*. New York: Arner Publications, 1972.

————. *Analysis of Lost Person Behavior*. Mechanicsburg, PA: Barkleigh Publications, 2000.

Tolhurst, Bill. *The Police Textbook for Dog Handlers*. Sharp Print, 1991.

————. *The Silent Witness*. Self-published, 2000.

White, Tim D., and Pieter A. Folkens. *The Human Bone Manual*. New York: Eslevier Academic Press, 2005.

About the Author

Vi Hummel Shaffer has 27 years experience as a volunteer K9 handler specializing in forensic human remains detection. She is also an instructor, speaker, and consultant in SAR/R, and is an associate instructor with Texas Forensic Associates. In 2002, Vi was appointed the national chairperson of the federal Disaster Mortuary Operational Response Team (DMORT) Mass Fatality K9 Standards and Requirements Committee by the director of the U.S. Office of Emergency Preparedness/National Disaster Medical Systems/Department of Health and Human Services. In addition, she was a four-year member of the FBI–Southeast Texas Evidence/Crime Scene Working Group and was a member of the National Volunteer Advisory Board/University of North Texas Forensic Services Unit Center for Human Identification from 2006 to 2014.

In 2003, her dog Mercy was recognized by the federal government as the first mass fatality K9 in the United States and as the inspiration for DMORT'S K9 program. As a logistics specialist, Vi was a DMORT member for 19 years and a two-term board member of Region 6. She is a life member of the Homicide Investigators of Texas, and although not law enforcement, was appointed to their board of directors, where she served for five years. She and her dog Mercy, at the request of the FBI, were a part of Operation Noble Eagle, the victim recovery team at the Pentagon in

Vi with her dogs True (left) and Spirit (right).

the aftermath of 9-11-01. Vi has also lectured at death investigation seminars, law enforcement conferences, and fire protection schools, and is a court-qualified subject matter expert witness.

She has received numerous federal, state, city, and county recognition for her work, including from the following:

- Parents of Murdered Children–North Texas Chapter
- United States Department of Health and Human Services/ Office of Emergency Preparedness/DMORT
- Division of Emergency Management/Texas Department of Public Safety
- National Disaster Medical Systems
- Federal Emergency Management Agency (FEMA)
- State of Oklahoma Offices of the Chief Medical Examiner
- Federal Bureau of Investigation (FBI)
- United States Police Canine Association/Region Three
- Department of the Treasury/Bureau of Alcohol, Tobacco and Firearms (ATF)